WOMEN'S
PATHS to POWER

WOMEN'S
PATHS to POWER

Female Presidents & Prime Ministers, 1960–2020

Evren Celik Wiltse & Lisa Hager

LYNNE
RIENNER
PUBLISHERS

BOULDER
LONDON

Published in the United States of America in 2021 by
Lynne Rienner Publishers, Inc.
1800 30th Street, Suite 314, Boulder, Colorado 80301
www.rienner.com

and in the United Kingdom by
Lynne Rienner Publishers, Inc.
Gray's Inn House, 127 Clerkenwell Road, London EC1 5DB
www.eurospanbookstore.com/rienner

Library of Congress Cataloging-in-Publication Data
Names: Çelik Wiltse, Evren, author. | Hager, Lisa, author.
Title: Women's paths to power : female presidents and prime ministers,
    1960–2020 / Evren Celik Wiltse and Lisa Hager.
Description: Boulder, Colorado : Lynne Rienner Publishers, Inc., [2021] |
    Includes bibliographical references and index. | Summary: "A
    comprehensive study of women's paths to political leadership,
    encompassing all of the women presidents and prime ministers around the
    world from the 1960s through 2020"— Provided by publisher.
Identifiers: LCCN 2020047203 | ISBN 9781626379282 (hardcover) | ISBN
    9781626379305 (paperback)
Subjects: LCSH: Women heads of state—History. | Women
    politicians—History. | Women—Political activity—History.
Classification: LCC HQ1236 .W475 2021 | DDC 352.23082—dc23
LC record available at https://lccn.loc.gov/2020047203

British Cataloguing in Publication Data
A Cataloguing in Publication record for this book
is available from the British Library.

Printed and bound in the United States of America

The paper used in this publication meets the requirements
of the American National Standard for Permanence of
Paper for Printed Library Materials Z39.48-1992.

5 4 3 2 1

Contents

Tables and Figures

Tables

Figures

Acknowledgments

We owe the inception of this book to April Brooks. Always a strong advocate for women and women's studies, she encouraged Evren to teach the women and politics class at South Dakota State University (SDSU). That class led to a conference paper on women leaders in Latin America at the Midwest Political Science Association Annual Convention, and that project subsequently led to our book contract. Sadly, we lost April Brooks on April 2, 2015. However, her legacy of women's empowerment and international engagement continues with the annual Women's Excellence Awards at our institution.

As our project evolved from a series of papers to a manuscript, we received support from several sources. SDSU and the College of Arts, Humanities, and Social Sciences provided us multiple dissemination grants. This allowed us to present our work at academic conferences and receive invaluable feedback from our peers. We appreciate the financial support from our home institution, as well as the insightful comments of our copanelists and conference attendees. The Women, Gender, and Sexuality Studies Program at SDSU also provided continued support, encouragement, and a platform to share our findings in the campus events they organized. Our students Allison Vinson and Carly Boder provided much-needed research assistance as we all delved into the personal stories of more than 100 world leaders. We appreciated the times when we got together to compare our coding and shared the intriguing facts we encountered while reading each leader's biography.

Our book developed over time, and we believe that each stage significantly improved the quality of our work. We appreciated the thoughtful and detailed comments and criticism from multiple anonymous reviewers. We revised our work substantially based on their input. We also would like to thank our publisher, Lynne Rienner. She provided incredibly helpful feedback on all stages of our work, starting from the initial book proposal to the final stage of production. We appreciate all the help Nicole Moore provided us by answering questions and clarifying aspects of the publication and review process. Lastly, we would like to thank our copyeditor, Jennifer Top, for her kind and careful reading of our entire book.

—Evren Celik Wiltse and Lisa Hager

* * *

Each book is an adventure, and so was this one. Thankfully, the joyful moments outweighed the stressful ones. First and foremost, I appreciate how my department head at the time, April Brooks, steered me toward this project with utmost support and encouragement. With her short silver hair and New Yorker attitude, she was a solid advocate of junior faculty and particularly of women. I do hope to carry on some of her principles. Supporting women and junior faculty could only make academia become a better place. When Lisa joined our department, I was quick to notice the gender and politics credentials on her resume. This led to our wonderfully productive coauthorship. Without her, I would still be reading bios of all these impressive women fighting uphill battles. In our meetings, I would bring up yet another heart-wrenching story, such as the leader who started her career as a street vendor, and she would patiently listen to me until I finished and finally ask, "Okay, how do we code her?" A great many thanks for her sharp focus and diligent work ethic.

I want to thank my immediate family for not complaining about my late nights and weekends at the office, and for bringing me dinner, treats, and big smiley faces. Life with them takes me to interesting places, from Scotland to Georgia, and Cabo to Cuba. I hope we can pursue that habit (Covid-19 permitting) and encounter more countries with women heads of state along the way. It takes a village to concentrate on a project of this scale, and it certainly would not have been possible if I had grumpy villagers at home. Dave, the boy, and Bestemor, you all are incredibly special.

I also want to express my gratitude to our publisher. Both Lisa and I were assistant professors when we proposed this project. Without the steady help and support from our publisher, I doubt that it would have been possible for us to navigate these waters. When sheer panic was about to take us over, the LRP staff's calm professionalism certainly helped us. I appreciated Lynne Rienner herself taking the time to read our work and provide clear and constructive criticisms. We are incredibly grateful for her insights and editorial expertise. Similarly, Nicole Moore was there any time we needed, promptly answering our questions, clarifying our confusions.

Finally, I want to thank all my mentors, colleagues, and students. Contrary to the cartoonish professor doing academic research in isolation while buried under papers, we are deeply social beings. Seeing my students and colleagues every day keeps me grounded. I feel lucky to have mentors who watch over me, and whom I can to turn to when in need. Without that dense and supportive network, I do not think I could produce any meaningful academic work. Thank you all for your continued support, friendship, and solidarity.

—Evren

Writing a book is no small feat, especially when it is your first one, and there are a few people I would like to personally thank. The first is my mentor, Chris Banks. Chris not only helped me successfully navigate graduate school, a dissertation, and the job market, but he has been an invaluable resource throughout my time here at SDSU. Chris is always available to answer questions regarding teaching, research, and service. I am very appreciative of this, and it is because of his support and mentorship that I was able to write this book.

I would also like to thank my coauthor Evren Celik Wiltse and my colleague at SDSU, Dave Wiltse. It was an absolute joy to be able to develop this book into what it is today with Evren. Evren was not only a fantastic coauthor but also a great mentor as I went through the book publication process for the first time. To both Dave and Evren, I appreciate your friendship and support. You made the transition from graduate student to faculty member a breeze. It is a delight for me to come to work every day with you as my colleagues.

Last but not least, I would like to thank my parents, Kim and Becky Hager. What a journey it has been since I decided to pursue a

PhD in political science. As I was growing up, they told me to find a career that I was passionate about, and I did. I never could have imagined all the places this career has taken me, but it is because of their love and support that I am where I am today. They have been there for the highs and lows, frustrations and celebrations, and there are not words to express what that means to me. This book is for them.

Shoutouts are also warranted for my dog Addy, my students and colleagues at SDSU, and my friends here in Brookings. If you know me, you know that Addy is technically my parents' dog, but I claim her as my own. I worked on this book numerous times with her lying on my lap sleeping. She is by far my favorite research assistant. Photos and her tail wags and kisses kept me going. Thank you to my students and colleagues at SDSU. My students make going to class every day a true pleasure. There is nothing I love better than watching them grow, succeed, and achieve their dreams. To my colleagues, thank you for the warm welcome from my very first day here and all your kind words and support throughout the book writing and publication process. I so appreciate all our conversations, and it meant a lot when any of you would take the time to ask how the book was going. My friends in Brookings would also often ask how the book was going, but more important they gave me an opportunity to take a break from writing and revising for some fun.

—Lisa

1

Women's Paths to Political Power

Politico: "Trump Pulls Off Biggest Upset in U.S. History" (Goldmacher and Schreckinger 2016). NBC News: "2016 Election: Donald Trump Wins the White House in Upset" (Arkin and Siemaszko 2016). *Washington Post*: "Donald Trump Wins the Presidency in Stunning Upset over Hillary Clinton" (Tumulty, Rucker, and Gearan 2016). "Upset" immediately became one of the media's choice words to describe 2016 election results. Why? Because before election night, polls and predictions pointed toward a Hillary Clinton victory. Once the initial shock wore off, Clinton's loss to Donald Trump led many to ask, why have US voters yet to elect a female president? The 2020 election has sparked renewed interest in this question. Multiple women presidential hopefuls ran in the primary races, but Joe Biden won the nomination and the presidency. Now, the closest a woman is to the Oval Office in this election is as vice president, with Biden naming California senator Kamala Harris as his running mate. One hundred years after women's suffrage, Senator Harris is only the third woman to run for the vice presidency in the United States and the first to capture the office.

Political commentators often seek to answer this question by focusing on voter sexism. For example, in the case of Clinton there was much debate in the media over whether voter sexism was the reason her extensive political career was not enough to beat Trump, a candidate labeled as politically inexperienced and anti-establishment (e.g.,

Bevan 2017; Cohen 2016; Peck 2017; Robbins 2017). However, sexism is present in the electorates of all the democracies around the world that *have* elected women as executives. From Brazil to Bangladesh, Liberia to Iceland, electorates granted access to women to serve as political executives, and in some cases for multiple terms. Scholars studying women presidents and prime ministers from across the globe have long since noted that voters possess gender stereotypes that serve as a substantial hurdle to women becoming executives (e.g., Kittilson 1999; Kittilson and Fridkin 2008; Sczesny et al. 2004). This has led to studies, notably Jalalzai (2013), that focus on how women overcome voter, but also institutional and cultural, sexism by examining the paths women executives take to office and the institutional and political characteristics of countries with women presidents or prime ministers.

The existing literature has identified three paths to executive positions: family, political activism, and political career. Women with male family members (i.e., fathers, brothers, or husbands) who hold political office or serve as high-ranking government officials are more likely to become executives (Hodson 1997; Jalalzai 2004, 2008; Jalalzai and Rincker 2018; Richter 1991). Similarly, oftentimes women become executives after having served in the legislature or holding a cabinet position (Jalalzai 2004, 2013; Whicker and Isaacs 1999). Other women executives have less traditional political experience, having gained notoriety as political activists, typically by participating in national independence or democratization movements (Hodson 1997; Jalalzai 2013; Katzenstein 1978; Richter 1991; Thompson 2002/2003). Across each of these three paths, the women are relatively highly educated (Jalalzai 2013). In general, the family path is most prominent in Asia and Latin America, whereas the political career path is common in Africa and Europe (Jalalzai 2013; Jalalzai and Rincker 2018). Interestingly, the political activism path occurs in each of these regions, with prominent activist politicians hailing from Iceland, Brazil, Malawi, and South Korea.

A related area of research examines institutional and political factors that increase the likelihood that women will become executives. Institutional factors focus on how much power is afforded to the executive and whether a nation has a dual executive (i.e., a president and prime minister) and/or a multiparty system. Political factors relate to the number of women serving in the legislative and executive branches, the nation's political stability, and historical trends involving the advancement of women's political rights, including suffrage and previous women executives. With respect to institutional factors, findings suggest that women are more likely to serve as executives in countries with dual-executive and/or multiparty systems (e.g., Hodson 1997; Jalalzai 2008, 2013, 2016a). However, the amount of power afforded to the executive does not influence whether women become presidents or prime ministers (Jalalzai 2013, 2016a). In other words, women are not more likely to serve in weak, or ceremonial, executive positions than strong, or head of government, posts. Mixed findings have been reported for political factors in which countries with more female legislators and previous women executives are more likely to have female presidents and/or prime ministers (Jalalzai 2013, 2016a). Conversely, women are less likely to lead nuclear power states (Jalalzai 2013). Interestingly, higher numbers of women cabinet members, political instability, and longer periods of women suffrage do not appear to influence whether women become executives (Jalalzai 2013, 2016a).

Women Executives: Remaining Questions and Research Opportunities

These two bodies of research—on the paths that women take to executive positions and the factors that increase the likelihood a country will have a woman executive—have developed separately. As a result, the literature provides an incomplete picture of how women can overcome voter, institutional, and cultural sexism to become presidents and prime ministers. Specifically, it is unclear which political and institutional factors lead women to take each path to executive office, and how the path a woman uses to reach executive office is influenced by the path(s) taken by her female predecessor(s). Do certain political and institutional factors cater to a particular path, or do they impact all types of women executives equally? Does a woman executive's path to office help or hinder future women from becoming presidents or prime ministers via the same or a different path? More work is needed to unpack the paths—and to examine the political and institutional factors that lead women to take each path to executive office and how a woman's ability to become president or prime minister is impacted by the path(s) her female predecessor(s) used to claim executive power.

Scope and Coverage

Other ways to expand the existing scholarship relate to how scholars have approached studying women executives. As also recognized by

Jalalzai (2013), most studies on the subject focus on one or a few cases or regions (e.g., Genovese 1993b; Montecinos 2017a; Opfell 1993; Richter 1991), provide qualitative in-depth descriptions of how women executives rose to power and behaved once in office (e.g., Genovese 1993b; Liswood 2007; O'Brien 2018; Opfell 1993; Skard 2014), and/or briefly examine women executives comparatively (e.g., Genovese 1993b). Consequently, there is a vast amount of research covering relatively short periods of time on individual and country-specific reasons that women have been able to capture executive posts. This simultaneously means that there is a dearth of work on the broader political and institutional factors that can explain over time whether countries have women executives and the paths women take to become presidents and prime ministers (Jalalzai 2013).

In order to identify patterns among countries that have had women executives and the paths they take to office, Jalalzai's (2013) groundbreaking study, which begins in 1960 with the first female executive, Sri Lankan prime minister Sirimavo Bandaranaike, and ends in 2010, uses a comparative global approach and presents both descriptive and statistical analyses. The time period of 2000–2010 for the statistical analyses covers just 31 percent of all women executives who assumed office prior to 2020. Since 2010, thirty-six women have assumed an executive office, thus the literature would benefit from extending the time frame of these analyses of political and institutional factors that predict whether a country has a female president or prime minister, and from additional quantitative analyses on the paths women take to office.

Research Design

Additional opportunities for further research stem from specific aspects of existing descriptive and/or statistical analyses in the women executives literature. First, some researchers code women as taking multiple paths to executive office (e.g., Jalalzai 2013). Yet, many women who reach executive positions have had long political careers, whereas some come from prominent families or start as activists and gradually engage in political parties, rise up in the ranks, serve as legislators, and finally reach the presidency or premiership. Should they be considered as taking the family path, political activist path, or political career path to power? Consequently, more work is needed on how best to characterize a woman's path to office, why multiple paths are dominant in several regions of the world, and why certain paths are common in one region but not another with similar political and institutional characteristics.

Second, studies exclude interim executives or those who stay in office for relatively short periods of time (e.g., Jalalzai 2013). Are these interim positions distributed randomly across the world, or are women serving in an interim capacity more in some regions than others? Additional research should examine the dynamics surrounding *all* female executives.

Third, studies include factors that directly and indirectly relate to whether women attain executive positions (e.g., Jalalzai 2013, 2016a). For example, proportional representation, quotas, and leftist parties are discussed as increasing the number of women in government and, consequently, the pool of potential women executives. Despite the role of parties in nominating executive candidates and/or selecting presidents and prime ministers (e.g., Jalalzai 2013, 2016a; Lovenduski 1993; Norris and Lovenduski 2010), the women under consideration are those who have already benefited from the party's emphasis on increasing female representation in government. Taken collectively, the literature would benefit from focusing on factors that directly help women reach executive positions.

Lastly, studies tend to use multiple indicators to measure essentially the same phenomenon. For example, previous work uses length of female suffrage, number of women in parliament, and number of women in the cabinet to assess the impact of women's representation in government on whether a country has a female executive (e.g., Jalalzai 2013, 2016a). Future studies adopting a parsimonious approach would help advance the body of work on women executives by providing a more concise explanation of how women become presidents and prime ministers around the world.

Additional Insights on Women Who Claim Executive Seats

Enhancing Prior Work on Women Executives

In order to add to this body of work on how women overcome voter, institutional, and cultural sexism to become executives across the globe, and to gain insight into how to break the glass ceiling of the US presidency, we enhance prior work through a global, mixed-methods analysis of women executives from 1960 to 2020. Each effort to enhance existing work will now be discussed in turn.

First, we follow Jalalzai's (2013) lead by providing a comprehensive analysis of all female executives who have taken office since the installment of the first one, Prime Minister Sirimavo Bandaranaike, in 1960 in Sri Lanka. In doing so, our descriptive and quantitative analyses cover eight and fifteen more years, respectively, than those found in Jalalzai's (2013) book. Furthermore, this time period covers more than 130 women executives and adds over 50 cases to Jalalzai's (2013) data. The expanded coverage of our book allows for more patterns to be uncovered over time regarding the paths that women take to executive office and the institutional and political factors that tend to give rise to female presidents and prime ministers. Additionally, it is possible that the inclusion of additional cases stands to influence conventional wisdom stemming from the results of the extant literature.

Second, in our analyses we coded women presidents and prime ministers as taking one path to office. The authors and two undergraduate research assistants read Jalalzai's (2013) biographies of women presidents and prime ministers to discern which path propelled each woman to an executive seat. Women with a familial tie to political power (i.e., a parent, spouse, or sibling holding federal political office prior to her involvement in politics) are automatically coded as taking the family path to office (e.g., Prime Minister Chandrika Kumaratunga of Sri Lanka). Women who participated in democratization, women's rights, or any other social or political movement prior to holding political office are coded as following the political activist path to her executive post (e.g., President Ellen Johnson Sirleaf of Liberia). Lastly, women who began their careers by running for lower political offices and continued to work their way up the government ranks are coded as taking the political career path to the presidency or premiership (e.g., Prime Minister Julia Gillard of Australia). Any coding disagreement was resolved by consulting a variety of online biographical sources that tended to be used by Jalalzai (2013) (e.g., *Encyclopedia Britannica* and the BBC). These same biographical resources were also consulted to code and resolve coding disagreements over women who assumed office since 2010. In an effort to build on Jalalzai's (2013) data, biographies for these women can be found in the appendix.

Third, rather than excluding female interim executives from some or all analyses, we include them in both descriptive and quantitative analyses in order to fully determine the differences among them and their elected and appointed counterparts. To ensure that the inclusion of interim presidents and prime ministers does not bias the results, the descriptive analyses unpack the results based on whether women are elected, appointed, or interim executives and the quantitative analyses control for women who served on an interim basis.

Fourth, we focus on political and institutional factors that the literature has identified as directly impacting whether a woman becomes a president or prime minister. These are characteristics that can be used to describe the political and institutional environment of a country, including the extent of democratic institutionalism, level of human development, presence of a multiparty system, type of executive system, and female representation in government. These factors contrast with (1) direct factors found to have no impact on a woman's ability to become president or prime minister, such as the position's level of power (see Jalalzai 2013, 2016a); (2) indirect factors, for example, party quotas that help women get elected to legislative office; and (3) factors that are cultural or unique to each country and/or woman, like religious-based views of women, terrorist attacks, or the woman's educational attainment.

Lastly, the descriptive and statistical analyses in this book are parsimonious in an effort to avoid multiple measures of the same concept. In particular, we use one measure of female representation in government: the percentage of women in parliament.

Research Questions and Advancing the Literature on Women Executives

In addition to enhancing the existing work on women executives in the specific ways mentioned above, this book advances the literature by exploring the following research questions: (1) What are the dominant paths to power for women in different regions of the world? (2) What factors allow each path to result in an executive position? (3) What conditions increase the likelihood that a country will have a female executive? (4) Does the path that a woman takes to executive office help or hinder future female executives? (5) What circumstances determine how long a woman holds executive office? (6) Do certain paths influence how long women serve as presidents and prime ministers? While exploring each of these questions, special attention is also paid to changes that have occurred over time and differences among women presidents and prime ministers who were elected, were appointed, or served on an interim basis.

Thus, this book builds upon previous studies by explaining (1) why certain paths are prevalent in certain regions; (2) how institutional and political factors determine the paths that women take to executive positions; (3) the impact a woman's path to executive office has on future women seeking presidencies and premierships; and (4) whether a woman's path to an executive position and the country's institutional and political environment dictate how long she stays in office.

Overall, the book contributes to the existing literature by offering additional insight into how women overcome various types of sexism (voter, institutional, and cultural) to become executives across the globe, how long female presidents and prime ministers remain in power, and the durability of the US presidency's glass ceiling. In the rest of this chapter we provide a more thorough review of the existing literature, highlight opportunities for additional research, and preview the remaining chapters.

Literature Review

Prior to Jalalzai's (2013) groundbreaking work on women presidents and prime ministers spanning 1960–2010, the literature on women executives was largely composed of case studies covering a relatively short time frame and/or a certain country or geographical region (e.g., Bauer and Tremblay 2011; Clemens 2006; Genovese 1993a, 1993b; King 2002; Murray 2010; Opfell 1993; Thompson and Lennartz 2006). These studies provided a wealth of information about women presidents and prime ministers, most notably that (1) women come to power in various different political contexts; (2) women possess different leadership styles; (3) women must overcome political stereotypes; and (4) "women's issues" are emphasized differently in each executive's policy agenda.

Additional scholars have concluded that a number of institutional, political, and cultural factors must be taken into account to explain a woman's ascension to power: electoral system, executive structure, quotas, parties, female representation in government, and economic development (e.g., Inglehart and Norris 2003; McDonagh 2009; Reynolds 1999). In an effort to draw generalizable conclusions from the findings of prior research, Jalalzai (2013) identifies three primary paths that women take to become president or prime minister: (1) family, (2) political activism, and (3) political career. Before Jalalzai's work, the existing literature had not utilized a global approach to comprehensively study a woman's path to power or factors that increase the likelihood that a country will have a woman president or prime minster. The next two sections review these two dominant strands of literature on women presidents and prime ministers in more detail and highlight opportunities to build on the work of Jalalzai and others addressed in this book.

Paths to Executive Power

Family path. Many scholars observe that the family path is utilized by women most often in patriarchal and/or politically less stable countries, such as those in Latin America and Asia (Hodson 1997; Jalalzai 2004, 2008, 2013; Jalalzai and Rincker 2018; Richter 1991). By capitalizing on familial connections to power, usually through husbands or fathers (Jalalzai and Rincker 2018), this path explains how women can reach executive seats in societies that are among the least favorable to women's civil rights and liberties. For example, Indira Gandhi's father, Jawaharlal Nehru, was among the founding fathers of India and had served as the first prime minister of the newly independent nation. Isabel Perón of Argentina, Mireya Moscoso of Panama, and Corazon Aquino of the Philippines all followed in the footsteps of their husbands to office. In patriarchal societies, especially those where women have recently gained suffrage, women must capitalize on their family name in order to overcome pervasive gender stereotypes that men are better suited for executive positions and to attain power (Baturo and Gray 2018; Fox and Oxley 2003; Huddy and Terkildsen 1993; Jalalzai and Rincker 2018; Sczesny et al. 2004). Women often take the family path to executive positions in politically unstable countries because power can be "inherited" or regained following regime changes often due to the assassination or imprisonment of male executives (Hodson 1997; Jalalzai 2013). Frequent turnover also benefits women as more feminine qualities, such as collaboration and consensus building, are viewed as ideal traits for executives who must be able to promote unity in these politically turbulent countries (Jalalzai 2008; Katzenstein 1978; Saint-Germain 1993).

Building on these insights into the family path, this book offers additional dimensions to add to the women executives literature. First, it is unknown whether there is any variation in the use of the family path over time. Second, we do not know the impact of a woman becoming president or prime minister via the family path on more women rising to power similarly, so we explore these questions in our study. Third, we examine why the family path is dominant in some regions of the world that have experienced political instability and/or are relatively patriarchal—Latin America and Asia—but not in others that could also be characterized in one or both of these ways— the Caribbean, Africa, or the Middle East. Furthermore, since none of these regions are static, the book will also shed light on whether the family path's historical dominance in a region means that it will endure in the future. Fourth, although political instability and multiple leadership changes are prevalent in countries where women reach executive office via the family path, studies have not examined how long these female presidents and prime ministers stay in power. Thus we address longevity of term questions. Lastly, outside of women recently gaining suffrage (Baturo and Gray 2018), it is unclear which political and institutional factors give rise to women executives who take the family path. Consequently, we explore the possibility that various political and institutional factors can explain a woman's path to power via family ties. For example, it is likely that women take the family path to appointed executive posts in dual-executive systems or interim positions.

Political activism path. Women in patriarchal and/or politically less stable countries also tend to take the political activism path to executive positions. In addition to Asia and Latin America, this path is also common in Africa and Eastern Europe (Jalalzai 2013). For example, Ellen Johnson Sirleaf of Liberia, Janet Jagan of Guyana, Agatha Barbara of Malta, and Megawati Sukarnoputri of Indonesia all participated in democratization and/or women's rights movements before assuming power. There have also been examples of activist women in Nordic countries, such as prime minister of Iceland Jóhanna Sigurðardóttir. Participation in an activist movement can help women launch political careers and eventually reach executive posts for a few reasons. First, as the movement gains momentum, a critical juncture may be reached in which representation in formalized political institutions is needed in order to realize additional change (Jalalzai 2013; Montecinos 2017b). Second, and relatedly, female leaders of activist movements running for political office to advance their political agenda already have voters mobilized on their behalf (Jalalzai 2013). Third, women are best able to capitalize on their political activist background by drawing upon stereotypes that they are maternal caretakers and peacebuilders to justify their political involvement, especially during or shortly after democratization movements (e.g., Geske and Bourque 2001; Jalalzai 2013; Salo 2010). Consequently, times of democratic transition have been advantageous for the rise of women executives.

Although these findings shed substantial light on how women reach executive positions using the political activist path, we add more insight into this path. First, it is unknown why this path is seen in Africa, Asia, Latin America, and Eastern Europe but not other regions characterized as patriarchal and/or politically less stable, such as the Middle East. We look at different factors leading to the activist path and thereby shed light on the cases/regions that are more conducive to it. Second, as is the case with the family path, the existing literature has not explored whether certain institutional and political factors, such as multiparty systems, lead women to take the activist path to executive office; therefore, we consider this possibility. Third, we address how it has not been determined whether a woman taking the activist path to executive office encourages future female presidents and prime ministers to do so as well. Fourth, and also similarly to the family path, studies have not addressed how long activist women executives stay in office. We do, in light of the literature discussing the presence of political instability that would likely lead to relatively short terms in office. Lastly, the literature categorizes women as taking multiple paths to office in which there is considerable overlap between the family and political activist paths. The issue of overlapping paths deserves closer scrutiny. After a closer reading of individual biographies, we focus on the initial path that launched and steered their career to an executive post. Coming from a political dynasty provides immense name recognition to women politicians. Consequently, we placed women with familial ties to political office in the family path, in order to provide more insight into the factors leading women to the activist path. This also helps to better isolate the prevalence of the activist path in certain regions of the world, and any changes in its use over time or among elected, appointed, or interim executives.

Political career path. Other women, especially those in Africa and Europe, become involved in politics and reach executive posts in a much more traditional fashion than their political activist counterparts by pursuing political careers and holding political office, such as serving as a cabinet minister and/or an elected representative at the local, regional, and/or national level (e.g., Bond, Covington, and Fleisher 1985; Genovese 1993a; Jalalzai 2004, 2013). For example, Luísa Dias Diogo of Mozambique held various positions in the Department of Budget in the Ministry of Finance, including minister of finance, before being selected as prime minister. Another case in point is Tarja Halonen, who was a member of the Helsinki City Council, the Parliament of Finland, and the cabinet as the minister of social affairs and health, justice, and foreign affairs before being elected president of Finland. Similar to men, prior political experience serves as a set of qualifications that legitimizes a woman's election or appointment. However, becoming a president or prime minister often requires women to wait for an opening, highlight their outsider status, and/or hold "masculine" cabinet positions that handle foreign affairs or national defense (e.g., Jalalzai 2013; King 2002; Thompson and Lennartz 2006). For example, Margaret Thatcher was considered an outsider for being a woman and of a lower socioeconomic status than her male counterparts in the Conservative Party and Tory network (King 2002).

Taken collectively, current descriptive and statistical research on the political career path by Jalalzai (2013) confirms the conclusions of existing case study research (e.g., Escobar-Lemmon and Taylor-Robinson 2009). However, more research, such as this book, is needed in order to understand fully the reasons why women take the political career path to executive office, and especially whether future female executives follow in the footsteps of their female predecessors and use this path to also reach the presidency or premiership.

The Covid-19 crisis illustrated the superior performance of women leaders (Aldrich and Lotito 2020; Huang 2020). Almost all the high-performing leaders, including Angela Merkel (Germany), Jacinda Ardern (New Zealand), Sanna Marin (Finland), and Erna Solberg (Norway), come from the political career path. While this book does not focus on the performance of the women after they took power, it may provide valuable insights for future research on the relationship between women leaders' paths to power and their performance while in office. The relatively underexplored question of paths to power could impact performance while in power.

We address these issues by first recognizing that, as was the case with the political activist and family paths, prior studies grouped any woman with prior political experience into this category. It is possible that removing activist women and those with major name recognition (family path) will better explain why the political career path is utilized most often in Africa and Europe, and any changes in this path over time. Second, we provide a clearer portrait of whether legislative or cabinet positions are more common before becoming president or prime minister. Closer scrutiny of individual biographies allows us to better chart the career paths of these women leaders. Our findings indicate cabinet positions are the more viable path for women, while most of the literature focuses on the legislative branch as a major pool for women leaders. Third, although it appears that the political career path is dominant in regions where the family and political activist paths are not (i.e., Latin American and Asia), we consider the possibility that certain institutional and political factors and the executive position itself influence whether a woman takes this path to power. For example, the political career path may be used most often in meritocratic and/or politically stable countries with dual executives in which qualified women in high-ranking cabinet positions have a better chance of being appointed prime minister than overcoming gender stereotypes to be elected president. Fourth, we acknowledge how the combination of qualified, politically experienced women in politically stable environments suggests that the political career path results in presidents and prime ministers who serve full terms in office and are well positioned for reelection or reappointment. Yet, current studies have not examined this possibility, so we do so by exploring how the political career path and various political and institutional factors influence a woman's length of time in executive office.

Factors That Facilitate a Woman's Rise to Executive Power

Electoral systems. Electoral systems have long been identified as crucial in promoting female representation in legislative government (e.g., Duverger 1955). In particular, multimember and proportional representation systems lead to more female legislators than single-member majoritarian districts (Darcy, Welch, and Clark 1994; Lovenduski and Norris 1993; Matland 1998a; Paxton 1997; Rule 1985; Rule and Zimmerman 1994; Salmond 2006; Yoon 2010).

The benefits of multimember districts depend on the number of seats available. Women are more likely to be elected from districts where several seats are available because there are more opportunities and parties are more conscious about putting male and female candidates on the ballot (Matland 1993; Rule 1985; Taagepera 1994). How much proportional representation increases the number of women elected to parliament depends on the extent to which women are organizing and demanding representation, voter views of party elites, and whether parties utilize closed or open lists (Matland 1998b; Matland and Taylor 1997; Rule and Zimmerman 1994; Salmond 2006; Valdini 2012, 2013). Women benefit from closed lists when voters have traditional views of party elites, whereas women are more likely to reach parliament via open lists when electorates have progressive views of party elites (Matland 1998b; Rule and Zimmerman 1994; Valdini 2012). Although the extent to which multimember and proportional representation systems increase the number of women in the legislature depends, respectively, on the number of seats available and closed versus open lists, both systems produce more politically experienced female politicians, which increases the likelihood that women will serve as president or prime minister (Jalalzai 2013; Reynolds 1999). Consequently, multimember and proportional representation systems indirectly impact whether women can attain executive power via female representation in parliament.

Executive structures. Women are best able to ascend to power as prime ministers, especially those who wield relatively less power, in parliamentary and semi-presidential systems for two reasons (e.g., Hodson 1997; Jalalzai 2008, 2013, 2016a). First, the appointment system is conducive to women taking the political career path to office in which they work their way up in the party and/or government (Hodson 1997; Whicker and Isaacs 1999). Second, presidents, who enjoy a substantial amount of independence and are only curtailed by the threat of impeachment and/or not being reelected, are often thought of in general, and by voters, in "masculine" terms. Presidents must be strong, quick decisionmakers who garner the respect necessary to be commander in chief. Female politicians are perceived to be more collaborative and consensual, which are ideal qualities for a prime minister who must facilitate cooperation within parliament to ensure the government runs smoothly while simultaneously avoiding being removed from office via a vote of no confidence or an unsuccessful party election (Duerst-Lahti 1997).

Quotas. Quotas do not directly impact a woman being elected or appointed president or prime minister. However, they influence the ability of women to reach executive office, especially those taking the political career path. Quotas seek to increase female representation in a nation's legislature or executive branch.

A few different methods may be employed at the legislative level: reserved seats, legislative quotas, or party quotas (see Krook 2009). Reserved seats provide women with a certain number or percentage of spots in the national legislature. Legislative quotas require political parties to nominate a specific percentage of female candidates. Party quota systems are adopted by parties themselves to ensure that a particular number or percentage of its candidates are women (Hughes, Paxton, and Krook 2017). Findings suggest that quotas are best able to create gender parity within a nation's legislature in proportional representation systems where multiple seats are available per district and parties use closed lists (Htun and Jones 2002). Quotas are also most successful in countries dominated by leftist parties, which are more supportive of advancing gender equality (Davidson-Schmich 2006; Kittilson 1999). Quotas tend to be ineffective for two reasons: (1) significant and immediate consequences are not attached to failing to meet the mandate, and (2) they are difficult to implement in light of current political institutions and candidate selection practices (Jones 1998; Krook 2009; Schmidt and Saunders 2004; Schwindt-Bayer 2009).

Executive quotas are most commonly found in Latin America but differ vastly from one another in terms of scope and design (Htun and Piscopo 2014; Paxton, Hughes, and Barnes 2020). Executive quotas can operate at the federal level (e.g., Costa Rica), municipal level (e.g., Honduras), or both (e.g., Ecuador) and typically require that women hold 30–50 percent of the positions (Htun and Piscopo 2014; Paxton, Hughes, and Barnes 2020). At the federal level, Costa Rica has gone so far as to require that at least one of the two vice presidential candidates be female although the position is largely ceremonial (Htun and Piscopo 2014). Since many executive quotas have only recently been instituted, they have been relatively understudied (Htun and Piscopo 2014). However, initial findings suggest that female influence is increasing across Latin America as a result, especially in

Costa Rica with the mandated selection of at least one female vice presidential candidate (Franceschet and Piscopo 2013; Htun and Piscopo 2014; Paxton, Hughes, and Barnes 2020; Pignataro and Taylor-Robinson 2019; Piscopo 2015). Similar to legislative quotas, executive quotas can also be ineffective due to loopholes and issues with oversight and enforcement (Htun and Piscopo 2014).

Parties. Parties have an indirect influence on a woman's ability to become a president or prime minister despite being tasked with officially nominating candidates. In order to be considered for an executive position, a woman must have already benefited from factors relating to a party's structure and ideology that help women advance their political careers at all levels. Findings indicate that more women candidates are nominated for all political offices if parties have more control over their local affiliates, more members to choose from, and candidate selection criteria that emphasize qualifications and electability instead of ethnic or regional ties and party-level experience, which favor men (Bjarnegård and Zetterberg 2019; Lovenduski 1993). Yet, leftist parties tend to nominate more women as gender equality is an important party platform (Davidson-Schmich 2006; Kittilson 1999).

In addition to a party's internal structure, a country's party system can also influence whether a woman can rise to executive power. Multiparty parliamentary systems are routinely found to increase the likelihood that a country has had a female executive (Jalalzai 2013, 2016a). This is often because a coalition government is in place. Coalition governments require the prime minister to bring the parties together by building consensus, which is a task considered best suited for females because they are more collaborative than their independent male counterparts (Jalalzai 2013).

Female representation in government. It is conventionally assumed that as female representation in government increases, so too do the odds that a country will have a female executive (e.g., Jalalzai 2013, 2016a; Reynolds 1999). Additionally, the longer that women have had the right to vote and the more women who serve in the legislature and the cabinet, the more likely it should be that women will eventually break the executive glass ceiling (e.g., Reynolds 1999). Jalalzai's (2013, 2016a) statistical results are mixed in that neither the number of female ministers nor the length of time that women have had suffrage increase the likelihood that a country will have a female executive. However, longer periods of female suffrage are associated with countries that have had multiple female executives (Jalalzai 2016a). Jalalzai (2013, 2016a) does find that women are more likely to become presidents and prime ministers in countries with high numbers of female legislators and previous women rulers.

Economic, human, and political development. A country's level of economic development is typically associated with the global power of the executive. Economically developed countries, and their executives, tend to have more influence over worldwide economic issues and foreign affairs (Jalalzai 2013). Since elites and voters stereotypically consider foreign affairs, economics, and defense "masculine" issue areas that require male leadership (e.g., Duerst-Lahti 2006; Huddy and Terkildsen 1993), this could partially explain why many female executives hail from less economically developed, less globally powerful countries, such as Jamaica and Panama. However, as Jalalzai (2013) points out, relatively little research has been conducted on the relationship between economic development and whether women are able to break the executive glass ceiling. Jalalzai's (2013) results suggest that a country's level of economic development does not impact whether it has a female president or prime minister. However, women are less likely to head countries with nuclear weapons, thus highlighting the gender stereotypes that make it difficult for females to secure executive positions with significant amounts of power over "masculine" policy areas (Jalalzai 2013).

Although societal gender parity does not always equate to political equality between men and women, it is often assumed that countries with higher levels of human development have more female representation in government and a higher likelihood of having a woman executive (e.g., Jalalzai 2013, 2016a). Jalalzai (2013, 2016a) does not find support for this assumption when it comes to whether countries have a female president or prime minister. However, countries with higher levels of gender parity are more likely to have multiple female executives (Jalalzai 2016a). Since women rise to power in a variety of political contexts, there are also questions about the relationship between a country's political development (i.e., level of democracy) and stability and whether it has a female executive. Again, Jalalzai (2013, 2016a) does not find that political development or stability influences whether a country has a woman president or prime minister. However, again, Jalalzai (2016a) finds that more democratic and unstable countries are more likely to have multiple women executives.

Unanswered questions. In examining the impact that development (economic, human, and political), political institutions, and female representation in government have on whether a country has a female executive, there are three areas ripe for additional research that we undertake in this book. First, we address how more work is needed on how a woman's path to executive office is dictated by factors that directly impact her rise to power—executive structure, multiparty system, female representation in government, and development—in contrast to those that are indirect and influence female representation in government—electoral systems, quotas, and parties. It is apparent how political institutions, such as the structure of the executive, are conducive to women taking the political career path to the presidency or premiership. However, it is unknown how these other direct factors impact women taking the family or political activist paths to executive office. For instance, women with family ties may have an advantage in a presidential system where name recognition helps offset voter stereotypes. When it comes to female representation in government and economic, human, and political development, it is less clear whether these factors facilitate women taking the political career path or the family and political activist paths. For example, developed countries with substantial female representation in government may be more conducive to women taking the political career path to reach executive office because they do not have to rely on dynastic political family ties or fight an uphill battle as political activists.

The second relatively underexplored issue we examine in this book relates to the relationship between each path to power and the tenure of women executives. Overall, it is unknown whether the path a woman takes to office influences how long she stays in power. For example, it is likely that women who take the family and political career paths to executive office serve for shorter periods of time than their counterparts who took the political career path because these paths are common in politically less stable countries; however, it is also possible that women who take the family path have lengthy tenures in office because their household name lessens the likelihood of efforts to overthrow the government. Similarly, activism can work both ways: it could result in shorter terms in office due to the politically tumultuous circumstances in the country, or it could result in extended time in office for the activist woman leader who manages to gain electoral support despite the tense political climate.

Finally, we expand upon findings, such as Jalalzai's (2013, 2016a), that it is easier for women to rise to executive power in countries that have had a female president or prime minister by examining how the path a woman executive takes to office impacts her successor(s). It is unknown whether women are constrained by the path of their predecessor(s). In other words, for any given path, it is unclear whether future women executives have to take the same path as their predecessor(s). This may be considered relatively unproblematic if women are taking the political career path to executive office. However, it is possible that women are impeded from taking the political career path to power in countries that have only had female presidents and prime ministers who took the family or political activist paths to executive office.

Taken collectively, we provide a better understanding of how development, political institutions, and female representation in government impact whether a country has a female executive and the path she takes to executive office. In doing so, we also offer more insight into differences observed in the extant literature based on time, type of executive (i.e., elected, appointed, and interim), and region. The next section provides an overview of the book's chapters.

Overview of the Book

The next three chapters lay out the three different paths to executive power: family, political activist, and political career. Throughout each chapter, descriptive analyses are conducted over the time period of 1960 to 2020 with special attention paid to political and institutional factors that lead women to take each path to executive office and changes in the path's use over time, across each region, and among elected, appointed, and interim executives. Chapter 2 explores the family path and discusses cases that highlight the descriptive results, such as Prime Minister Benazir Bhutto of Pakistan, President Janet Jagan of Guyana, and Prime Minister Khaleda Zia of Bangladesh. Key findings of this chapter relate to the path's historical prevalence and regional concentration. Chapter 3 focuses on the political activist path. Case studies are presented to underscore the findings regarding the different sources of mobilization and activism that occur under various political and institutional contexts. Some of the cases that are highlighted include President Dilma Rousseff of Brazil, President Ellen Johnson Sirleaf of Liberia, and President Vigdís Finnbogadóttir of Iceland. Chapter 4 examines the most conventional and frequently used path to power: the political career path. Results show commonalities among women taking this path to executive power regarding their personal backgrounds (e.g., business, law, or government) and the offices they held prior to claiming executive office, in particular serving in parliament or the cabinet. Consequently, Chapter 4 also discusses the hierarchies between various cabinet positions (e.g., the Ministries of the Economy or Defense versus the Ministries of Culture or Women's Affairs). Cases highlighting these results include Prime Minister Tansu Çiller of Turkey, Prime Ministers Helle Thorning-Schmidt and Mette Frederiksen of Denmark, and Prime Minister Kamla Persad-Bissessar of Trinidad and Tobago.

The next three chapters statistically analyze women executives in terms of their paths to power, prevalence in countries around the world, and length of time in office. Chapters 5 and 6 statistically test whether the patterns identified in Chapters 2, 3, and 4 and the women executives literature systematically explain (1) the path women take to executive office, and (2) whether a country has a female president or prime minister, especially one taking each path to the presidency or premiership. Chapter 6 also addresses how a woman's path to office impacts her predecessors. Throughout both chapters, the time period under analysis is 1990–2015 due to data availability.

Chapter 7 focuses on how long a woman executive stays in office. The chapter begins with a statistical analysis exploring the impact that a woman's path to power and various political and institutional factors have on a woman's length of time in office. In order to uncover additional insight into a woman executive's tenure, the second half of the chapter presents descriptive analyses with case examples that focus on factors often included in research on women presidents and prime ministers: time, region, path to office, and type of executive (i.e., elected, appointed, and interim).

Chapter 8 is premised upon the notion that in order to fully understand how women reach executive office, it is important to examine women who were unable to obtain these positions. Consequently, the chapter examines the failed presidential candidacies of two globally renowned politicians: Hillary Clinton of the United States in 2008 and 2016 and Marine Le Pen of France in 2012 and 2017. Despite the global scope of this book, these two women from globally powerful Western nations were chosen for two reasons. First, Clinton and Le Pen are the most prominent women to fail multiple times to reach an executive post near the end of the time period covered by this book: 1960–2020. Second, each woman's failed campaigns received substantial media coverage in global media outlets, and political commentators and scholars alike sought to explain their losses. Chapter 8 adds to this conversation by using the results of the previous chapters and advancing the argument that the family path is not a viable way to reach executive posts in democratic or meritocratic countries. This is supported by our findings that illustrate a strong congruence between certain paths and political and institutional characteristics. In particular, while some political settings repeatedly have women executives from the family path, others never have. In other words, hailing from a prominent political family appears to have served as a liability for these two women as Clinton attempted to follow in the footsteps of her husband, former president Bill Clinton and Le Pen sought the same office her father, Jean-Marie Le Pen, was unable to capture throughout his extensive career as the founder and president of Front National and a member of the European Parliament.

Chapter 9 concludes the book by beginning with a summary of the findings from the qualitative and quantitative chapters (Chapters 2–7). The conclusions from Chapter 8's case studies on Hillary Clinton and Marine Le Pen are discussed along with how our findings can be used to explain the failed candidacies of other women across the globe. The chapter ends with a discussion of opportunities for future research. The suggestions provided are based on the book's findings and the applicability of the conclusions to other executive positions, such as mayors or governors.

2

The Family Path

The candidacy of Senator Hillary Clinton in the US presidential races in 2008 and 2016 and her losses in each of those attempts to a male candidate generate interesting puzzles for the gender and politics literature (Carroll and Fox 2018; Jalalzai and Krook 2010; McThomas and Tesler 2016). Clinton was one of the most recognized political figures in the United States and around the world. Yet, in both attempts, this did not deliver her the victory. The names of Michelle Obama and Ivanka Trump are mentioned as viable candidates in the future, both of whom can take advantage of their family legacy to break the formidable glass ceiling in the United States. This leads to a variety of questions: What is the role of family in women's political success? Can women from dynastic political families ascend to executive power more or less easily? Is the glass ceiling easier to break for women with a recognizable last name? Can the family path carry women to an executive seat around the world? If the family path is salient for women globally, why did it not work for Hillary Clinton? Rather than being a political asset, can family name be a liability for women in certain contexts?

Research on the paths women take to executive positions has identified the family path as one of the most common ways for women to reach the presidency or premiership (Adler 1996; Jalalzai 2013, 2016a; Jalalzai and Krook 2010; Thompson, 2002/2003). In fact, the very first woman who served three times as the prime minister of Sri Lanka starting in the 1960s, Sirimavo Bandaranaike, was the wife of Sri Lankan prime minister Solomon Bandaranaike. He was serving his term that started in 1956 when he was assassinated by a Buddhist monk in 1959, thus effectively starting Sirimavo Bandaranaike's political career (Jalalzai 2013, 197). Commonly referred to as the "widow's effect" or "widow's succession" in the literature, numerous women presidents and prime ministers around the world reached executive office by succeeding their assassinated husbands (Folke, Rickne, and Smith 2020).

As Figure 2.1 illustrates, in the first two decades after Bandaranaike's success, ten countries placed women in their executive offices across the globe. Of these, three of them came from established political families: Sirimavo Bandaranaike of Sri Lanka, Indira Gandhi of India, and Isabel Perón of Argentina. Bandaranaike and Gandhi ended up serving multiple terms. Being wives and daughters

Figure 2.1 Earliest Women Executives and Their Paths to Power, 1960–1988

1960	1966	1969	1970	1971	1974
Sri Lanka	India	Israel	Sri Lanka	India	Argentina
Bandaranaike	Gandhi	Meir	Bandaranaike (2)	Gandhi (2)	Perón
FAMILY	FAMILY	Activist	FAMILY	FAMILY	FAMILY

1975		1979			1980		
CAR	UK	Portugal	Bolivia	India	Dominica	Iceland
Domitien	Thatcher	Pintasilgo	Gueiler Tejada	Gandhi (3)	Charles	Finnbogadóttir
Career	Career	Career	Career	FAMILY	Career	Activist

1981	1982	1984		1986	1988
Norway	Malta	Yugoslavia	Guinea-Bissau	Philippines	Norway	Pakistan
Brundtland	Barbara	Planinc	Pereira	Aquino	Brundtland (2)	Bhutto
Career	Activist	Career	Activist	FAMILY	Career	FAMILY

Source: Jalalzai (2013).

of prominent politicians certainly played a decisive role in the political careers of all three of them. Between 1981 and 1988, seven more women gained access to executive office (Figure 2.1). Of these, two of them took the family path: Corazon Aquino of the Philippines and Benazir Bhutto of Pakistan. An empirical study of women and men in the legislative branch in twelve democratic nations from 1945 to 2016 illustrates that women benefit more from dynastic family ties than their male counterparts. This is largely because of the "imperfect information" regarding the quality of the candidates (Folke, Rickne, and Smith 2020). Folke, Rickne, and Smith (2020, 6) argue that "dynastic ties are more helpful for women than men because they help women overcome an informational disadvantage in the evaluation of their competence on the part of parties and voters."

Our data on all women executives indicate that the family path is the second most common path to political office. Starting in the 1960s, it was the earliest path for women to power, and it is still relevant as the pro-democracy protests in Belarus in 2020 coalesce around the candidacy of opposition leader Svetlana Tikhanovskaya. Calling herself an "ordinary person, a housewife," Tikhanovskaya's political life began instantly, when her husband, Sergei Tikhanovsky, was jailed right before the elections.[1]

Consequently, this path requires greater scrutiny. While Jalalzai (2013, 94–114) offers one of the most comprehensive analyses of the paths to power, she combines the family path with the political activist path, which makes it harder to pinpoint the conditions that give rise to the family path. Other studies focus only on a single region, such as Asia (Thompson 2002/2003) or Latin America (Chaney 2014 [1979]; Htun 2016; Schwindt-Bayer 2011). However, the dynastic family path is not exclusive to certain regions. Early work on widowed women in the US Congress (Kincaid 1978) and more recent work on the legislative branches of democratic nations (Folke, Rickne, and Smith 2020) illustrate a distinct familial dynastic bias that favors women, especially when the overall political system has fewer women politicians. Consequently, this path is not confined to certain regions but is more widely spread across the world, including Europe.

A more comprehensive analysis of the family path as a separate category from the political career and political activism paths could also offer some insights about the lackluster performance of Hillary Clinton in the 2008 and 2016 US presidential races (as explored at length in Chapter 8). Most research on Hillary Clinton tends to focus on US politics and the Clinton case alone (Carroll and Fox 2018; McThomas and Tesler 2016). However, placing the United States and Hillary Clinton in a larger, global context can shed more light on her two failed attempts to become the first female US president. Looking at a single case may not be helpful to easily identify larger structural dynamics. Thus, there is a need to examine a large number of cases, to look for similarities and differences.

History of the Family Path

Women have been progressively pushing for greater political rights for more than a century, but executive office seems harder to access in comparison to other branches of government. In the United States, the first women who were able to crack the glass ceiling of executive office did so at the state level as governors because of the family path to power; women got elected as governors of Wyoming (1925), Texas (1925), and Alabama (1967).[2] In all three cases, the women governors succeeded their husbands into office. In Wyoming, the governor died in office, and the Democratic Party rallied behind his wife, Nellie Tayloe Ross, to "continue her husband's work." In Texas, Miriam Ferguson was a substitute for her husband, who was convicted of corruption and impeached. Forty years after the first two women governors, Lurleen Burns Wallace also served as a stand-in for her husband because he could not run for office in Alabama due to term limits (Dolan et al. 2016, 233–234)

Historically, women have been able to gain access to political power in the executive branch, first and foremost, through the family path. Eventually, women were able to reach executive posts by participating in political activist movements or pursuing political careers in the bureaucracy or elected branches of government. The signs of increasing diversity in the paths to executive power and the gradual dominance of the political career path can be observed in Figure 2.1. However, regardless of the particular approach used to code a woman's path to power (i.e., ours or that of Jalalzai [2013]), the family path is historically the earliest and to this day remains the second most frequently observed path to power for women executives.

As Figure 2.2 illustrates, the family path to power is not randomly distributed across the world. This path is most prevalent in Asia and

Figure 2.2 Global Distribution of the Family Path to Executive Power, 1960–2020

Key: ■ Family Path

Latin America; however, there are some interesting outliers, such as Moldova and Switzerland. Table 2.1 lists all the women executives who reached power through the family path. This table includes the year these executives came to power and how long they served. These details provide important insights into the women presidents and prime ministers who came to power through the family path. Some of the patterns derived from the data in Table 2.1, such as the length of time in office, were not uncovered by the quantitative analyses (see Chapters 5–7). However, a closer, qualitative breakdown of the data can reveal noteworthy trends, as will be seen in the case of family path executives and their endurance in office in Chapter 7.

Finally, data on the country's level of political development and gender equity are included for each of these cases. In particular, Freedom House ratings of democracy are used, which look at political rights and civil liberties. This index classifies countries into one of three categories: free, partly free, or not free. We opted to use the most recent data for the democratic status, instead of the country score at the time of the woman leader's ascendance to power. This helps us look at all the cases at the same point in time, instead of having the scores scattered across decades. We hope the most recent democracy score also provides a better way to observe relative democratic progress. In order to measure gender equity, Table 2.1 includes the 2020 rankings of each of the countries in the Global Gender Gap Report developed by the World Economic Forum. The Gender Gap Report is a composite of economic opportunities, educational attainment, health scores, and political empowerment of women in 153 countries. As such, it also provides some insights into a country's level of socioeconomic development.

Some of the findings in this chapter, such as the inverse relationship between levels of development and the use of the family path, are also verified in the corresponding quantitative chapter (see Chapter 5). The quantitative findings show a statistically significant relationship between low levels of development and frequency of the family path. While low levels of development increase the chances of women ascending to political power through the family path, in countries with very high levels of development, the family path becomes the least likely route to office. In many ways, these results concur with those of Folke, Rickne, and Smith (2020). They argue that in societies where women are rarely seen in the political marketplace, both parties and voters are highly risk averse and thus avoid female candidates. Under these circumstances, voters use the strong

Table 2.1 Family-Path Women Executives, 1960–2020

Name	Country	First Year in Office	Elected Appointed Interum	Total Time in Office	Terms Served	Family Connection	Democratic Status (Freedom House 2019)	Gender Equality Status (2020 Ranking)
PM Sirimavo Bandaranaike	Sri Lanka	1960	Appointed	17 years, 5 months	3	Wife	Partly free	102
PM Chandrika Kumaratunga	Sri Lanka	1994	Appointed PM; elected PRES	15 years, 3 months	2	Daughter	Partly free	102
PM Indira Gandhi	India	1966	Elected	15 years, 10 months	3	Daughter	Free	112
PRES Corazon Aquino	Philippines	1986	Elected	6 years, 4 months	1	Wife	Partly free	16
PRES Gloria Macapagal-Arroyo	Philippines	2001	Elected	9 years, 5 months	2	Daughter	Partly free	16
PM Benazir Bhutto	Pakistan	1988	Elected	4 years, 9 months	2	Daughter	Partly free	151
PM Khaleda Zia	Bangladesh	1991	Elected	10 years	2	Wife	Partly free	50
PM Sheikh Hasina	Bangladesh	1996	Elected	~15 years	3	Daughter	Partly free	50
PRES Megawati Sukarnoputri	Indonesia	2001	Elected	3 years, 3 months	1	Daughter	Partly free	85
PM Yingluck Shinawatra	Thailand	2011	Elected	2 years, 9 months	1	Sister	Not free	75
PRES Park Geun-hye	South Korea	2013	Elected	4 years	1	Daughter	Free	108

continues

Table 2.1 Continued

Name	Country	First Year in Office	Elected Appointed Interum	Total Time in Office	Terms Served	Family Connection	Democratic Status (Freedom House 2019)	Gender Equality Status (2020 Ranking)
PRES Eveline Widmer-Schlumpf	Switzerland	2012	Elected	2 years	2	Daughter	Free	18
PM Natalia Gherman	Moldova	2015	Interim	38 days	1	Daughter	Partly free	23
PRES Isabel Perón	Argentina	1974	Appointed	1 year, 8 months	1	Wife	Free	30
PRES Cristina Fernández	Argentina	2007	Elected	8 years	2	Wife	Free	30
PM Janet Jagan	Guyana	1997	Appointed PM; elected PRES	2 years, 5 months	2	Wife	Free	NA
PRES Mireya Moscoso	Panama	1999	Elected	5 years	1	Wife	Free	46

Sources: For biographies of women executives, see Jalalzai's (2013) appendix for the period 1960–2010. For the women executives between 2011 and 2020, see the appendix of executive biographies at the end of this volume. For democratic status, see Freedom in the World 2019 Map, https://freedomhouse.org/explore-the-map?type=mit&year=2020. For gender equality status, see the Global Gender Gap Report from the World Economic Forum, https://reports.weforum.org/global-gender-gap-report-2020/the-global-gender-gap-index-2020/results-and-analysis/.

reputation and name recognition of a dynastic family as a shortcut to judge the qualifications of female candidates. However, as more women are recruited into the political system, or as gender quotas are introduced, the importance of a dynastic family tie diminishes (Folke, Rickne, and Smith 2020, 30).

The Power of Dynasty

> *Benazir Bhutto, 40, obtained her political clout the old-fashioned way: she inherited it. In South Asia, wealthy families still play a conspicuous role in national politics. The Bhuttos in Pakistan, the Nehru-Gandhi clan in India, the Zias in Bangladesh and the Bandaranaikes in Sri Lanka are tenacious dynasties that make the Kennedys look like office temps. Despite the male domination of their respective societies, each family has produced a female prime minister.*
> —Russell Watson, *Newsweek*

Looking at the list of women who came to power using family ties, Asia as a whole dominates the picture. According to Jalalzai (2017, 71), nearly 80 percent of all women executives in Asia have some ties to prominent political families. According to Thompson (2002/2003), women in this region are able to reach executive positions despite having strong traditions of patriarchy and direct opposition to their candidacy. In Bangladesh, Indonesia, and Pakistan, conservative Muslim leaders have attempted to block the rise of women executives, arguing that female leadership violates Islamic principles (Thompson 2002/2003). Yet, despite this hostility from some clergy, almost all majority-Muslim nations in Asia and South Asia have had a woman head of state.

Family ties provide important advantages for women candidates, particularly in societies with weak democratic institutions and strong clientelistic networks. "Dynastic succession is a 'natural' outgrowth of such family-based political networks" (Thompson 2002/2003, 538). It provides name recognition and public trust before women even enter the political arena or campaign. These women are socialized in politically astute families, and it is an established fact that many of them, such as Indira Gandhi and Benazir Bhutto, served as disciples and confidantes of their fathers, who were larger than life figures as the founders of their respective nations. Corazon Aquino of the Philippines "came from a political dynasty whose power base was vast tracts of land. . . . Patron-client relations between landlords and their tenant farmers have prolonged political power over generations, creating an elite class that until present day continues to dominate Philippine politics" (Mendoza and Lao 2017, 206).

In one of the earliest empirical studies of women politicians in Chile and Peru, Chaney (2014 [1979], 115–117) states that about 51 percent of survey respondents said their fathers or mothers have been the main influence in their political socialization, while another 14 percent said their husbands played a critical role. Together, nearly 65 percent of women politicians in these two Latin American countries expressed that their families have been the critical factor that launched them into politics. The role of family is so strong in the political socialization of these early women politicians that some even call politics a "hereditary vocation" (Chaney 2014 [1979], 115–117).

We avoid employing culture or region as a catch-all explanation. Neither culture nor region alone can explain the use of the family path without explicitly highlighting underlying factors and causal mechanisms that are likely present elsewhere. In fact, more often than not, catch-all explanations lead to tautologies. For example, consider statements like, "The Asian region or culture leads women executives to take the family path," or vice-versa, "The family path is dominant in Asian societies." If the family path is specific to Asia, why is this path also seen in places like Argentina, Moldova, and Switzerland? Or attempted in the United States and Belarus? Moreover, this approach also disregards the vast cultural diversity of Asia. From India to Indonesia, the Philippines to South Korea, women executives are observed in majority Hindu, Muslim, Catholic, and Buddhist societies with very different levels of socioeconomic development. Lumping them all together and calling the family path the predominantly Asian path does not offer tangible answers to why women take the family path to office. Consequently, the question still remains: *Why* is the family path used in some regions but not others?

Another important question with the family path involves its evolution over time. Scholars highlight the recent erosion of the family path in certain regions, particularly across Latin America (Jalalzai 2013; Morgan and Buice 2013). While Latin America has had its fair share of women executives from the family path, it is increasingly electing female executives with distinguished political careers, such as Laura Chinchilla of Costa Rica and Michelle

Bachelet of Chile. Montecinos (2017b) argues that Bachelet's presidency was groundbreaking for Chile. The openly feminist executive with a gender agenda was the embodiment of Chile's transition from authoritarianism, militarism, and patriarchal anachronisms toward a democratic Chile that respected women's rights (Montecinos 2017b, 141–142). In the cases of President Dilma Rousseff in Brazil and President Violeta Chamorro in Nicaragua,[3] women with strong activist backgrounds also got elected as presidents. Empirical studies on Latin America show that attitudes of male voters in the region are not permanent. Instead, they are contingent on elite cues and may change easily when it comes to the issue of female leadership. Furthermore, severe political crisis and the discrediting of establishment politicians (who are mostly male) also make the public, especially male voters, more likely to support female candidates across Latin America (Morgan and Buice 2013). On the other hand, Baturo and Gray (2018) highlight the importance of women's suffrage. They conclude that if women have had voting rights for an extensive period of time and societies have normalized the presence of women in politics, then the family dynasty path is much less likely. The diversity of cases within the family path and its evolution over time, particularly across Latin America, calls for a closer scrutiny of this path.

Prevalence of Violence

The subgroup of women executives who reach political power through the family path seem to have certain shared life experiences: the prevalence of political violence and assassinations in their families. In fact, in some cases, the trend seems to continue from generation to generation. The first woman prime minister of Sri Lanka in 1960, Sirimavo Bandaranaike, not only lost her husband to assassins, but her daughter, Chandrika Kumaratunga, who came to power in 1994, also lost her husband due to a political assassination. This family misfortune can also be observed in multiple cases from Asia. Indira Gandhi was assassinated by Sikh extremists in 1984, and her son, Rajiv Gandhi, would suffer the same fate after he came to power (Thompson 2002/2003, 539). Gandhi's other son, Rajiv's brother, had managed to survive an assassination attempt in 1977 while he was on the political campaign trail but died in a plane crash in 1980.

In all these cases, assassinations and violent deaths accompanied these dynastic families.

Pakistan also had its fair share of political violence. Its only woman executive to date, Benazir Bhutto, took the mantle of political leadership from her father, Zulfikar Ali Bhutto, after he was executed by the military regime of General Zia-ul-Haq. Before being toppled by a military coup, Zulfikar Ali Bhutto was serving as the prime minister of Pakistan. Unfortunately, the family could not escape this grim legacy. Benazir Bhutto was assassinated on the campaign trail in 2007 when a suicide bomb killed her and dozens of other people escorting her. Benazir Bhutto had survived another suicide bombing attempt in October of the same year, when two bombs hit her convoy, killing at least 130 people (BBC 2007).

Examining the biographies of the women executives on the family path shows that political violence is a strikingly common trait in many cases. The number of military coups, house arrests, executions, suicide bombs, and assassinations is astonishingly high. Across Asia, almost all women executives shared a tragic past. In Thailand, Yingluck Shinawatra gained party leadership and subsequently got elected to serve as the prime minister only after her brother was deposed by a military coup. Unfortunately, she also shared the same fate as her brother and was deposed by the military in 2014 (BBC 2017). Both Bangladeshi women prime ministers have had assassinations in their families. Khaleda Zia's husband and Sheikh Hasina's father were both assassination victims. In the Philippines, Corazon Aquino started mobilizing against the political regime when demonstrations began during the funeral procession of her assassinated husband, Benigno Aquino. In Indonesia, President Megawati Sukarnoputri's father was deposed and imprisoned. In short, the heavy-handed suppression or politically motivated murders of these women's male predecessors seem to have played an important role in legitimizing their rise to executive office. These women executives became "powerful moral symbols . . . whose noble motives were now beyond doubt" (Thompson 2002/2003, 542–543) (see Table 2.1 for the women executives' relationships to their male kin who previously held office).

Political violence was also a factor across the ocean in Latin America. In the case of Juan and Isabel Perón's Argentina, the 1970s were known for turmoil. Juan Perón was forced into exile in Europe before returning and claiming the presidency again at seventy-eight years old. Upon his death in office, his wife and vice president,

Isabel Perón, succeeded him. Her rule was marked with notorious death squads and disappearances of political dissidents. Eventually, she too was forced into exile in Spain. Guyanese president Janet Jagan also experienced political violence and coercion. She was jailed alongside her husband, who served as president before her until his death, for being pro-independence activists while Guyana was under British colonial rule (Jalalzai 2013).

Why the Family Path?

Women's ascendance to executive office is still rare enough that it compels researchers to carefully chart the conditions that pave the way to political success. A long list of variables has been tapped, including but not limited to the basic political rights and liberties of women (i.e., the right to vote, ability to hold elected office, etc.), public opinion on gender equality, the implementation of gender quotas, party systems, prior experience in legislatures and cabinets, and the role of mentors. Broadly speaking, everything matters in improving the chances of women: having good mentors, supportive party gatekeepers, quotas, proportional representation, prior experience in legislative and powerful cabinet positions, and favorable public opinion. However, if everything matters, it is hard to estimate what exactly matters the most under which conditions. Consequently, our focus is on the paths so that we can isolate the conditions that are critical to women becoming executives.

For the family path, we ask some key questions: (1) Why does this path seem to be salient in some regions and not in others? (2) How can the gradual marginalization of the family path in Latin America be explained over time? (3) Why is the family path rare in socioeconomically developed regions? These questions diverted us away from exclusively cultural explanations and led to more structural answers; the vast cultural variation within Asia and Latin America compels social scientists to seek different answers. Both Asia and Latin America have immense diversity of cultural, religious, linguistic, and ethnonational traditions. Billions of people live in Asia, and more than half a billion live in Latin America. Culture as a catch-all category invites more questions than answers. For example, if the family path is salient in Latin America, why has its use declined in the last decades but not in similar cultural contexts?

Studies that compared women's paths to political office with those of men from 1960 to 2010 also highlight the importance of political family dynasties (Baturo and Gray 2018; Jalalzai 2013). It is well established that women need significantly more resources, connections, and political capital than men to get to executive office (Jalalzai 2013). "Those resources most frequently take the form of being part of political dynasties, particularly when women are not present in politics more broadly. However, family dynasties are less important the longer women have been active in political life more generally" (Baturo and Gray 2018, 695). The findings of Baturo and Gray illustrate the progressively diminishing role of dynastic families as societies become more inclusive of women in politics. In fact, the authors state that "women leaders benefit from family ties when women are scarce in political life generally, but as their participation in politics becomes normalized, family ties become less important (Baturo and Gray 2018, 695).

Prominent social theorists predicted that socioeconomic modernization in the form of industrialization and urbanization would likely trigger significant changes in sociopolitical attitudes. Comte, Durkheim, Weber, and Marx all assumed that the fading away of religion and, along with it, traditional ways of thinking would occur as modernity, rationality, and science replaced the core principles around which societies organized themselves. While there has not been a shortage of criticism of this approach, which is broadly referred to as the modernization theory, recent empirical studies provide further evidence of its relevance in the contemporary era.

Norris and Inglehart (2011) delve into the vast data from the World Values Survey, which covers nearly eighty societies in four waves from 1981 to 2001. Accordingly, they argue that there is solid empirical support for the secularization trend the social theorists predicted long ago. Industrialization, urbanization, and higher levels of health and educational attainment all weaken religious institutions and traditional bonds. Modernization positively contributes to human development, which means improvement in education, nutrition, access to clean water, a basic social safety net, and health care. All of these in turn reduce the existential threats to survival. However, this change is not "deterministic" as early theorists predicted, but rather "probabilistic" (Norris and Inglehart 2011, 53–54).

Table 2.2 illustrates the steady decline of religion as societies become more developed. Norris and Inglehart state that "religious

Table 2.2 Religious Participation and Levels of Development

Religious Participation	Agrarian Societies	Industrial Societies	Postindustrial Societies
At least weekly attendance at services of worship	44%	25%	20%
Pray every day	52%	34%	26%
Religion is very important	64%	34%	20%

Source: Norris and Inglehart (2011, 58).

participation is twice as strong in poorer than richer societies" (2011, 58). In traditional societies, women's opportunities for education and participation in the paid labor force are limited as they have a short list of tasks to perform, most of which revolve around motherhood and family (Norris and Inglehart 2011, 23).

Inglehart and Norris (2003, 169) also developed a three-tiered categorization of nations according to their levels of development. The twenty most developed nations in the world are classified as the postindustrial societies. They have a GDP per capita of approximately $30,000 (by the early 2000s), predominantly high-skilled labor force, service industry, and high level of affluence. The second group is the industrial societies, composed of fifty-eight nations with moderate levels of development and GDP per capita income of approximately $6,000. The least developed group of countries are the agrarian nations, with GDP per capita income averaging $1,100. Ninety-seven countries fall in this category (Inglehart and Norris 2003, 169).

It is expected that most of the countries where women frequently use the family path are agrarian societies. Bangladesh, India, Indonesia, Pakistan, and Moldova are all categorized as agrarian nations by Inglehart and Norris (2003) (see Table 2.3). As such, these nations have the highest levels of traditional values and a predisposition to family ties. Inglehart and Norris state that when it comes to women's rights, "agrarian societies proved to be the least egalitarian" (2003, 35). If these societies are less favorable to seeing women in charge, then the family path becomes effectively the only route to political, especially executive, office. A predisposition to traditional family ties and close connections to strong male political figures likely help aspiring women executives when meritocracy and activism are not viable options. In fact, three of the countries with family-path female

Table 2.3 Family-Path Countries in Inglehart and Norris's
          Socioeconomic Development Categories

Agrarian Societies	Industrial Societies	Postindustrial Societies
Bangladesh	South Korea	Switzerland
India	Philippines	
Indonesia	Argentina	
Pakistan		
Moldova		

Source: Inglehart and Norris (2013, 34).
Note: Panama and Thailand were not included in the World Values Surveys, so they were not included in the table.

executives—Pakistan, India, and Sri Lanka—also rank the lowest on the Global Gender Parity Index (see Table 2.1). Sri Lanka is ranked at 102, India at 112, and Pakistan at 151, which demonstrates that the political cultures in these societies are not friendly toward women in political leadership positions.

Existential Security and Development

International organizations, such as the World Bank and the United Nations Development Programme, and global initiatives, like the UN's Millennium Development Goals, all rely on a basic premise: that socioeconomic development improves human security. Very briefly, human security is defined as "freedom from various risks and dangers" (Norris and Inglehart 2011, 14). In poor agrarian nations, the likelihood of premature death is greater since there is less access to nutrition, clean water, decent housing, education, health care, and social safety nets. These conditions progressively improve as poor agrarian nations move toward moderate industrial societies. Urbanization allows for better sanitation, health care, and education for boys *and* girls. Greater levels of affluence are associated with postindustrial nations where existential threats and gender differences are minimal.

Looking at the World Development Indicators, the gap between boys and girls in educational attainment remains wide in countries that frequently have women executives who use the family path. As of 2017, the number of girls of primary school age who were not enrolled in school was 3.2 million in Pakistan, 935,000 in India, 1.37 million in Indonesia, and 130,618 in Bangladesh (World Bank 2019). In short, millions of elementary school–aged girls were denied access to education in these four countries that, combined, had five women executives use the family path who served for a combined eleven terms. Interesting questions of substantive representation arise within these countries based solely on the many numbers of girls who are deprived of schooling despite the fact that multiple women have reached the highest executive office.

Scholars point at the role of dynastic families as a force to counterbalance these structural disadvantages against women candidates (Baturo and Gray 2018; Folke, Rickne, and Smith 2020). Some of these women presidents and prime ministers had entire municipalities named after them (e.g., the Municipality of Gloria in the Philippines) before they ran for executive office in the nation. Consequently, association with a politically dynastic family provides name recognition, a network, and political capital to female candidates, who would otherwise have to face a highly asymmetrical race vis-à-vis their male counterparts. For female candidates, a prominent family name can signal stronger qualifications to the voters as well as to the party elites.

In Latin American and European countries where women executives have taken the family path to office, albeit much less so recently, there are fewer school-aged girls who are out of school: Argentina with 26,385, Panama with 26,862, Moldova with 7,668, and Switzerland with 422 (World Bank 2019). When compared to Asia, this variation within countries that have had women reach executive office via the family path suggests the presence of a long-term trend. Improved educational outcomes for girls can be considered a manifestation of generally improved socioeconomic development and changing political culture. In fact, most countries in Latin America are categorized as industrial according to Inglehart and Norris (2003). The Latin American countries in this category (Argentina, Panama, and Guyana) rank much higher on development, gender parity, and democratization indexes as compared to those in Asia, such as Pakistan, Bangladesh, and the Philippines (see Table 2.1). The solid progress in girls' educational outcomes in some regions yet their stagnation in others can illustrate which regions will likely maintain the family path and which ones will likely see the political career or activist paths become dominant.

Conclusion

Contemporary research on modernization theory highlights the persistence of existential concerns in less developed, agrarian societies (e.g., Norris and Inglehart 2011). Individuals in these societies feel less secure, largely because they remain at the mercy of unpredictable, natural forces (Norris and Inglehart 2011, 19–20). If a natural disaster hits those regions, they are more vulnerable because they do not have the infrastructure and effective bureaucracy to respond accordingly. Higher existential threats lead to discretion toward authority, tradition, religion, and the status quo. On the other hand, in industrial and postindustrial societies, people can feel more "in charge." Life is more predictable, and there are mechanisms in place should there be an unexpected disaster. Strong social safety nets and steady, stable household incomes "diminish the need for absolute rules, which contributes to the decline of traditional religious rules" (Norris and Inglehart 2011, 19). When existential threats are low at the personal and community levels, there is greater functional differentiation from traditional gendered patterns of division of labor.

The protracted problems of existential security and the exclusion of women from the political domain contribute to the salience of the family path. As Table 2.1 illustrates, countries in this category tend to have lower levels of democratic development (most categorized as partly free by Freedom House) and rank relatively low on gender parity indexes. Prominent development economist Amartya Sen (1990) used the expression "missing women" when referring to the systematic discrimination toward women in less developed societies. Girls are selectively aborted and receive fewer resources and less education than boys as children, and they are systematically pushed behind men in their adult lives.

As will be discussed in Chapter 4, the predominant path for women to executive seats is the political career path. Women reach executive posts by moving up in the rank and file of the party network, legislature, cabinet, and/or bureaucracy. However, this scenario of self-made women on the political career path is neither as common nor even as feasible in less developed, traditional, agrarian societies. This is especially the case when looking at the first women executives in Sri Lanka and India or even those who followed later in Bangladesh, Indonesia, and the Philippines. Relatively low levels of development and systematic exclusion of women from the social, economic, and political spheres reduce opportunities for female political leadership. Furthermore, heightened threats of existential security further undermine the chances of switching from male to female leadership when political violence and assassinations are frequent.

Despite the structural inequities, dynastic political families close the gender education gap among their children in countries where the family path dominates. One common thread among the women in the family path is that they all come from elite families who provide top educational opportunities for their daughters and wives. In most cases, these women receive education from prominent institutions in the United States or Europe. When elite families effectively close the education gap among their children, they significantly improve the chances that their daughters and wives will participate and succeed in politics.

The political cultures women emerge from also impact their political success. Yet these cultures do not take shape in a vacuum, nor do they stay frozen over time or across generations. Social and economic institutions play an important role (Inglehart and Norris 2003). Folke, Rickne, and Smith's (2020) study on the role of family ties in the legislative branch in twelve advanced democracies confirms that the dynastic family bias favored women politicians until around 1980. However, after the 1980s as these countries increased the pool of women in their parliaments, the impact of coming from a dynastic family diminished for women. This is one reason that we also illustrated that historically powerful political family dynasties across Latin America may no longer have as much room to maneuver in the contemporary political landscape. While women's empowerment is alive and well across the Americas, the family path might increasingly become a relic of the past. This could have potential implications for the women candidates who come from strong political dynasties in North America, including the United States. In Chapter 8 we address this issue in greater detail.

Overall, women in countries where the family path is the dominant route to executive power face substantial amounts of cultural, voter, and institutional sexism. In particular, voters' and political elites' preference for male candidates for executive office in these countries is rooted in its culture, which is linked to its level of socioeconomic development. Lesser developed countries experience more existential threats and cannot respond to them effectively, so they seek stability in authority, tradition, and religion, all of which systematically shut women out of politics. However, as this chapter has shown, women can overcome these barriers to office, especially voter and cultural sexism, by relying on their dynastic family ties. Additionally, as countries attain higher levels of economic and political development, tradition and religion become less dominant influences over politics and society, which leads to less frequent use of the family path, as was shown in the regions of Latin America and Europe. In order to continue examining how women overcome sexism in order to become presidents and prime ministers, in the next chapter we explore another common route to power, the political activist path.

Notes

1. Bernard-Henri Lévy, "Belarus's Unlikely Opposition Leader," *Wall Street Journal*, September 4, 2020, https://www.wsj.com/articles/belaruss-unlikely -opposition-leader-11599246962.

2. National Governors Association database, https://www.nga.org/former -governors/.

3. We had slight difficulty placing President Violeta Barrios de Chamorro of Nicaragua. Referred to as *reina-madre* in impeccable white dress suits, most of the literature highlights her political career starting after the assassination of her husband, and her conservative, antifeminist policy preferences upon becoming president. These qualities initially resonate with the family path. However, closer scrutiny reveals the following: All seventeen names on our list in the family path (Table 2.1) had male relatives who actually held political office. President Chamorro's husband was a well-known journalist and was never elected to political office. Upon his assassination in 1978, she took over the newspaper and gradually built a movement and her political reputation. Despite her initial support for the Sandinistas, over time she became a vocal force for opposition. We believe the fact that her husband never held elected office, and her more than a decade of activism prior to her election are important factors that deviate from the traditional family-path characteristics. Consequently, we discuss President Chamorro as taking the activist path (Chapter 3).

3

The Activist Path

The existing literature identifies three relatively distinct paths to power for women who occupy executive seats: family, political career, and political activism (Adler 1996; Jalalzai 2013). Compared to the first two groups, the last group, which is the focus of this chapter, is a less traditional path to political power. Women executives in this last group share a solid track record of political activism. They have participated in national fights for independence (e.g., Prime Minister Maria Adiatu Dialó Nandigna of Guinea-Bissau and Prime Minister Golda Meir of Israel), advocated for democracy (e.g., Prime Minister Han Myeong-sook of South Korea, Prime Minister Yulia Tymoshenko of Ukraine, and President Violeta Chamorro of Nicaragua), stood up against military regimes (e.g., President Michelle Bachelet of Chile and President Dilma Rousseff of Brazil), and fought for women's rights (e.g., Prime Minister Jóhanna Sigurðardóttir of Iceland) and environmental rights (e.g., President Zuzana Čaputová of Slovakia) in the early stages of their political careers. Consequently, many of them paid a heavy personal price. Some survived torture; others were exiled or placed under house arrest for many years. Additionally, many witnessed brutal civil wars or military coups.

In this chapter, our focus is on women who were propelled to executive seats in their respective countries largely due to their extensive political activism. According to Jalalzai's (2017, 70) classification, nearly a third of women executives between 1960 and

43

2010 "gained experience as activists prior to their presidencies and prime ministries." Across Latin America and the Caribbean, women participated in movements to protest gross human rights violations by the government. In Europe, they mobilized for gender parity. In Africa, women acted as peacemakers and advocated for greater women's participation in politics. Overall, these executives built up their reputation and name recognition through effective political activism. For example, in Liberia, women activists played a key role in mobilizing grassroots movements to advance the overall cause, and the number of women registered voters increased by 30 to 50 percent in 2005 when Ellen Johnson Sirleaf was elected president (Jalalzai 2017, 22–24).

Women who are classified as taking the political activist path to executive power also attain success in more conventional forms of politics. In fact, almost all women who reach the executive seats with an activist background also have impressive political careers in party leadership, parliament, and/or the cabinet. However, these women cannot be classified as taking the political career path to power because they have vastly different backgrounds than those women who rose through the party or political ranks. The existing literature on women executives has recognized this and separates activists from their political career counterparts. For example, activists are usually referred to as outsiders (Dolan et al. 2016). Examining the individual biographies of women who took the political activist path to power reveals not only a strong track record of political activism but also that their outsider status as an activist began in the early parts of their career. These women build a reputation and political capital—largely as a result of their commitment, feistiness, and resilience—and their activist nature becomes part of their identity. For example, president of Slovakia Zuzana Čaputová came to be known as the Erin Brockovich of Slovakia before taking office due to her effective campaigning against the toxic landfill in her hometown. She initiated a legal battle that involved Greenpeace and was appealed all the way to the Supreme Court of Slovakia (see appendix for more details). Without a doubt, the earlier political activism of these women presidents and prime ministers played a key role in their political ascendance to executive seats. Consequently, rather than the political career or family paths, they are categorized under the political activist path.

In this chapter we tackle some important but underexplored research questions. First, what are the similarities among the women executives who were able to gain access to political power in vastly different parts of the world using the political activist path? It is important to highlight general trends in women's executive political leadership despite the difficulty of generalizing cases that come from multiple geographical regions spanning Brazil to Bangladesh. Despite regional variation, it is likely that similar psychological or institutional factors are at work that help launch women activists to executive seats. Focusing on the factors that stimulate and motivate the political activism of these women executives might help us discover a shared thread among otherwise seemingly random cases.

Second, as we will briefly tackle here and in more detail in Chapter 7, how stable is the political activist path to power? By definition, political activism is perilous (Della Porta 2006; Tarrow 2011). If it did not involve any personal risks, then this would be a much more common path to executive office. Long imprisonments, physical torture, political stigma, and years spent in political exile are frequently mentioned in the biographies of these women presidents and prime ministers. Given the perilousness of this path to office, it is unknown what the stability of their tenure is once they come to power. Compared to the other paths, how long do women executives who come to office through the activist path manage to stay in power? Can they stay long enough to execute their agenda, or are they toppled soon after claiming an executive seat? Answers to these questions could potentially illustrate the viability of this path.

Analyzing Women Presidents and Prime Ministers Around the World

Before analyzing women who took the political activist path to office, it is important to discuss how this chapter is part of the larger effort of this book to enhance and build upon the existing research on women presidents and prime ministers by (1) presenting a global analysis and (2) classifying women as taking one path to executive office. In doing so, in this section we highlight how our book differs from existing research, its contributions to the work on women presidents and prime ministers, and the unique challenges presented by analyzing women on the political activist path because many do also have political experience.

Adopting a Global Approach

Many scholars are hesitant to draw generalizations from the existing universe of women executives. Montecinos (2017a, 1) argues that the universe of women executives is as of yet "small and highly diverse"; therefore, the potential of new cases added to this pool might have significant chances to "alter the existing patterns." However, initial attempts to identify common paths to power for women executives did so with as few as twenty-five cases (Adler 1996). Despite certain methodological precautions, numerous studies tried to cast a wider net and conduct their analysis of women executives on a global scale (Jalalzai 2013; Martin and Borrelli 2016; Watson, Jencik, and Selzer 2005). Examining the distribution of cases worldwide, it appears that no region is left without a woman occupying an executive seat. These large-N studies also highlight some common paths to power among women presidents and prime ministers. Thus, we continue in this fashion by devoting an entire chapter to each path to office in an effort to find out more about them.

Given the frequency and the distribution of cases across the world's regions, it is possible to observe some distinct patterns as to where and how women can claim executive seats. While some women executives come from a privileged pedigree due to their link to a dynastic political family (see Chapter 2), in most cases, female presidents and prime ministers emerge from distinguished political careers. They tend to display impressive records of success as professionals, technocrats, or elected politicians (see Chapter 4). In many cases, it is possible to observe the overlapping of multiple paths and qualities, such as a woman executive having a successful political career *and* coming from a politically well-connected family (e.g., Prime Minister Benazir Bhutto of Pakistan).

Classifying Women Executives on Seemingly Overlapping Paths

In order to clarify the distinctions among different paths, in this book we focus on identifying the main political capital that propelled these women into the initial stages of their political careers. In some cases, there were women executives whose family members were persecuted or assassinated, which had significant consequences for the rest of the family, including political exile. In other cases, women executives pursued successful political careers simultaneously with their politically active spouses. Such cases seemed to straddle multiple paths, such as family and political career or family and political activism. Instead of categorizing these women executives in more than one path, we look at the earliest stages of their political careers. What was the initial impetus that drew these women into politics? Was it their activism, or was it their intimate personal ties to political power? While it could be difficult to untangle family ties from the career steps of these women, the advantage of working with such high-profile cases is that there is an abundance of biographical data available. In most cases, biographical information and prior academic works on any given female president or prime minister provided clear guidance as to which path the woman took to office. Only in very rare cases do we differ from the existing literature.[1]

The Fight to Power

The ability of women to forcefully push their way into politics and achieve high-profile political positions remains a relatively underexplored subject. However, more insight can be gained through research on activist women in executive positions. In fact, this process is not confined to the modern era either. As early as the 1700s, women are documented as leading armies to success. In an edited volume on women in Caribbean politics, scholars highlight women leaders fighting against British imperialism (Barrow-Giles 2011). For example, Gottlieb (2011, 4) states the following about Jamaica's Queen Nanny:

> From any point of view, Queen Nanny's political and military achievements are remarkable. Leading a half-starved, sometimes rag-tag band of no more than 500 Africans, fleeing the fires, guns, dogs and soldiers with the might of the British Empire behind them, she successfully defeated the British and their allies time and again, her guerilla army battling 5,000 and 10,000 at any given time.

Consequently, both contemporary and historical evidence shows that women are not novices to fighting for freedom and progress, nor are they strangers to leadership positions in such fights.

The biographies of women executives in this book show that there is a distinct group of women who had to *fight* their way to power. Women who chose the political activist path dedicated their political careers to causes such as national independence, democracy, labor rights, human rights, women's rights, or LGBT rights in their nations. As Figure 3.1 shows, about 13 percent of all women executives (18 out of 136) take the political activist path to office. While ten were elected to their posts through competitive elections, the rest were appointed, with two serving in an interim capacity. Almost all women executives on the political activist path (seventeen out of eighteen) were forced into exile at some point in their lives.

In addition to identifying the women executives who started their political careers on the political activist path, it is important to explore regional patterns; distinguish between women who were elected, were appointed, or served in an interim capacity; and examine how long they stay in power. Although almost all regions in the world have had both elected and appointed women executives on the political activist path, those in Africa were mostly appointed while those in Europe, Latin America, and the Caribbean were both elected and appointed.

More insight is gained into the political activist path to executive power when we examine how women come to power and the length of time they stay in office. As Table 3.1 illustrates, interim office-holders tend to stay on the job the shortest amount of time at approximately four months on average. This is to be expected since most of these women executives are handpicked as reliable trustees for a brief period of time. They often serve until a constitutional crisis is

Figure 3.1 Comparing the Political-Activist Path to the Political-Career and Family Paths

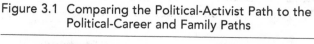
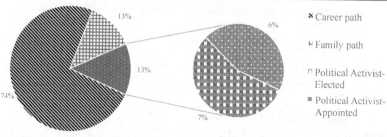

Source: Jalalzai (2013); *Encyclopedia Britannica*; and the official government websites of each country.
Note: Women executives who served multiple terms are only counted once (n=136).

Table 3.1 Political-Activist-Path Women Executives, 1960–2020

Name	Country	Region	First Year in Office	Elected Appointed Interum	Total Time in Office	Democratic Status (Freedom House 2019)
PRES Carmen Pereira	Guinea-Bissau	Africa	1984	Interim	2 days	Partly free
PRES Ellen Johnson Sirleaf	Liberia	Africa	2006	Elected (2 terms)	12 years	Partly free
PRES Joyce Banda	Malawi	Africa	2012	Appointed	2 years, 1 month	Partly free
PM Aminata Touré	Senegal	Africa	2013	Appointed	10 months	Partly free
PM Golda Meir	Israel	Middle East	1969	Elected	5 years, 3 months	Free
PM Maria de Lourdes Pintasilgo	Portugal	Europe	1979	Interim	4 months	Free
PRES Vigdís Finnbogadóttir	Iceland	Europe	1980	Elected (4 terms)	16 years	Free
PM Jóhanna Sigurðardóttir	Iceland	Europe	2009	Elected	4 years, 3 months	Free
PRES Agatha Barbara	Malta	Europe	1982	Appointed	5 years	Free
PRES Zuzana Čaputová	Slovakia	Europe	2019	Elected	June 2019–present	Free
PRES Ruth Dreifuss	Switzerland	Europe	1999	Elected	1 year	Free
PM Yulia Tymoshenko	Ukraine	Europe	2005	Appointed (2 terms)	2 years, 10 months	Partly free

continues

Table 3.1 Continued

Name	Country	Region	First Year in Office	Elected Appointed Interum	Total Time in Office	Democratic Status (Freedom House 2019)
PRES Lidia Gueiler Tejada	Bolivia	Latin America	1979	Interim	8 months	Partly free
PM Eugenia Charles	Dominica	Caribbean	1980	Elected (3 terms)	15 years	Free
PRES Violeta Chamorro	Nicaragua	Latin America	1990	Elected	6 years, 8 months	Not free
PRES Michelle Bachelet	Chile	Latin America	2006	Elected (2 terms)	4 years and 2014–present	Free
PRES Dilma Rousseff	Brazil	Latin America	2011	Elected (2 terms)	5 years, 8 months	Free
PM Han Myeong-sook	South Korea	Asia	2006	Appointed	11 months	Free

Source: Jalalzai (2013); *Encyclopedia Britannica*; BBC; *The Guardian*; *The Independent*; *Los Angeles Times*; Jewish Women's Archive; and the official government websites of each country.

averted (e.g., President Carmen Pereira of Guinea-Bissau) or new elections are held (e.g., President Lidia Gueiler Tejada of Bolivia). While the appointed executives tend to stay in office longer than those serving on an interim basis at just shy of two and a half years, it is clear that the elected executives stay in power the longest at approximately eight years, which indicates that these women executives are often reelected. These findings and others pertaining to the length of time women presidents and prime ministers spend in office will be discussed more in Chapter 7.

Why Activism?

Women executives with activist backgrounds were usually engaged in what Tarrow (2011, 2) calls "contentious collective action," or movements caused by conventional politics or established political institutions that do not address citizen demands effectively. Many of the women who took the political activist path to the presidency or premiership not only took part in but founded these movements.

In an attempt to define social movements, Tarrow (2011, 4) identifies four key attributes of such movements: common purpose, collective challenge, solidarity, and sustained interaction with elites, opponents, and authorities. What motivates these women to take this rather risky path to power rather than following a safer path with a career in politics? Why challenge the political establishment and the authorities instead of working within the system? Three theoretical approaches may answer this question. While some of them prioritize psychological motivations as the driving force, others highlight the availability of resources, such as funds, networks, and so forth that can give rise to collective activism. A third approach brings in political variables, by emphasizing the role of critical political openings that generate a window of opportunity for activism to thrive.

Psychological Model

This model highlights emotional distress, outrage, or bursts of feelings as the main factors that activate women. This outburst could be caused by turmoil in a given society due to severe conflict or war, which then might lead to an increasing sense of confusion and isolation. Similarly, rapid economic development or industrialization may also trigger psychological reactions, such as feelings of alienation. Citizens then react to these emotionally distressing developments by coming together and fighting collectively in order to pursue a sense of normalcy (Henderson and Jeydel 2014, 40). According to Henderson and Jeydel (2014, 36–52), an example of the psychological model was when Nigerian women activists, outraged by exploitation at the hands of Chevron, took over the oil plant and stripped naked until their demands were met.

The best examples of this category among women presidents and prime ministers include President Violeta Chamorro of Nicaragua, President Ellen Johnson Sirleaf of Liberia, President Carmen Pereira of Guinea-Bissau, and President Joyce Banda of Malawi. In almost all of these cases, these executives operated in incredibly polarized, traumatized, and war-torn nations. They were faced with civil wars, gruesome guerrilla warfare, exile, and imprisonment. Their ability to rise to the occasion under such extreme and psychologically distressing circumstances makes each one of them rather strong activist leaders and executives. Furthermore, their skill at providing peace and normalcy after turmoil was widely praised. Although President Pereira of Guinea-Bissau had a rather brief tenure, her colleagues in this category from Nicaragua and Liberia remained in power for extensive periods of time.

Popularly referred to as the Great Conciliator, President Chamorro's husband was assassinated by the Samosa dictatorship in Nicaragua in 1978. While her husband Pedro Chamorro was a prominent journalist from an established family, he never held any elected political office. The political situation in Nicaragua progressively worsened upon Pedro Chamorro's assassination. Yet, Doña Violeta continued publishing her dissident newspaper and advocated for a return to democracy in her country torn apart by guerrilla warfare. The intensity of conflict and social trauma in Nicaragua reached epic proportions as civil wars claimed more than 30,000 lives. The polarization between the Sandinistas and anti-Sandinistas penetrated all the way into Doña Violeta's family with two of her children identifying as staunch Sandinistas while the other two were avid anti-Sandinistas, thus creating unique personal challenges that she needed to reckon with (Chamorro 1996).

Previous works have categorized President Violeta Chamorro as an executive who came to power riding on the coattails of her martyred husband, who belonged to a dynastic political family in

Nicaragua (Adler 1996, 143). However, a closer reading of Doña Violeta's biography reveals a committed political figure fighting for democratic ideals alongside her husband. In fact, she continued to publish the newspaper and advocate for democracy years after her husband's death and at great personal peril. Consequently, it would be inappropriate to credit her husband for the independent accomplishments she achieved after he was deceased. All seventeen leaders classified as taking the family path in our book had male relatives who held the highest office in their respective nations. However, Doña Violeta's journalist husband never held elected office. Hinojosa (2012) aptly points out that there are plenty of male politicians who come from politically well-connected families and reach executive seats, yet scholars do not automatically credit their families for the success of these male executives. Thus, all the credit should not be given to family ties for women executives.

Similarly, President Ellen Johnson Sirleaf in Liberia presided over a war-torn, traumatized nation that had suffered through a civil war. Before claiming her executive seat, she was imprisoned twice and came very close to political execution. She had to flee to exile for over a decade (Jalalzai 2013). Below is an excerpt from her biography that vividly illustrates the hardships she went through:

> Johnson escaped death in 1980 when all four cabinet ministers were executed when Samuel Doe overthrew the government of President William Tolbert. . . . After the coup, Johnson Sirleaf began protesting Doe's government. These activities eventually led her to flee Liberia. While working for Citibank during her exile in Kenya, she continued agitating for democratic transition in her country. In 1985, she returned to Liberia to run for Senate and was placed under house arrest for several months; when she was released again, she went into exile in Kenya. (Jalalzai 2013, 187)

In 2011, she received the Nobel Peace Prize as the first elected woman president in Africa who made substantial contributions to women's rights, nonviolence, and peacebuilding. The severity of political conflict in both Nicaragua and Liberia played an important role that mobilized both women to take action. Similarly, the electorate in both contexts found a semblance of calm and normalcy in the women's personal integrity and relatively reconciliatory personalities. That likely explains why Chamorro and Sirleaf served for nearly seven and twelve years, respectively.

Resource Mobilization Model

This model emphasizes the importance of material and nonmaterial resources in order to realize a viable movement. People, funds, and space, as well as a strong support network and alliances with other powerful actors are key factors that help the formation of social movements. According to Tarrow (2011), both ideology and organizational structures are crucial components of the resource mobilization model. As such, this model emphasizes both formal and informal institutions that can be mobilized to advance a certain cause. Strong unions, progressive social movements, or an established labor party could all serve as platforms that facilitate a woman's rise to power.

A common example of this model is the rising feminist movement in the United States during the 1960s and 1970s. This movement was mostly initiated by middle-class women who were well educated and had financial security, which served as useful material resources for mobilization. However, their mobility aspirations were hampered since they were expected to fulfill stereotypical gender roles as wives and mothers (Henderson and Jeydel 2014, 41). Improved economic conditions in the United States in the post–World War II era, President Kennedy's initiatives for gender equality, and the rising awareness for equal rights across the nation all helped provide substantial material and intellectual resources for the feminist activists of this era.

Among women presidents and prime ministers, President Dilma Rousseff of Brazil, President Michelle Bachelet of Chile, President Agatha Barbara of Malta, and President Ruth Dreifuss of Switzerland can all be considered women activists who came to power by utilizing a strong network of resources. Probably the two cases that best fit under this category are from Iceland: President Vigdís Finnbogadóttir and Prime Minister Jóhanna Sigurðardóttir. In both of these Icelandic cases, the interplay of individual activism and the supportive role of material and nonmaterial resources available in the nation can be observed.

President Vigdís Finnbogadóttir of Iceland, who remained in power for sixteen years, had an extensive track record of activism early on. In the 1970s, she participated in the protests against NATO military bases in Iceland. She also pushed for women's rights, environmental rights, cultural rights, and rights for single women. At the age of forty-one, she was the first single woman in Iceland to adopt a child. In many ways, Finnbogadóttir's initial election was made possible by the enormous influence of a one-day women's strike in 1975. Shops, offices, banks, schools, newspapers, restaurants, and theaters closed for the day, and men had to look after the children to prove how much society depended on women (Adler 1996, 146). Feminist activism was alive and well in Iceland in the 1970s, and Finnbogadóttir was at the front lines. This large-scale collective activism certainly helped fuel substantial political support for her candidacy. In her words, "the atmosphere created by the strike certainly helped me to be elected. It gave people the idea that a woman as leader would be a valuable thing" (Adler 1996, 146).

Iceland has an impressive legacy of women's activism. Women pushed for and gained suffrage as early as 1882 (albeit initially only for widows and women with independent wealth). They established all-women newspapers, campaigned for all-women party lists, and ran for local council elections during the 1920s. The organizational capacity of Icelandic women was remarkable. They reached out to all enfranchised women, held large meetings, and acted as a well-organized and effective political party when such an organization hardly existed in the first half of the twentieth century (Styrkársdóttir 2013, 128).

This steady push for women to participate in local and parliamentary elections in Iceland has led to a gradual increase in the percentage of women in city councils and the parliament, particularly from the 1970s on. The percentage of women in both levels of representative government increased from about 5 percent in the 1960s to about 45–50 percent in 2010.

The strength of the women's movement in Iceland provided, in Tarrow's (2011) terms, both ideological and organizational support for a woman candidate in the presidential race. President Finnbogadóttir states this explicitly when she said, "I am president today as a result of the women's strike in 1975" (Styrkársdóttir 2013, 124). Moreover, she expresses her active role in this process of social transformation: "I am at the same time part of this process of change" (Styrkársdóttir 2013, 124).

Another woman, Prime Minister Jóhanna Sigurðardóttir, was able to follow in the footsteps of President Vigdís Finnbogadóttir and claim an executive position. Prime Minister Sigurðardóttir was elected as the first openly gay executive in Iceland. In both cases, it is important to note that neither woman was a lone warrior. Iceland has a strong tradition of feminist movements since the turn of the century. Women have effectively participated in local politics and national parliament since the 1920s, and Iceland has had a feminist political party since the early 1980s. As such, Iceland ranks as the number one nation in the 2020 Global Gender Gap Report by the World Economic Forum. These dense organizational networks and the general strength of a feminist ideology in the larger society played a key role in elevating certain high-profile activists to executive seats in Iceland. Consequently, it is no surprise that another woman, Prime Minister Katrín Jakobsdóttir, emerged as the new prime minister in 2017.

Malta's president Agatha Barbara could also be included as a case for the resource mobilization model. A trailblazer and activist from an early age, President Barbara had a long career in the Labor Party. Due to her participation in demonstrations, she was sentenced to hard labor when she was young. She founded the Women's Branch of the Labor Party and later served as minister of labor, culture, and welfare. While in office, she pushed for workers' rights, equal pay, and maternity leave. Her early activist career as well as the political and organizational network of the Labor Party inevitably played an important role when she was appointed to the presidency in 1982. As previously discussed, appointed presidents do not seem to have extended tenures in office. However, Barbara served in that capacity for five years and, thereby, was the longest serving appointed president who took the political activist path to power (Scicluna 2018).

The region of Latin America and the Caribbean has achieved significant progress in terms of gender equality, despite its long association with a typically *machismo* political culture. Fifteen countries in the region have adopted quotas for women in their legislative branches, ranging from 20 percent in Paraguay up to 50 percent in Bolivia, Costa Rica, Ecuador, Mexico, Nicaragua, and Panama (Htun 2016, 15). Public opinion surveys in the region show surprisingly little difference in the political preferences of men and women, which highlights the gradual closing of the gender gap in political attitudes. On the question of whether "men are better political leaders than women," Booth and Bayer Richard (2015, 141–142) state that "both sexes took a nonsexist position, but women did so more strongly" across Latin America. Based on these public opinion surveys of the region, scholars cautiously conclude that while the results do not confirm the "death" of *machismo*, they do display a "greater openness toward female leadership" in Latin America (Booth and Bayer Richard 2015, 141–142).

Historically, Latin American countries had women in the highest executive seats as early as the 1970s. However, starting with Argentina's Isabel Perón, who succeeded her husband Juan Perón in 1974, the earliest women executives were almost exclusively members of dynastic political families (Adler 1996; Hinojosa 2012). Consequently, the family path dominated the region. In her seminal work that focused on the paths women take to political power, Jalalzai (2013) agrees that family ties were salient in Latin America and Asia. However, in her later work, Jalalzai (2016) also mentions that the paths used in Latin America have changed since the 1990s. Even though it is much harder for women to win competitive seats as powerful executives of presidential regimes, on multiple occasions they were able to do so in Latin America and the Caribbean, and were even reelected, such as in the cases of President Michelle Bachelet in Chile and President Dilma Rousseff in Brazil. As such, Jalalzai (2016, 3) argues that women presidents in Latin America "led the way in defying the prevailing patterns."

As previously mentioned, two female executives who were reelected from Latin America stand out for their strong credentials as political activists: Chile's Michelle Bachelet and Brazil's Dilma Rousseff. During their youth, both women were active in progressive movements and severely penalized by the authoritarian regimes in their respective countries (Macaulay 2017; Montecinos 2017b). While Bachelet lost her father to state torture and had to flee to exile, Rousseff was tortured by the military regime for nearly three years. Her activist background and the torture remained as defining features of President Rousseff throughout her political career. During her impeachment proceedings, right-wing members of the Brazilian Chamber of Deputies praised the military and the specific torture centers that she was detained in even though the official reason behind her impeachment was federal budgetary misconduct (Macaulay 2017, 137).

Both women had distinguished careers prior to being elected president, Bachelet as a medical doctor and Rousseff as a technocrat. Their earlier activism certainly played a significant role as they climbed the ranks in center-left, progressive political parties (Jalalzai 2016). These parties nominated both women to cabinet positions that were traditionally reserved for men. Rousseff served as the energy minister, and Bachelet, after serving as the health minister, became the first woman defense minister in Chile and Latin America (Macaulay 2017; Montecinos 2017b). As such, the leftist parties served as important resources to help both women get elected to executive seats in their respective nations.

Overall, in countries as diverse as Iceland, Chile, Brazil, and Malta, the existence of strong progressive parties and social movements provided critical material resources for activist women politicians to rise up among the ranks. These political parties appointed women in critical positions, which subsequently helped them build credentials for higher office. The expansive scale and scope of the social movements delivered substantial votes for these executives, who were in almost all cases running against the conventional social norms.

Political Context/Opportunity Model

Not all psychologically motivated and/or resourceful activists can launch effective social movements. This third model highlights the critical importance of being at the right place at the right time. Timing is crucial when activists try to launch social movements. The political climate "needs to be amenable" to activism and protest (Henderson and Jeydel 2014, 43). In many cases, times of intense political turbulence can help the activists. When the status quo is shaken and the establishment political actors cannot resolve gridlock, this can create a window of opportunity for nontraditional actors. Such circumstances might be "amenable" to activist women leaders as well. Scholarship on the third wave of democracy in Africa, Latin America, Asia, and Eastern Europe illustrates how democratic transitions brought many women executives to power. Nearly two-thirds of "women [65 total] accessed office during transition to democracy" (Jalalzai 2017, 69).

Examples include Prime Minister Maria de Lourdes Pintasilgo of Portugal, Prime Minister Yulia Tymoshenko of Ukraine, and President Lidia Gueiler Tejada of Bolivia. The common thread for each of these three cases is the critical moment of a transition in the political systems. Both Pintasilgo and Tejada, for example, were called in to oversee upcoming elections (Jalalzai 2017, 69). This often occurs when authoritarian regimes are on their way out but new political actors have not yet established a new system, so nontraditional actors are asked to step in. Transitions from a military regime to civilian authority or from a dictatorship to a democracy create a slim window of opportunity for women executives who might have had strong activist backgrounds. While the system may not be welcoming to political activists under normal circumstances, these extraordinary circumstances make it possible for a woman on the political activist path to claim an executive post.

For example, Portugal's prime minister Maria de Lourdes Pintasilgo was considered a pioneer activist in both the political arena and the business world. Her obituary praises her as a progressive leader who pushed for significant improvements in women's rights while remaining a committed Catholic. Even though she had an interest in philosophy, she received an engineering degree in industrial chemistry in order to show her competence in a "man's subject," she later said in an interview (*The Independent* 2004). The opportunity that rewarded her lifelong political activism came with the collapse of the Salazar regime. As a Catholic who had good relations with the church and strong progressive activist credentials, she was a credible candidate for both sides of the political spectrum. She served a brief period of four months as a caretaker prime minister and also served as the minister of social affairs, making significant progress on health care, education, and labor rights (*The Independent* 2004).

Conclusion

Previous research shows that presidential systems are more difficult institutional structures for women to reach an executive seat when compared to a parliamentary setting. While parliamentary systems on average give women an 8 percent chance of being in an executive position, in presidential systems this average drops down to 2 percent (Jalalzai 2013, 50–51). Several factors are likely at play here. In parliamentary systems, once women become leaders of their parties, they almost automatically become the prime minister if their party wins the election. However, in presidential systems women have to run multiple individual races, first within the party and then at the national level against opposing candidates. This could be one of the key factors behind the lackluster performance of Hillary Clinton against Obama in 2008 and Trump in 2016 (Jalalzai 2018; and see

Chapter 8) and the disappointing outcomes for multiple women senators from the 2020 Democratic Party primary.

Since presidential races pit a woman candidate directly against a man, making gendered voter behavior even more salient, proportional representation systems in parliamentary systems with an emphasis on the party (rather than the candidate) are likely more conducive for women who are seeking executive office. Additionally, presidential systems have more rigid terms. Once elected, a president is expected to serve the entire presidential term (from four to six or seven years) unless they are impeached, which is a mechanism triggered only under rather extraordinary circumstances. However, if a prime minister cannot secure the vote of confidence from the legislative branch, they could be brought down immediately. This rigidity of presidential terms might be another reason that makes it more difficult for women to reach executive office in presidential systems.

Despite the extra challenges that presidential systems pose for women, both the quantitative findings (see Chapter 5) and in-depth analysis of individual cases in this chapter illustrate that the political activist path seems to be an effective and viable alternative for women to become presidents and prime ministers. While it is rather rare for women to reach powerful executive positions through competitive elections, the findings demonstrate that if a woman has a proven track record of activism and can either mobilize sufficient institutional resources (such as progressive political parties or social movements) or is in the right place at the right time (i.e., during transitional periods when the status quo is weakened), they can break the proverbial glass ceiling much easier. Tripp (2001) highlights the role of increased women's activism in Africa during the 1990s as a key factor that empowered women to seek and claim executive offices. While women rarely ran for executive office in their countries prior to the 1990s, this changed as a result of new forms of women's activism. Unlike the earlier forms of women's mobilization, these new women's movements were independent of single-party structures and patronage networks and advocated strongly for women's rights rather than just developmental issues. Women coming from these movements "often have strongly opposed sectarianism, in contrast with other political leaders who have exploited ethnicity, race, or religion" (Tripp 2001, 151). Women executives with activist backgrounds ran for president in Kenya, Rwanda, and Liberia. Out of the eighteen females who became presidents and prime ministers using the political activist path, four of them were from Africa: Guinea-Bissau, Liberia, Rwanda, and Senegal (see Table 3.1). These high levels of mobilization also carried women into other positions of power in the legislatures; for example, Ethiopia, Lesotho, Uganda, Zimbabwe, and South Africa had women speakers or deputy speakers in their parliaments.

In addition to highlighting the strengths of these women who took the political activist path to power, it is also important to note the institutional factors that are in effect. Table 3.2 includes the top ten countries that have the highest scores in gender equality in 2020. Both Iceland and Nicaragua, which have had women executives take the political activist path to office, rank among the top five most gender-equal nations in the world. In the last fifty years, Iceland had a woman executive for twenty-two years and Nicaragua for seven years. Both countries have completely closed the educational attainment and health and survival gaps between women and men. Another striking aspect in the top ten most gender-equal countries is the disappearance of the family path. It would be safe to expect the impact of dynastic political families to attenuate as societies achieve more gender parity.

Table 3.2 Top Ten Gender-Equal Countries in 2020 and Women Executives

Rank	Country	Executive (Path)	Total Women Executives
1	Iceland	PRES Vigdís Finnbogadóttir (political activist path) PM Jóhanna Sigurðardóttir (political activist path) PM Katrín Jakobsdottír (political career path)	3
2	Norway	PM Gro Harlem Brundtland (political career path) PM Anne Enger (political career path) PM Erna Solberg (political career path)	3
3	Finland	PRES Tarja Halonen (political career path) PM Anneli Tuulikki Jäätteenmäki (political career path)	4

continues

Table 3.2 Continued

Rank	Country	Executive (Path)	Total Women Executives
		PM Mari Kiviniemi (political career path)	
		PM Sanna Marin (political career path)	
4	Sweden	N/A	0
5	Nicaragua	PRES Violeta Chamorro (political activist path)	1
6	New Zealand	PM Jenny Shipley (political career path) PM Helen Clark (political career path) PM Jacinda Ardern (political career path)	3
7	Ireland	PRES Mary McAleese (political career path) PRES Mary Robinson (political career path)	2
8	Spain	N/A	0
9	Rwanda	PM Agathe Uwilingiyimana (political career path)	1
10	Germany	CHAN Angela Merkel (political career path)	1
	Average number of women executives per country:		1.8

Source: Global Gender Gap Report 2020, World Economic Forum.

Studies show that the public becomes less sexist if a country has had a female president or prime minister. In Latin America, when comparisons are made between six countries that had women presidents (Argentina, Costa Rica, Chile, Nicaragua, Panama, and Brazil) and the rest of the continent, citizens from these six nations showed a "higher approval of women political leaders" and exhibited more egalitarian attitudes (Booth and Bayer Richard 2015, 143). Booth and Bayer Richard (2015, 143) state that experiencing a woman executive affects men more so than women. Therefore, it is not a coincidence to observe countries that have already had a woman executive continuing to have more women presidents and prime ministers. The positive correlation between having a woman executive and the prospects of future women presidents and prime ministers is discussed in detail in Chapter 6.

In short, women executives are shaped by the sociopolitical contexts in which they emerge, but, simultaneously, their tenure also makes significant changes in the national political culture. Unlike the family path, which seems to gradually attenuate, the frequency of the political activist path seems to stay steady or slightly increase over time. Since women presidents and prime ministers who took the political activist path to office constitute 13 percent of all women executives, they deserve special attention. Their biographies show that their struggles were geared toward achieving equal pay, career opportunities, political rights, health care, maternity leave, cultural rights, nonsectarianism, and sexual rights in many nations. As such, these women faced cultural, voter, and institutional sexism, but they were able to overcome these barriers to executive office using their activist experience. For example, women on the political activist path are able to get elected despite voter sexism because many citizens are already supporters from during their time as activists. Similarly, women are able to get appointed if there is an opening conducive to an outsider who can be viewed as a caretaker, such as during a transition from an authoritarian regime to a democracy. In order to continue understanding how women overcome voter, cultural, and institutional sexism to reach executive office, the next chapter examines the most common route to power, the political career path.

Note

1. The single case that is coded differently than the extant literature is that of President Violeta Chamorro of Nicaragua. She is categorized as taking the political activist path to office rather than the family path. Adler (1996, 143) categorizes her under the family path with the following statement: "Nicaraguans elected Violeta Chamorro president more than 12 years after the assassination of her politically prominent journalist husband." Upon careful reading of her autobiography (Chamorro 1996) and works about her, crediting her husband for the hard work and perseverance would downplay her own achievements. Even though she was not politically active until her husband's death, she was a very effective, well-known, and highly respected political activist for twelve years after his death. Furthermore, her husband never held any elected office as a politically influential journalist, whereas all the other women executives in the family path had husbands, fathers, or brothers who held high, if not the highest, political office in the nation. Her persistence in a nation torn by civil war for twelve years after the death of her husband illustrates the breadth of her commitment to her cause.

4

The Political
Career Path

Women executives do not operate in institutional vac-
uums. In any given polity, they must navigate multiple institutional
settings on their way to power. While some of these institutional
arrangements help speed up women's political careers, such as quotas, others might pose greater challenges and barriers to executive
office, such as presidential regimes and majoritarian electoral systems. In this chapter we focus on women prime ministers and presidents who had lengthy careers in politics prior to reaching executive office. Some of them have a long track record in elected office,
usually as legislators. Over half of the women executives in this
category (53 of 100) held elected office as parliamentarians, either
as federal representatives or senators. Others served as successful
career diplomats (e.g., President Sahle-Work Zewde of Ethiopia),
competent bureaucrats (e.g., Prime Minister Jacinda Ardern of New
Zealand and Prime Minister Rosario Fernández of Peru), or judges
on the high courts with a staunchly independent, nonpartisan reputation (e.g., Presidents Vassiliki Thanou-Christophilou and Katerina
Sakellaropoulou of Greece). The shared characteristic of the women
executives who took this path to office is their impressive political
careers. As such, this path is the focus of this chapter, which differs
from the female executives who came from established political
dynastic families (see Chapter 2) or those with a strong activist past
(see Chapter 3).

Institutionalism and its various subcategories (new institutional-ism, neoliberal institutionalism, [neo]Marxist institutionalism, or formal-legal institutionalism) have been a strong theoretical tradi-tion in political science and comparative politics. Defined briefly as "the rules of the game," institutions are the norms, rules, and widely accepted standard operating procedures in a political system. They "create elements of order and predictability." They also impact the actors by enabling or constraining their behavior (March and Olsen 2011, 160–162). In a sense, they set the stage and shape the condi-tions for political actors to operate under.

A significant portion of the political science literature focuses on what March and Olsen (2011) refer to as "concrete political institu-tions." These refer to the legislative, executive, and judicial branches; the bureaucracy; and the electoral system. The gender and politics lit-erature extensively addresses the impact of each of these formal insti-tutions and their role in widening or bridging the gender gap in poli-tics. However, much ink is also spilled on informal institutions and their role in women's ascendance to political power. Usually referred to as gender norms, these informal institutions include the established beliefs, values, and attitudes about gender in a given society (Borrelli and Martin 1997; Inglehart and Norris 2003).

In their seminal works, Inglehart and Norris (2003; Norris and Inglehart 2011) highlight the strong relationship between levels of development and political values and attitudes. When societies are less developed, individuals have greater deference to religion, tradition, and gendered divisions of labor. Such a normative setting tends to dis-criminate against women and makes it harder for women executives to emerge. If the population associates masculine traits, such as assertive-ness and decisiveness, with the executive branch and automatically assigns feminine traits, like compassion and nurturing, to women, it makes it harder for women to be judged based on their merits. While women can at times benefit from these stereotypical female attributes, usually under the conditions of social crisis or distress (Morgan and Buice 2013), in general these gender norms undermine the political chances of women executives.

Studies on political communication and campaigns of women for executive seats across the world, including in France, Canada, the United States, and Germany, also illustrate gender stereotyping as a significant hurdle for women (Murray 2010). In many cases, women suffer from problems of the "double bind." When women present themselves as assertive candidates ready to take on hard issues like the economy or defense, the public accuses them of looking too masculine, aggressive, and not feminine enough. When they express themselves as cooperative and collaborative leaders, then they look too soft. In short, informal institutions in a society, particularly gender norms, can have a significant impact on women's political careers. Gender stereotyping can dominate public debates and diminish the chances of women to be judged based on their skill and merit.

When examining the impact of formal institutions on women executives who take the political career path, several key findings from the literature stand out. These relate to the role of electoral institutions (Kittilson and Schwindt-Bayer 2012), the implementation of gender quotas (Franceschet, Krook, and Piscopo 2012; Kittilson and Schwindt-Bayer 2012), executive systems (Jalalzai 2013), the proportion of women in cabinets (Bego 2014; Escobar-Lemmon and Taylor-Robinson 2005, 2009), and the intrabranch contagion, or the mobility of women from one branch of government to another (Thames and Williams 2013). Most of these institutional factors are discussed in detail in the quantitative chapters of this book (see Chapters 5 and 6). In many ways, the quantitative findings in the following two chapters, based on a database from 1990 to 2015, largely confirm and enhance the existing literature. However, in other ways, our findings in this book offer some novel insights and advance the scale and scope of the findings expressed in the works of Jalalzai (2004, 2008, 2013, 2016a, 2017).

In this chapter, we focus on women's use of the political career path to reach the presidency or premiership from a qualitative perspective in an effort to shed light on underexplored aspects of the extant literature. As seen in Figure 4.1, the political career path stands out as the predominant path that takes women to an executive seat. It is also the most widespread around the globe with cases from all world regions. Its frequency is progressively increasing over time as seen in Figure 4.2. In the last ten years (2010–2020), the number of women executives using the political career path more than doubled.

The political career path is by far the most popular route to power for women presidents and prime ministers, with over 100 individual cases. While the quantitative analyses (see Chapters 5 and 6) look at a variety of political and institutional factors that lead women to consistently take this path to executive office, this chapter complements those findings with a more detailed, qualitative approach.

Figure 4.1 Number of Women Executives from the Family, Activist, and Political-Career Paths to Power, 1960–January 2020

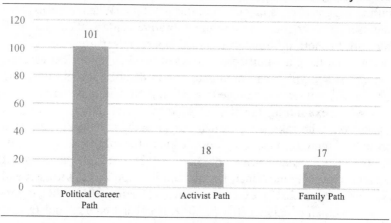

Figure 4.2 Number of Women Executives from Political-Career Path, 1960–January 2020

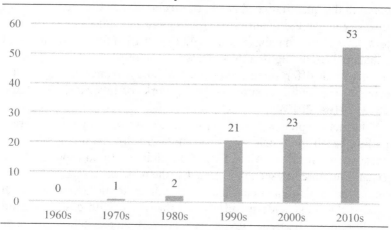

We uncover shared characteristics found in the biographies of these women presidents and prime ministers based on their specific career trajectories. In particular, the following questions are addressed: Do they mostly come from the public or private sectors? What is the role of the legislative branch in terms of supplying eligible women to executive office? Did women executives have cabinet positions prior to becoming presidents or prime ministers? If so, what was the nature of these cabinet positions? Were they mostly "feminine" posts, like to the Ministry of Women and Social Welfare? Or do more women hold "masculine" cabinet positions such as in the Ministry of Finance, Justice, or Foreign Affairs? It is important to answer these questions because there is a relative disconnect between the institutions literature and work on the paths women take to executive office. Consequently, throughout this chapter, we make an effort to identify which conditions and institutional settings tend to pave the way for women executives to take each career trajectory within the political career path.

The Legislative Path

In consolidated democracies, clear political career paths exist that run from the national legislature to the national executive, and prior experience in the legislature is often a norm for running for executive office.

—Leslie Schwindt-Bayer and
Catherine Reyes-Housholder,
*Women Presidents & Prime Ministers
in Post-Transition Democracies*

Incumbency is a potent asset for all politicians. Many studies on women and politics highlight the importance of the legislative branch as paving the way for women's advancement in politics (Escobar-Lemmon and Taylor-Robinson 2014; Schwindt-Bayer and Reyes-Housholder 2017). A progressively growing number of countries, especially those across Europe and Latin America, have endorsed quotas for women in a deliberate attempt to increase women's participation in the legislative branch. The basic argument for quotas is that it would expand the pool of qualified experienced women for other political positions, particularly president or prime minister (Franceschet, Krook, and Piscopo 2012; Htun 2016, 15–16). In other words, women from one branch of government could then "spill over" to the others (Thames and Williams 2013).

Latin America provides ample empirical support for the positive role of incumbency and quotas, particularly in the legislative branch. During the 1990s, national legislatures across Latin America had only 13 percent women on average. In 2010, this increased to 21 percent, and in 2014 one in four (25 percent) legislators were women. How-ever, there was significant variation within the region. While Brazil had less than 10 percent women in the legislative branch, Argentina and Nicaragua had nearly 40 percent women. The answer, according to Htun (2016), is the implementation of national quotas for this branch of the government. When quotas are implemented, the share of women representatives increases, whereas when they are not put in place, the percentage of women representatives remains in the single digits (Htun 2016, 27).

In the case of Europe, the European Parliament and especially left-wing, progressive parties were praised for granting better access to women legislators. Scholars found the European Parliament more women-friendly, "primarily because the hours are more structured, committee work involves discussions rather than debates and the pol-itics in general is less confrontational" (Luhiste and Kenny 2016, 628). While there was some controversy as to whether the "quota women" were qualified enough, empirical studies have illustrated that these new members of the legislative branch could carry their own weight and they were not in any way inferior to their colleagues (Allen, Cutts, and Campbell 2016).

In general, the literature highlights the importance of institutional settings and strong contagion effects in increasing the number of women in legislative bodies while cautioning how variation in the effectiveness of these endeavors can occur due to differing levels of development. However, despite vast differences in terms of socioeco-nomic development, it is possible to encounter similar trends in other regions outside of Latin America and the European Parliament. For example, Rwanda and Sweden both have implemented relatively high quotas for women. According to the Rwandan constitution, women have 30 percent of reserved seats, while Swedish political parties have voluntarily endorsed the zipper method (i.e., candidates on party lists alternate back and forth between males and females) to create a 50 percent party quota. Consequently, both Rwanda and Sweden have very high percentages of women in the legislative branch, 69 percent and 45 percent, respectively (DEA Gender Quota Database 2020). Other findings related to political institutions include the greater suc-cess of women politicians in proportional representation systems compared to majoritarian systems. However, this relationship holds mostly in developed countries as statistical findings are less robust for less developed or developing countries (Rosen 2013).

While the literature highlights the legislative branch as a critical gateway to political office, especially the presidency or premiership (e.g., Jalalzai 2013), the biographies of 100 women executives illustrate a slightly different trajectory. Using the biography of each woman executive to code their individual political-career steps shows that while the legislative path is clearly very important, the predominant path to the executive branch seemed to pass first and foremost through cabinet membership as shown in Figure 4.3. Of the 100 women executives who took the political career path to office over the course of 1960 to January 2020, 72 of them, or approximately 70 percent, had ministerial experience prior to assuming executive office. The legislative path was also important, but it was the second most frequently traveled path. Among the 100 women presidents and prime ministers who used the political career path,

Figure 4.3 Political Backgrounds of Women Executives Who Took the Political-Career Path, 1960–January 2020

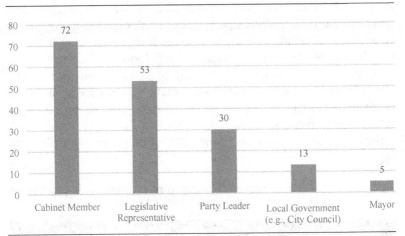

Source: Jalalzai (2013); *Encyclopedia Britannica*; and official government websites.

Notes: The total number of women using the political career path in our database was 100: 72 of them held cabinet positions, including the vice presidency; 53 served as parliamentarians or senators, including in the European Parliament; 30 of them held a leadership position in their political party; 13 of them came from local elected positions, such as city council; and 5 of them were mayors. Since many women held more than one position throughout their political careers, the sum of the five categories above is higher than 100. For example, women may serve as the general secretary of their party while also serving in the parliament and, later, may hold a position as minister of finance. See Table 4.1 for details of individual cases.

about half of them (53 of 100) served in the national legislature as parliamentarians or senators prior to assuming executive office. It is possible that this number is even higher because the biographies of these women executives are not always complete or consistent, even when cross-checked with multiple sources. Regardless, despite possible undercounting, cabinet experience did stand out across all regions and at all levels of development. While 71.2 percent of the women executives had prior cabinet experience before assuming office, 52.4 percent came from the legislative branch.

Since some women occupied both legislative and cabinet positions, it is important to gauge the degree of overlap between them by looking at individual cases. Figure 4.4 illustrates the strong degree of overlap between these two career trajectories. Out of eighty-one women executives, forty-four of them (72 percent) held both cabinet and legislative branch positions. This finding illustrates the mutually reinforcing nature of these top two pathways to executive posts as well as the importance of cabinet experience for women who later become presidents and prime ministers. Similar to the findings of Rosen (2013), our database of women executives until 2020 also revealed that the legislative path tends to be dominant in developed countries, particularly in Europe, whereas it is less frequent in Africa and the Caribbean. The literature also highlights parliamentary systems as the more women-friendly path to executive power (Jalalzai 2013). This is because, first, parliamentary systems are seen as less confrontational and less zero-sum than presidential regimes. Second, party leadership can also help women because they can test their leadership skills at the party level and later claim the premiership once

Figure 4.4 Political-Career-Path Women Executives with Legislative and Cabinet Experience, 1960–January 2020

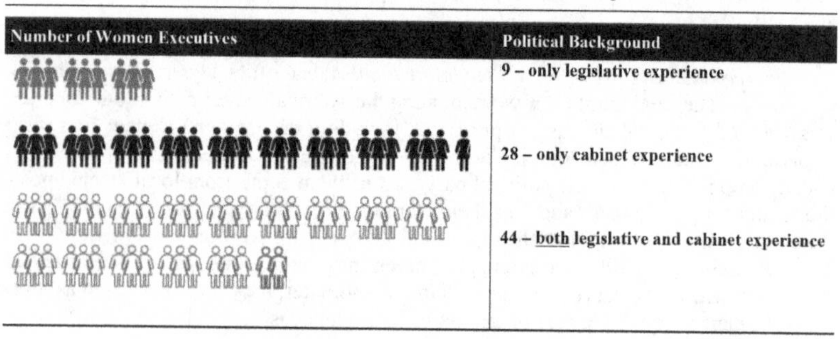

Number of Women Executives	Political Background
	9 – only legislative experience
	28 – only cabinet experience
	44 – **both** legislative and cabinet experience

they gain an electoral plurality. This track seems to be particularly viable for women in Northern Europe and Scandinavia, as the cases of Germany (Chancellor Angela Merkel), Norway (Prime Ministers Gro Harlem Brundtland, Anne Enger, and Erna Solberg), Finland (Prime Ministers Anneli Tuulikki Jäätteenmäki and Mari Kiviniemi), and Denmark (Prime Ministers Helle Thorning-Schmidt and Mette Frederiksen) illustrate. Therefore, it is expected that there is a steady trajectory of women executives moving from party leadership to parliaments and then to the executive branch.

In contrast to expectations, the biographies of women executives who took the political career path to office (see Table 4.1) did not show a vast number of women in party leadership positions. Out of 100 women executives, 30 of them served as the leaders of their party in the form of party presidents, spokespersons, and/or party chairs or vice chairs. This means 70 percent of the women executives using the political career path did not serve as the leaders of their party prior to becoming presidents and prime ministers. However, this does not mean party leadership is a marginal position. If anything, it seems to be more established in Northern Europe and Scandinavia. Out of the thirty women who did hold a party leadership position prior to becoming president or prime minister, nineteen of them—nearly two-thirds—hailed from Northern Europe and Scandinavia. Prime ministers from Denmark (Thorning-Schmidt and Frederiksen), Finland (Jäätteenmäki and Kiviniemi), Iceland (Jakobsdottír), Norway (Brundtland and Solberg), the United Kingdom (Thatcher and May), and Germany (Chancellor Merkel), served as the chairpersons of their respective political parties (see Table 4.1). Particularly in Germany and the United Kingdom, establishing clear leadership over the party rank and file seems to be a prerequisite to progress to higher office. However, the party leadership step prior to assuming the presidency or premiership is not uniformly replicated across the world. Out of the eighteen women executives who used the political career path in Africa, only four of them served in party leadership positions. Similarly, in Latin America, only three of the sixteen women who came to power via the political career path served as top leaders in their respective political parties.

Finally, it was unexpected to see the relative lack of local political experience considering it would likely be assumed that women on the political career path to executive power would have worked to gradually build their political credentials. Of the 100 women executives using the political career path, only 5 of them had previously

Table 4.1 Political-Career-Path Women Executives, 1960–2020

Name	Country	First Year in Office	Professional Career	Party Leadership	Elected Office	Cabinet Membership
PM Sylvie Kinigi	Burundi	1993	Bureaucrat			
PM Elisabeth Domitien	Central African Republic	1995	Business	Vice president of ruling party		
PRES Catherine Samba-Panza	Central African Republic	2014	Corporate lawyer		Mayor	
PRES Sahle-Work Zewde	Ethiopia	2018	Diplomat			
PRES Rose Francine Rogombé	Gabon	2009	Lawyer		Local representative; senator; president of senate	
PM Maria Adiatu Djaló Nandigna	Guinea-Bissau	2012		Government spokesperson		Minister of culture, youth and sports; minister of foreign affairs
PM Cécile Manorohanta	Madagascar	2009				Minister of defense
PM Cissé Mariam Kaïdama Sidibé	Mali	2011	Civil servant			Minister of planning; minister of agriculture; minister of rural development
PRES Monique Ohsan Bellepeau	Mauritius	2012	Journalism; media	President of Labor Party	Parliamentarian	Vice president
PRES Ameenah Gurib-Fakim	Mauritius	2015	Chemist; dean			
PM Luísa Dias Diogo	Mozambique	2004	Bureaucrat; finance			Minister of finance

continues

Table 4.1 Continued

Name	Country	First Year in Office	Professional Career	Party Leadership	Elected Office	Cabinet Membership
PM Saara Kuugongelwa-Amadhila	Namibia	2015	Bureaucrat		Member of the Lower Chamber	Minister of finance
PM Agathe Uwilingiyimana	Rwanda	1993	Teacher; bureaucrat			Minister of education
PM Maria das Neves Ceita Batista de Sousa	São Tomé & Príncipe	2002	Civil servant, finance			
PM Maria do Carmo Silveira	São Tomé & Príncipe	2005	Governor of the national bank			Minister of finance
PM Mame Madior Boye	Senegal	2001	Civil servant, judiciary			
PRES Ivy Matsepe-Casaburri	South Africa	2005			Provincial government	Minister of communication
PRES Pratibha Patil	India	2007	Lawyer	Political party chief	Positions in local and national governments	Minister of tourism; minister of social welfare; minister of housing; minister of education
PRES Roza Otunbayeva	Kyrgyzstan	2010	Diplomat	Head of party parliamentary caucus		Minister of foreign affairs
PM Nyam-Osoryn Tuyaa	Mongolia	1999			Parliamentarian	Minister of foreign affairs
PRES Bidhya Devi Bhandari	Nepal	2015		Vice chair of the Communist Party	Parliamentarian	Minister of environment; minister of defense

continues

Table 4.1 Continued

Name	Country	First Year in Office	Professional Career	Party Leadership	Elected Office	Cabinet Membership
PRES Halimah Yacob	Singapore	2017	Legal services		Parliamentarian; Speaker of Parliament	Minister of community development, youth and sports; minister of state on social and family development
PRES Tsai Ing-wen	Taiwan	2016	Lawyer; legal scholar		Mayor	Minister of mainland affairs
PRES Đặng Thị Ngọc Thịnh	Vietnam	2018			Parliamentarian	Vice president
PRES Dalia Itzik	Israel	2007	Teacher		Deputy mayor; Knesset member; Speaker of the Knesset	Minister of environment; minister of industry and trade
PM Kim Campbell	Canada	1993	Lawyer			Minister of Indian affairs; minister of justice; defense minister; attorney general
PM Julia Gillard	Australia	2010	Lawyer		Parliamentarian	Deputy prime minister; minister of education and employment
PRES Hilda Cathy Heine	Marshall Islands	2016	Teacher; counselor		Parliamentarian	Minister of Education
PM Jenny Shipley	New Zealand	1997	Teacher	Leader of the National Party	Parliamentarian	Minister of women's affairs; minister of social welfare; minister of transportation
PM Helen Elizabeth Clark	New Zealand	1999	Lecturer		Parliamentarian	Minister of health; minister of housing; minister of conservation; deputy prime minister

continues

Table 4.1 Continued

Name	Country	First Year in Office	Professional Career	Party Leadership	Elected Office	Cabinet Membership
PM Jacinda Ardern	New Zealand	2017	Bureaucrat	Party leader		Minister of culture; minister of social policy; minister of national security, and intelligence
PM Cynthia Pratt	Bahamas	2005	Teacher; Protestant minister		Parliamentarian	Deputy prime minister
PM Mia Mottley	Barbados	2018	Lawyer	Opposition leader	Senator	Minister of education, youth affairs, and culture; attorney general
PRES Jeanine Áñez	Bolivia	2019	Law; media; journalism		Senator, Senate vice president	
PM Ertha Pascal-Trouillot	Haiti	1990	Lawyer; judge			
PM Claudette Werleigh	Haiti	1995	Education; NGOs			Minister of social affairs; minister of foreign affairs
PM Michèle Pierre-Louis	Haiti	2008	Education; NGOs			Minister of justice and public security
PM Florence Duperval Guillaume	Haiti	2014	Health worker			Minister of public health and population
PM Portia Simpson-Miller	Jamaica	2006		Ruling party president	Parliamentarian	Minister of defense, development, information, and sports; minister of labor, social security, and sports; minister of tourism and sports; minister of local government
PM Kamla Persad-Bissessar	Trinidad & Tobago	2010	Lawyer	Opposition leader	Parliamentarian	Attorney general; minister of education

continues

Table 4.1 Continued

Name	Country	First Year in Office	Professional Career	Party Leadership	Elected Office	Cabinet Membership
PRES Paula-Mae Weekes	Trinidad & Tobago	2018	Lawyer; judiciary			
PRES Laura Chinchilla	Costa Rica	2010	Consultant		Parliamentarian	Minister of public security; minister of justice
PRES Rosalía Arteaga	Ecuador	1997	Bureaucrat			Vice president
PM Beatriz Merino Lucero	Peru	2003	Lawyer; ombudsman		Senator	
PM Rosario Fernández	Peru	2011	Lawyer; bureaucrat			Minister of justice
PM Ana Jara	Peru	2014	Lawyer		Congresswoman	Minister of women and vulnerable populations; minister of labor and employment
PM Mercedes Aráoz	Peru	2017	Economist; scholar; bureaucrat		Congresswoman	Minister of foreign trade and tourism; minister of economy and finance
PRES Doris Bures	Austria	2016	NGOs		President of the Lower House	Minister for women, media, and public service; minister of transport, innovation, and technology
CHAN Brigitte Bierlein	Austria	2019	Lawyer, judge			
PM Sophie Wilmès	Belgium	2019	Finance		City council; parliamentarian	Minister of budget; minister of civil service
PM Reneta Indzhova	Bulgaria	1994	Bureaucrat			
PM Jadranka Kosor	Croatia	2009	Law; media; journalism	Party vice president	Member of the House of Representatives	Deputy prime minister; minister of family and veterans' affairs
PRES Kolinda Grabar-Kitarović	Croatia	2015	Diplomat			Minister of EU affairs; minister of foreign affairs

continues

Table 4.1 Continued

Name	Country	First Year in Office	Professional Career	Party Leadership	Elected Office	Cabinet Membership
PM Helle Thorning-Schmidt	Denmark	2011		Party leader; main opposition leader	European Parliament member; parliamentarian	
PM Mette Frederiksen	Denmark	2016	Union organizer	Party spokesperson; party leader	Parliamentarian	Minister of employment; minister of justice
PRES Kersti Kaljulaid	Estonia	2016	Business; banking; bureaucrat			
PRES Tarja Halonen	Finland	2000	Lawyer		City council; parliamentarian	Minister of justice; minister of foreign affairs; minister of social affairs and health
PM Anneli Tuulikki Jäätteenmäki	Finland	2003	Lawyer	Chairwoman of the Center Party	Parliamentarian; European Parliament member	Minister of justice
PM Mari Kiviniemi	Finland	2010	Politician	Chairwoman of the Center Party	Parliamentarian	Minister of public administration and local government; minister of trade and development; minister of interior
PM Sanna Marin	Finland	2019	Public service; NGOs		Parliamentarian	Minister of transport and communications
PM Édith Cresson	France	1991			Mayor; European Parliament member	Minister of agriculture; minister of foreign trade; minister of European affairs
PRES Nino Burdzhanadze	Georgia	2003	Law		Parliamentarian; Speaker of Parliament	
PRES Salome Zourabichvili	Georgia	2018	Diplomat			Foreign minister
PRES Sabine Bergmann-Pohl	East Germany	1990	Physician		Lower Chamber representative	Minister for special affairs

continues

Table 4.1 Continued

Name	Country	First Year in Office	Professional Career	Party Leadership	Elected Office	Cabinet Membership
CHAN Angela Merkel	Germany	2005	Physics PhD	Party chairwoman	Parliamentarian	Minister for women and youth; minister for environment and conservation
PM Vassiliki Thanou-Christophilou	Greece	2015	Law; judiciary			
PRES Katerina Sakellaropoulou	Greece	2020	Judge; technocrat			
PM Katrín Jakobsdóttir	Iceland	2017	Media; journalism	Party chair	Parliamentarian	Minister of education; minister of culture; minister of Nordic cooperation
PRES Mary McAleese	Ireland	1997	Lawyer; legal scholar			
PRES Mary Robinson	Ireland	1990	Lawyer; legal scholar		City council; parliamentarian	
PRES Atifete Jahjaga	Kosovo	2011	Law; law enforcement; director of Kosovo police			
PRES Vaira Vike-Freiberga	Latvia	1999	Psychology PhD; scholar			
PM Laimdota Straujuma	Latvia	2014	Economist			Minister of agriculture
PM Kazimira Danutė Prunskienė	Lithuania	1990	Economics professor; director		Parliamentarian	Deputy prime minister
PRES Dalia Grybauskaitė	Lithuania	2009	Lecturer of economics; bureaucrat			Minister of finance

continues

Table 4.1 Continued

Name	Country	First Year in Office	Professional Career	Party Leadership	Elected Office	Cabinet Membership
PM Irena Degutienė	Lithuania	1999	Physician		Parliamentarian; Speaker of Parliament	Deputy minister of health care
PM Radmila Šekerinska	Macedonia	2004	Engineering; law	Opposition leader	City council; parliamentarian	Deputy prime minister
PRES Marie-Louise Coleiro Preca	Malta	2014	Public notary	Assistant general secretary of party	Parliamentarian	Minister of the family and social solidarity
PM Zinaida Greceanîi	Moldova	2008	Bureaucrat		Parliamentarian	Vice prime minister; minister of finance
PM Maia Sandu	Moldova	2019	Economist; bureaucrat			Minister of education
PM Sibel Siber	Northern Cyprus	2013	Physician		Speaker of Parliament	
PM Gro Harlem Brundtland	Norway	1981	Medicine	Head of party	Parliamentarian	
PM Anne Enger	Norway	1998	Bureaucrat			Minister of culture
PM Erna Solberg	Norway	2013	Bureaucrat	Party leader	Parliamentarian; city council	Minister of local government and regional development
PM Hanna Suchocka	Poland	1992	Law; legal scholar		Parliamentarian	Minister of justice; attorney general
PM Ewa Kopacz	Poland	2014	Medicine		Local council member; Speaker of the Lower House	Minister of health
PM Beata Maria Szydło	Poland	2015	Academic	Party vice chair	Mayor; parliamentarian	Deputy prime minister
PM Viorica Dăncilă	Romania	2018	Engineer	Party leader	Parliamentarian	
PM Nataša Mićić	Serbia	2002	Lawyer; judge	Party vice president	Speaker of Parliament	

continues

Table 4.1 Continued

Name	Country	First Year in Office	Professional Career	Party Leadership	Elected Office	Cabinet Membership
PRES Slavica Đukić Dejanović	Serbia	2012	Physician; hospital director	Party vice president		Minister of family care
PM Ana Brnabić	Serbia	2017	MBA			Minister of public administration
PM Alenka Bratušek	Slovenia	2013	Civil servant, finance	Party president	City council; parliamentarian	
PM Iveta Radičová	Slovakia	2010	Academic	Party spokesperson	Parliamentarian	Minister of labor
PRES Micheline Calmy-Rey	Switzerland	2007	Book distribution business		Local and federal representative	Foreign minister
PRES Doris Leuthard	Switzerland	2010	Lawyer		Local and federal representative	
PRES Simonetta Sommaruga	Switzerland	2015		Pianist; bureaucrat	Local and federal representative	Minister of justice; vice president
PM Tansu Çiller	Turkey	1993	Economist; scholar		Local and federal representative	Deputy prime minister; state minister on economy; foreign minister
PM Margaret Thatcher	United Kingdom	1979	Lawyer	Party leader	Parliamentarian	Secretary of state for education and science
PM Theresa May	United Kingdom	2016	Banking	Party leader	Parliamentarian	Shadow secretary positions; secretary of state for the Home Department
PM Milka Planinc	Yugoslavia	1982	Bureaucrat			Minister of education

Sources: For executives from 1960 to 2010 see Jalalzai (2013); for executives between 2010 and 2020, see global media sources, including BBC, *The Guardian*, Reuters, *Time*, *Encyclopedia Britannica*, and http://www.councilwomenworldleaders.org, and official government webpages.

served as mayors and only eleven were elected to city councils and/or other forms of local/municipal governance bodies. Consequently, it would be safe to say that in order for women to reach an executive position, starting from local elected office may not be the most viable way (see Table 4.1 for details of individual executives and countries).

The Cabinet Path

Many of the women executives who served in cabinet positions were also parliamentarians. Therefore, these two tracks cannot be considered as analytically separate entities. In fact, empirical studies show that having more women in the legislative branch has a positive impact on the gender balance at the cabinet level (Thames and Williams 2013). A study by Escobar-Lemmon and Taylor-Robinson (2005) on eighteen countries in Latin America shows that higher percentages of women in the legislature increase the likelihood of more women in the cabinet. Higher levels of socioeconomic development and having more left-wing, progressive parties are also correlated with more women in cabinet positions. Finally, there are also robust signs of international diffusion in which having more women in the cabinets around the world also increases the chances other women will reach those posts (Escobar-Lemmon and Taylor-Robinson 2005).

Once women reach the cabinet, they tend to receive gendered positions. Specifically, they are more likely to be placed in ministries of social welfare, youth, or women's affairs, which are considered to be stereotypically feminine domains. Consequently, not being placed in more impactful cabinet positions, such as justice, foreign affairs, or economy and finance, further inhibits the upward mobility prospects of women politicians. Studies on Latin America illustrate that while women have been generally confined to feminine cabinet positions, there has recently been a change and more are receiving prestigious, impactful ministries. Intense party competition also helps qualified women get access to the prized cabinet positions. As parties try to appeal to swing women voters, they feel compelled to nominate strong women to influential cabinet positions (Escobar-Lemmon and Taylor-Robinson 2005, 2009).

Of the 100 women executives who took the political career path to office, nearly 70 percent had served in a cabinet position. Many of them served multiple times as ministers, usually in different ministries, before becoming presidents or prime ministers. As Table 4.2 shows, the findings regarding the ministries led by future women executives are mostly in line with the extant literature. Women executives tend to have more experience in high-prestige cabinet posts, prior to claiming executive positions.

Different countries have slightly different names for cabinet posts that more or less perform similar functions. One example of this is the attorney general in the United States and the minister of justice and interior minister in most parliamentary regimes. They are usually in charge of the judiciary and federal law enforcement. In some cases, there are different ministries, but they are engaged in a similar policy area. That is why, for example, the Ministry of Finance

Table 4.2 Cabinet Positions Women Executives Held on the Political-Career Path

Name of Ministry	Frequency
Minister of justice; justice and public security; attorney general; interior minister	16
Minister of foreign affairs; EU affairs; mainland affairs; Nordic cooperation	12
Deputy prime minister; vice president	12
Minister of finance; industry and trade; trade and development; foreign trade; state minister on economy	12
Minister of women, family, and social welfare; women's and veterans' affairs; women and vulnerable populations	11
Minister of education; science and education	9
Minister of housing; housing and planning; public administration and local government; community development	6
Minister of tourism; culture, youth, and sports	6
Minister of health; public health and population	5
Minister of environment; environment and conservation	4
Minister of transportation; transportation and technology; communication	4
Minister of agriculture; rural development	4
Minister of defense	3
Minister of labor; labor and employment	3
Minister of Indian affairs; special affairs	2
Total	109

Note: See Table 4.1 for details. The sum of all ministries is more than 100 since some women executives served in 2, 3, or 4 cabinet positions prior to becoming presidents or prime ministers.

is combined with the Ministry of Trade and other economic-related ministries. In short, similar ministries are grouped under one category in order to take a more concise approach to analyzing the data. Overall, there were 109 total ministerial positions that seventy-two executives served in.

When examining the list of cabinet posts in Table 4.2, it is clear that the top three most frequent cabinet positions for women presidents and prime ministers are all high-prestige ministries, such as the Ministry of Justice, Ministry of Foreign Affairs, and the position of deputy prime minister or vice president. Minister of justice was the most frequently occupied cabinet position for women who subsequently became presidents and prime ministers. Thus, these findings affirm those of prior studies (Escobar-Lemmon and Taylor-Robinson 2005, 2009) that highlight the hierarchy of different cabinet positions. If women serve as ministers of local government and public administration, ministers of agriculture, or ministers of communication, they are much less likely to make the leap to the executive seat due to the low visibility of these ministerial posts.

The allocation of cabinet positions for women executives tends to overlap with their professional backgrounds. Figure 4.5 displays the frequency of professional backgrounds of 100 women executives using this path to reach office. Probably one of the most interesting qualitative findings of this section is the potency of a legal career for women's ascendance to power. Women with law school training seem to have a distinct advantage to acquire impactful cabinet positions related to their professional backgrounds. The second largest group includes women from the public bureaucracy and civil service.

Prime Minister Kim Campbell of Canada, Prime Minister Rosario Fernández of Peru, President Tarja Halonen of Finland, Prime Minister Anneli Tuulikki Jäätteenmäki also of Finland, and Prime Minister Hanna Suchocka of Poland all have law degrees. Their legal backgrounds helped them as they built their careers in the Ministry of Justice to later move up to the executive position. Prime minister of Trinidad and Tobago Kamla Persad-Bissessar also took this track by serving as her country's attorney general. Serving as the minister of justice or the attorney general seems to be an effective path for women to later claim the post of president or prime minister. Thus, they are the most common cabinet positions to hold prior to getting an executive seat.

Figure 4.5 Professional Backgrounds of Women Executives from the Political-Career Path, 1979–January 2020

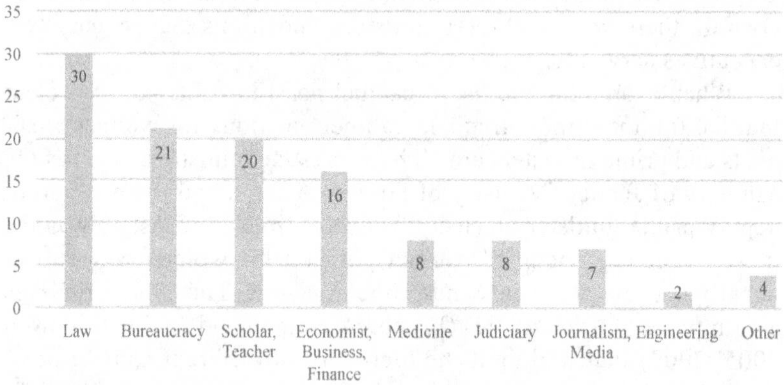

Note: See Table 4.1 for details. The total number of professions is more than the number of women executives because some of the women held more than one career, such as when a lawyer subsequently became a judge.

In general, at the cabinet level, there is a degree of meritocracy and efficiency of allocation in which the professional backgrounds of these women executives are taken into account when they are selected for a ministry position. If they were civil servants in finance-related posts, such as the directors of the national bank, or if they have academic training in economics, they tend to get the Finance Ministry or a related position. This was the case in Mozambique (Prime Minister Luísa Dias Diogo), Lithuania (President Dalia Grybauskaitė and Prime Minister Kazimira Danutė Prunskienė), Turkey (Prime Minister Tansu Çiller), and São Tomé and Príncipe (Prime Ministers Maria das Neves Ceita Batista de Sousa and Maria do Carmo Silveira). While only a few of the women executives had a medical background, in most cases they served in cabinet positions that were related to their professional background, such as the Ministry of Health. This was the case in both Lithuania (Prime Minister Irena Degutienė) and Poland (Prime Minister Ewa Kopacz). If they were diplomats, like President Roza Otunbayeva of Kyrgyzstan or President Kolinda Grabar-Kitarović of Croatia, they were appointed as ministers of foreign affairs or EU affairs. It was not uncommon for those with teaching or academic backgrounds to get the Ministry of Science or Ministry of Education (see Table 4.1).

Case Studies and the Role of Gatekeepers

In general, executive offices, including governors and mayors, are harder for women politicians to access in comparison to legislative or judicial offices. Across Latin America and the Caribbean, women governors and mayors constituted only 5 percent of the overall office holders in 2001 (Htun 2016, 27–28). Within a decade, that share increased to 9 percent, while women's share in the legislative branch was 21 percent by 2010 (Htun 2016, 27–28). Serving in a high-profile cabinet position, particularly if it is relevant to the professional career of a woman politician seems to be an effective way to overcome institutional barriers to an executive seat. The case of Prime Minister Tansu Çiller of Turkey is illustrative in this regard. Çiller studied economics in college and received her PhD in economics from the University of Connecticut. Subsequently, she returned to Turkey and taught at Boğaziçi University, eventually becoming a full professor; however, she remained in contact with political elites, particularly those in the center-right parties. The party gatekeeper that helped launch Tansu Çiller's political career in the center-right True Path Party (Turkish acronym, DYP) was the party leader and later president Süleyman Demirel. "Demirel brought in Çiller to engender the urban sectors' confidence in the party by showing that it was truly liberal. What made her accession extraordinary was that she was not only the first woman elected to the top leadership of a political party in Turkey, but to a right-wing party where top cadres were always occupied by male politicians" (Cizre 2002, 88–89). After leading the DYP, she served in several cabinet positions as the state minister in charge of the economy and the minister of foreign affairs before becoming the prime minister of a coalition government in 1993. Most analysts agree that without then Prime Minister Demirel's pivotal intervention and her powerful ministerial positions, the political career of Tansu Çiller would not have flourished like it did.

Compared to the Turkish case where the party gatekeeper(s) made a critical difference in a woman's ascendance to power, in the case of Denmark's first woman prime minister, somewhat different dynamics are observed. Examining the career trajectory of Prime Minister Helle Thorning-Schmidt, a much more gradual path is seen rather than a sudden interjection into the party's leadership by a male gatekeeper. After studying political science in college, Thorning-Schmidt joined the Social Democratic Party and began working for trade unions. Gradually, she moved up within the party rank and file and became the Social Democratic Party's representative at the European Parliament. Subsequent women executives in Denmark, such as Prime Minister Mette Frederiksen, also followed a similar path. Frederiksen studied social sciences in college, joined the union movement and the Social Democratic Party, became the youngest member of parliament at twenty-four years old, and served in two key ministerial positions—employment and justice—before becoming the prime minister in 2016 (see appendix for more detailed biographies of all women executives taking office from 2011 to 2020).

The strength of the women executives around the world who held cabinet positions also shows the mutually reinforcing trend that more women serving as presidents and prime ministers leads to more women in cabinet positions. Both qualitative and quantitative findings from this book illustrate that if a country had a woman president and/or prime minister take a certain path to office, it tends to have more executives who use similar paths. In fact, many women display similar backgrounds and career tracks as their predecessor(s). Finland, for example, had four women executives take the political career path since 2000: President Tarja Halonen, Prime Minister Anneli Tuulikki Jäätteenmäki, Prime Minister Mari Kiviniemi, and Prime Minister Sanna Marin. Norway had three women executives since 1981, all of them following successful political-career tracks as parliamentarians, party leaders, and prime ministers: Gro Harlem Brundtland, Anne Enger, and Erna Solberg.

Research on the gender composition of the cabinets of women presidents in Latin America shows that when they are not constrained, they are more likely to appoint women ministers in their cabinets than their male counterparts. Reyes-Housholder (2016, 3) adds that "in addition to breaking the highest glass ceiling, women presidents in Latin America often do improve women's presence in the executive branch." Examining the cabinet positions occupied by women executives who took the political career path to office around the world shows an increasing presence of women, particularly in high-prestige ministerial positions, such as in the foreign affairs, justice, and economy ministries. Consequently, cabinets serve as an effective pipeline to an executive position while simultaneously benefiting from having more female representation. The qualitative findings in this chapter that include 100 women executives testify to these facts. Nearly 70 percent of women come to executive power with prior experience as cabinet members; more often than not, they serve in high-profile ministries, like justice or foreign affairs, or hold the vice presidency or deputy prime minister positions.

Conclusion

Formal and informal institutions play crucial roles in shaping women's ascendance to executive power. Prior political careers at the local, regional, and national levels, or as in the case of Europe, at the supranational level, seem to be the most frequently traveled paths for women who claim executive political posts (Bond, Covington, and Fleisher 1985; Genovese 1993a; Jalalzai 2004, 2013). Three out of four, or nearly 75 percent of all women executives have achieved impressive political careers prior to assuming executive office in their nation, whereas the family path and the political activist path are used by about 13 percent of all women presidents and prime ministers. Moreover, the political career path is much more broadly spread across the globe and is now almost a prerequisite for women to succeed in Europe (Jalalzai 2013).

Our examination of the biographies of 100 women executives who used the political career path to assume power supports the existing literature on women and political institutions. There is strong evidence of the contagion effect (Thames and Williams 2013). Women from the legislative and judicial branches of government often move into an executive seat (50 percent of female executives come from the legislative branch while fewer than 10 percent come from the judicial branch). Serving in the legislative branch or the cabinet seemed to be the two most frequently followed paths to executive seats. It was unexpected to find that an overwhelming majority (71.2 percent) of women executives served in cabinets rather than the legislatures (52.4 percent). These findings affirm the warnings of Schwindt-Bayer and Reyes-Housholder (2017) that it should not be assumed that there is an automatic contagion effect between the legislative and the executive branches. These authors suggest observing "if it is the same person" who moves up from one branch to the other (Schwindt-Bayer and Reyes-Housholder 2017, 90). As shown in Figure 4.3, it is clear that the contagion effect from the legislative branch is not as large as many in the empirical literature predicted.

However, it is much larger in the cabinets, which is also the executive branch.

Another key point raised in the literature was the importance of leadership positions, particularly in leftist parties. Our findings showed that on a global scale, party leadership seemed to be a key step in advancing through European parliamentary systems, but it was less common across the globe. Overall, only 30 percent of the women executives using the political career path also held top party leadership positions. Experience as mayors or representatives on local councils only marginally helped women executives reach the presidency or premiership. This was the least frequently traveled track for women presidents and prime ministers using the political career path to reach executive power as only about 10 percent of the women had this type of experience.

In terms of women's experience at the cabinet level before claiming an executive seat, the "masculine," or high-prestige, ministries stood out compared to all others. Again, this qualitative finding was in line with the literature and most of the empirical studies that illustrated the gendered nature of cabinets. The top four cabinet positions among women presidents and prime ministers who had extensive prior political careers were in the Ministry of Justice or Interior/attorney general, Ministry of Foreign Affairs, Ministry of Economy or Finance, and deputy prime minister or vice president. Our study also illustrates the advantages of being a high-ranking bureaucrat or having a legal background as a lawyer or judge in order to claim a high-prestige cabinet position. These findings, particularly the importance of the cabinet path, could be useful for future research that examines systematically underperforming women candidates in US presidential races. Rather than seasoned senators, women candidates with strong executive experiences such as governors or secretaries of state might have slightly better chances.

The political career path is the most widely distributed path across the world. The work of Jalalzai (2013) also confirms this finding and adds that it is particularly well established in Europe and Africa. However, our results suggest a small caveat because when examining the political career tracks of women presidents and prime ministers in Europe and Africa, a couple of important points stand out. First, while both regions had highly qualified women executives with strong credentials, those in Africa tended to have shorter tenures. One important reason for this is the high frequency of temporary or interim appointments to the position of presidency. In Gabon (President Rose Francine Rogombé), Guinea-Bissau (President Carmen Pereira), South Africa (President Ivy Matsepe-Casaburri), and Central African Republic (President Catherine Samba-Panza), women served only in an interim capacity. Secondly, many of these women executives with solid political careers had their tenure abruptly interrupted. In particular, in Burundi (Prime Minister Sylvie Kinigi), Mali (Prime Minister Cissé Mariam Kaïdama Sidibé), and Madagascar (Prime Minister Cécile Manorohanta), women executives had to prematurely vacate their posts due to military coups.

While the political career path seems to have provided a steady stream of women executives across Europe and Latin America, with reelection victories and relatively long tenures in the executive office, this success is not uniformly distributed around the world. Levels of socioeconomic development and, particularly, overall political stability matter significantly. Not all women who reached office via the political career path can enjoy long and peaceful tenures as presidents and prime ministers. Especially in the cases from Africa, significant hurdles cause women to prematurely vacate their posts. The qualitative analysis presented here and in the preceding chapters on the political activist and family paths can offer some insights. Regardless, institutional political structures, such as parliamentary systems, and the experience provided by "masculine" cabinet positions help women overcome voter, cultural, and institutional sexism. In particular, women can avoid sexist voters by being appointed prime minister or gain the necessary experience in the cabinet to demonstrate that they would be an effective president on "masculine" policy issues like foreign affairs and the economy.

Women executives around the world are still rare. Yet, between 2010 and 2020, fifty-three new women presidents and prime ministers took office and nearly doubled the sample size (see Figure 4.2). As of 2020, 16 out of 193 (8 percent) of world leaders are women. Yet they illustrated exceptional success when confronting the global Covid-19 pandemic.[1]

Further research and the addition of more women executives can certainly provide insight into why and how women can break the glass ceiling in some cases but not in others. In order to continue enhancing and advancing the existing literature on women executives, in the next chapters we statistically analyze whether the factors that predict whether a country has a female president or prime minister impact the path they take to office, and how the path a woman takes to executive office impacts the path(s) used by those following in her footsteps.

Note

1. While we focus on women's paths to power, their length in office, and not necessarily on the performance of leaders while in office, we wanted to briefly draw attention to the grade book of world leaders in the face of Covid-19. While all leaders were faced with the exact same challenge, the Covid-19 pandemic, women leaders decisively outperformed their male counterparts. Scholars, journalists, and lay people highlight the efficient, competent, and caring ways in which women leaders in New Zealand, Germany, Taiwan, and Denmark tackled the problem. Most of them from the career path, these women were better at processing scientific evidence and taking precautionary measures ahead of the curve. Chancellor Merkel's approach was referred to as the Merkel effect, as she calmly explained the reproduction pace of the virus (R0) to the German citizens in a rare public address. Early on criticized for taking too drastic measures, Jacinda Ardern effectively kept the virus out of her island nation. While these cases might be anecdotal, further research on women's paths to power and their subsequent success while in office could provide valuable insights on the performances of women leaders. See Amanda Taub, "Why Are Women-Led Nations Doing Better with COVID-19?" *New York Times*, May 15, 2020, https://www.nytimes.com/2020/05/15/world/coronavirus-women-leaders.html; Sebastian Ocklenburg, "The Merkel Effect: How Leadership Reduces COVID-19 Anxiety," *Psychology Today*, June 3, 2020, https://www.psychologytoday.com/us/blog/the-asymmetric-brain/202006/the-merkel-effect-how-leadership-reduces-covid-19-anxiety.

5

The Impact of Political and Institutional Dynamics

Thus far we have examined the three paths women take to executive office: family, political activist, and political career. These qualitative analyses have revealed patterns relating to the use of each path: (1) over time; (2) regionally; (3) in different institutional and political contexts; and (4) by elected, appointed, and interim executives. Additionally, numerous cases were presented to show tangible examples of the findings. In this chapter we build on these findings by statistically testing which political and institutional factors lead women to take each path to executive office. In doing so, we also continue to advance the literature on women executives and offer additional insight into how women overcome various types of sexism (voter, institutional, and cultural) to become presidents and prime ministers. We proceed by developing hypotheses and discussing the results of each analysis in turn.

The Dynamics of the Paths Women Take to Executive Office

Democratic, Economic, and Human Development

Politically unstable countries are often characterized by regime changes that occur because of coups and/or the assassination or imprisonment of the current executive. Since power can be inherited or gained via other undemocratic means, women can often become executives using their family name (Hodson 1997; Jalalzai 2013; Jalalzai and Rincker 2018). Similarly, some women gain notoriety by participating in activist or democratization movements in these politically unstable, undemocratic countries. This allows them to launch a political career and eventually become a president or prime minister (Jalalzai 2013). Women are also able to overcome gender stereotypes that men are best suited for executive positions because politically unstable countries look toward women to serve as peacemakers and consensus-builders after politically tumultuous periods in history (Geske and Bourque 2001; Jalalzai 2008, 2013; Katzenstein 1978; Saint-Germain 1993; Salo 2010). In light of these findings from prior research, the following hypothesis can be derived:

> *H1: Women in countries with low levels of democratic institutionalism are more likely to take the family or political activist path to become a president or prime minister.*

Two other political factors often mentioned in the women-executives literature are patriarchy and a country's level of economic development. In patriarchal societies, women need family ties or an activist background in order to launch political careers that eventually lead to an executive position (e.g., Baturo and Gray 2018; Hodson 1997; Jalalzai 2004, 2008; Jalalzai and Rincker 2018; Richter 1991). Both paths help women overcome gender stereotypes that view men as better suited for executive positions that must handle "masculine" issue areas, such as national defense (Fox and Oxley 2003; Huddy and Terkildsen 1993; Sczesny et al. 2004). Put differently, women are able to gain political legitimacy through their dynastic family ties or by highlighting the need to be involved in formal political structures to advance the movement and/or serve as a caretaker and peacebuilder during politically tumultuous times (Baturo and Gray 2018; Beckwith 2000; Geske and Bourque 2001; Jalalzai 2013; Jalalzai and Rincker 2018; Salo 2010). Similarly, women struggle to break the glass ceiling in economically developed countries because they typically have more worldwide influence over "masculine" issue areas, such as the global economy and foreign affairs (Jalalzai 2013). However, women on the political career path are best situated to overcome this hurdle to executive power because they are often able to gain experience in these "masculine" policy areas within the cabinet or legislature (e.g., Jalalzai 2013). The research and the fact that economic development and patriarchy influence a country's level of human development—or its economic growth coupled with the extent to which citizens have freedom of opportunity and the ability to improve their well-being— suggest the following hypothesis:

> *H2: Women in countries with low levels of human development are more likely to take the family or political activist path to executive office, while women in countries with high levels of human development are more likely to take the political career path to executive office.*

Political Institutions

The extant literature has identified a number of factors related to political institutions that impact whether a country has a female executive. Political structures that indirectly enable a woman to reach executive office will be excluded from the analysis. In particular, those that increase the number of women in government and, consequently, the pool of women qualified to become president or prime minister: electoral systems featuring multimember districts and/or proportional representation systems, quotas, and leftist parties (Darcy, Welch, and Clark 1994; Davidson-Schmich 2006; Htun and Jones 2002; Htun and Piscopo 2014; Jalalzai 2013; Kittilson 1999; Lovenduski and Norris 1993; Matland 1993, 1998a; Paxton 1997; Paxton, Hughes, and Barnes 2020; Reynolds 1999; Rule 1985; Rule and Zimmerman 1994; Salmond 2006; Yoon 2010).

The first political institutions–related factor that directly explains whether a country has a female executive that will be examined in this analysis is the executive structure itself. It is easier for women to come to power in parliamentary and semi-presidential systems because they can be appointed and the duties of a prime minister are conducive to the stereotypical perceived strengths of women (Duerst-Lahti 1997; Hodson 1997; Jalalzai 2013, 2016a; Whicker and Isaacs 1999). Presidents are typically thought of in "masculine" terms because as commanders in chief, they must be quick and authoritative decisionmakers. However, prime ministers must be collaborative and consensual to unify parties in the legislature and work toward a common policy agenda (Duerst-Lahti 1997). In addition to valuing "feminine" governing styles in parliamentary and semi-presidential systems, appointment-based systems allow women to work their way up while bypassing voters who possess gender stereotypes. Overall, this body of literature suggests the following hypothesis:

> *H3: Women are more likely to become executives via the political career path in countries with semi-presidential and parliamentary executive structures.*

Multiparty systems are the remaining political institutional factor directly related to the rise of female executives. Multiparty systems typically occur in countries with parliamentary executive structures where the resulting coalitional government often requires a prime minister who possesses stereotypical "feminine" leadership skills, or those that focus on consensus-building and collaboration (Jalalzai 2013). Since prime ministers are often members of parliament, party leaders, and/or former cabinet members, it is expected that women in multiparty systems took the political career path to office. This expectation is summarized in the following hypothesis:

> *H4: Women are more likely to become executives using the political career path in countries with multiparty systems.*

Female Political Advancement

The literature also recognizes that it is easier for women to become presidents and prime ministers the longer women have had the right to vote, when there are multiple women serving in the national government, and/or when a woman has already broken the executive glass ceiling (e.g., Jalalzai 2013, 2016a; Reynolds 1999). This is because (1) voting rights facilitate women becoming involved in politics and launching political careers; (2) there is an ample number of women for parties and/or voters to nominate and/or select for an executive position; and (3) parties and voters have overcome gender stereotypes in the past. Since length of suffrage indirectly impacts whether a country has a female president or prime minister by increasing the number of women in government and the pool of potential women executives, it will be excluded from the analysis. Regardless, it appears that, in general, women have a better chance of becoming presidents and prime ministers as more females hold government positions; consequently, in order to be considered, women must be on the political career path to executive office. Yet many former political activists will launch political careers to further their cause, so it is also possible that these women benefit from more female representation in government (Jalalzai 2013). Additionally, women taking the family, political activist, or political career paths to executive office should also be better able to reach the presidency or premiership by following in the footsteps of a previous woman executive who has already defied gender stereotypes. These expectations are summarized as follows:

> H5: An increased number of women in national government positions increases the likelihood that a woman will take the political career or political activist path to executive office.

> H6: Having a previous female executive will lead women to take the family, political activist, or political career path to executive office.

Data and Methods

The above hypotheses will be tested by examining all women who assumed office as a president or prime minister at any point starting in 1990 through 2015. This time period was selected because these are the first and last years that the data for all of the variables included in the analysis are available.[1] Although the first woman to serve as an executive was Sri Lankan prime minister Sirimavo Bandaranaike in 1960, relatively few women immediately followed in her footsteps. Consequently, the time frame of this study covers 85 percent of all women who have assumed executive posts by the end of 2015. Only 79 percent of all women executives can be analyzed, however, because of issues related to data availability (see below). Regardless, this enhances prior research that is restricted to a relatively short time period, a few regions, or select cases (e.g., Genovese 1993b; Jalalzai 2013; Liswood 2007; Opfell 1993; Richter 1991). Each female president and prime minister is included once unless she served nonconsecutive terms (e.g., President Ivy Matsepe-Casaburri of South Africa) or changed positions (e.g., Chandrika Kumaratunga, who went from serving as prime minister to president of Sri Lanka), in which case, the women are included multiple times in the data set. The remainder of this section will discuss the data and methods used in this study.

Dependent Variables

The dependent variables in this analysis are the paths that women take to office: family, political activist, or political career. Unlike previous research (e.g., Jalalzai 2013), women are coded as taking one path to office. This was accomplished by the authors' and two undergraduate research assistants' reading of Jalalzai's (2013) biographies of women executives to determine which path propelled a woman to the office of president or prime minister. As such, any woman with a familial tie to political power (i.e., a parent, spouse, or sibling holding federal political office prior to her involvement in politics) is automatically coded as taking the family path to office (e.g., Prime Minister Chandrika Kumaratunga of Sri Lanka). Women who participated in democratization, women's rights, or any other social or political movements prior to holding political office are coded as following the political activist path to executive posts (e.g., President Ellen Johnson Sirleaf of Liberia). Lastly, women who began their careers by running for lower political offices and continued to work their way up the government ranks are coded as taking the political career path to the presidency or premiership (e.g., Prime Minister Julia Gillard of Australia). Any coding disagreement was resolved by consulting a variety of other online biographical sources frequently used by Jalalzai (2013) (e.g., *Encyclopedia Britannica* and the BBC). These same biographical resources were also consulted to code and resolve coding disagreements over women assuming office since 2010. In an effort to build on Jalalzai's (2013) data, biographies for these women can be found in the appendix. For each path, a dichotomous variable is created in which women are coded as 1 on the variable corresponding to the path taken to office and 0 on all others. Female executives who did not take any of the three dominant paths to power are coded as 0 on each of these three variables.[2]

Independent Variables

The independent variables correspond to the aforementioned hypotheses regarding political and institutional factors that should impact which path a woman takes to executive office. Beginning with variables measuring democratic, economic, and human development, *Democratic Institutionalism* is measured as the country's political Freedom House score—which ranges from 1, or most free, to 7, or least free—in the year each female executive took office, because this is a common way to measure the level of democratic institutionalism in a country (Coppedge et al. 2011).[3] *Human Development* is measured as the country's Human Development Index (HDI) score—which ranges from 0 (low human development) to 1 (high human development)—in the year the woman took office[4] because it recognizes that economic growth (i.e., gross national income) is just one aspect of a country's level of development along with health (i.e., life expectancy) and knowledge (i.e., the average number of years of schooling for adults over the age of twenty-five and the expected number of years of schooling for children entering school).[5]

Variables that measure political institutions expected to impact the path a woman takes to executive office will be discussed next. *Executive System* is measured using data from Robert Elgie's *The Semi-Presidential One* blog through a series of dummy variables that code women as 1 on the variable that represents her country's executive system when she took office and 0 on all others: presidential, parliamentary, and semi-presidential.[6] *Multiparty System* is measured as a dichotomous variable following Martin and Swank's (2008) approach[7] using data from the Constituency-Level Election Archive (CLEA) Effective Number of Parties and Party Nationalization data set (Kollman et al. 2018), the Democratic Electoral Systems Around the World data set (Bormann and Golder 2013), and the Election Indices data set (Gallagher 2018) in which women from countries that consistently have more than three effective parties during general elections (as calculated using the measure developed by Laakso and Taagepera [1979]) are coded as 1 and all others as 0.[8]

Two additional variables measure the extent of female political advancement in countries with women executives. *Female Representation in Government* is measured as the percentage of women in parliament the year each woman executive took office using data from the Inter-Parliamentary Union (as collected by Paxton, Green, and Hughes [2008]) from 1990 to 2003 and the World Bank from 2004 to 2015 because there are limited data available on the percentage of women in a country's cabinet.[9] *Previous Female Executive* is a dichotomous variable that is coded as 1 if the woman is *not* the first female president or prime minister in her country and 0 otherwise.

Control Variables

This analysis includes controls for region and type of executive: appointed, elected, or interim. Since each path to office is common in certain regions of the world (e.g., the family path is used in Latin America and Asia; see Jalalzai [2013]), it is important to control for region. During the time period under analysis, there are multiple instances in which certain paths are only used once or never used in each region, so a set of dummy variables cannot be used because certain regional variables would be omitted for predicting failure or success perfectly.[10] Consequently, the *Global South* variable[11] is created using data from the United Nations Statistics Division in which countries considered developing regions (i.e., most in Africa, Asia, the Middle East, and Latin America) are coded as 1 and developed regions are coded as 0.[12]

Type of executive is also controlled for because, first, the literature recognizes that women may be better able to attain executive posts through an appointment rather than an election, since prime minister positions are more conducive to female leadership styles and voters who possess gender stereotypes can be circumvented (e.g., Duerst-Lahti 1997; Hodson 1997; Jalalzai 2013; Whicker and Isaacs 1999). Second, many studies exclude women who are appointed to serve on an interim basis for relatively short periods of time (e.g., Jalalzai 2013); however, it is important to include them in order to fully understand the dynamics surrounding which path a woman takes to office. As such, a series of dummy variables are created for each type of executive: *Elected Executive*, *Appointed Executive*, and *Interim Executive*, in which female presidents and prime ministers are coded as 1 on the appropriate variable and 0 on all others.[13]

Methods

The dependent variables are dichotomous indicators of which path a woman took to executive office (see Table 5.2 for descriptive statistics), so logistic regression analysis is needed to test the aforementioned hypotheses (Menard 1995). The diagnostic tests did not reveal any issues with multicollinearity.[14] The chi-square statistics in Table 5.1 achieve standard levels of statistical significance and indicate that the independent variables accurately explain whether women take each path to executive office. In terms of explanatory power, the Nagelkerke (1991) *r*-square statistics reveal that the family path and

Table 5.1 Logistic Regression Results on Paths to Executive Office

Variable	Family Path			Political Activist Path			Political Career Path		
	Coefficient	Standard Error	z score	Coefficient	Standard Error	z score	Coefficient	Standard Error	z score
Democratic Institutionalism	0.83†	0.47	1.76	0.04	0.52	0.07	-0.34	0.32	-1.04
Human Development	-0.17	3.16	-0.06	-3.38	4.32	-0.78	1.42	2.87	0.50
Executive System—Semi-Presidential	-3.40*	1.56	-2.17	-4.37**	1.56	-2.80	4.30**	1.20	3.60
Executive System—Parliamentary	-0.59	0.94	-0.63	-5.31**	1.91	-2.78	2.89**	1.01	2.86
Multiparty System	-0.24	0.85	-0.28	-0.61	1.09	-0.56	0.34	0.76	0.45
Female Representation in Government	-0.04	0.04	-1.01	0.03	0.04	0.79	0.04	0.03	1.29
Previous Female Executive	2.31**	0.87	2.66	0.17	0.82	0.21	-1.47*	0.65	-2.26
Global South	0.84	1.37	0.61	-3.31†	1.74	-1.90	0.25	1.04	0.24
Appointed Executive	-1.23	0.93	-1.33	1.33	0.88	1.52	-0.15	0.76	-0.20
Interim Executive	-2.70*	1.27	-2.13				2.26*	0.99	2.28
Constant	-2.37	3.59	-0.66	4.56	4.41	1.03	-3.07	3.26	-0.94
N	100			100			100		
Model chi-square	38.24**			18.23*			44.66**		
Reduction in error	27.78%			9.09%			38.71%		
Nagelkerke r-square	.52			.33			.51		

Notes: Omitted categories were Executive System—Presidential and Elected Executive. †$p < .1$, *$p < .05$, **$p < .01$ (two-tailed tests).

Table 5.2 Summary Statistics

Variable	Mean	Standard Deviation	Minimum– Maximum	Mode
Dependent Variables				
Family Path	.18	.39	0–1	0
Political Activist Path	.11	.31	0–1	0
Political Career Path	.69	.46	0–1	1
Independent Variables				
Democratic Institutionalism	2.15	1.36	1–6	1
Human Development	.70	.17	.20–.95	
Executive System— Semi-Presidential	.46	.50	0–1	1
Executive System—Parliamentary	.37	.49	0–1	0
Executive System—Presidential	.17	.38	0–1	0
Multiparty System Female	.72	.45	0–1	1
Representation in Government	18.66	11.14	1.80–42.90	
Previous Female Executive	.48	.50	0–1	0
Control Variables				
Appointed Executive	.32	.47	0–1	0
Elected Executive	.47	.50	0–1	1
Interim Executive	.21	.41	0–1	0
Global South	.58	.50	0–1	1
N	100			

political career path models have relatively good explanatory power, which is not the case for the political activist path model. Additionally, the models tend to underestimate whether a woman takes each path to become president or prime minister albeit much more so for the political activist path than the family path and political career path. Nevertheless, the next section discusses the effects various factors have on the path women take to executive posts.

Results

Family Path

The results of the statistical analyses explaining the conditions under which women take different paths to executive office are shown in Table 5.1. Starting with the family path, 18 percent of women executives took this path to the presidency or premiership, and the results reveal some support for the aforementioned hypotheses. As predicted, women from countries with low levels of democratic institutionalism are more likely to take the family path to executive office (supports H1).[15] As shown in Figure 5.1, women from countries with high levels of democratic institutionalism (i.e., a Freedom House political rights score of 1) have less than a 1 percent likelihood of taking the family path to executive office.[16] The likelihood that women will become executives via the family path increases to 1.2 percent and 2.6 percent in countries with moderate levels of democratic institutionalism (i.e., Freedom House political rights scores of 2 and 3). As countries become less democratic (i.e., Freedom House political rights scores of 4 or higher[17]), women have between a 5.8 percent to 24.6 percent likelihood of utilizing the family path to reach executive office. Overall, the results indicate that women in undemocratic countries are best able to become presidents and prime ministers by taking the family path to power.

Although the results do not indicate that women are more likely to take the family path to executive posts in countries with low levels of human development (rejects H2), having had a female predecessor does facilitate taking this path to power (supports H6). Figure 5.2 shows how having a female predecessor affects whether women take the family path to power given different levels of democratic

Figure 5.1 Reaching Executive Office via the Family Path: The Impact of Democratic Institutionalism

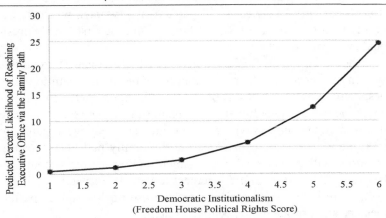

Figure 5.2 Reaching Executive Office via the Family Path:
The Impact of a Female Predecessor

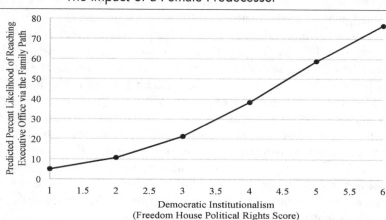

institutionalism. In countries with high levels of democratic institutionalism (Freedom House Political Rights scores of 1 and 2), the
likelihood women will take the family path to executive power after
the executive glass ceiling has already been broken is relatively low:
between 5 percent and 11 percent. At moderate levels of democratic
institutionalism (Freedom House Political Rights scores of 3 and 4),
the likelihood women will become presidents and prime ministers via
the family path and follow in the footsteps of a previous female executive is between 21.5 percent and 38.5 percent. As countries become
less democratic (Freedom House Political Rights scores of 5 or 6[18]),
it becomes very likely (over 55 percent) that women will take the
family path to executive office if they are not the first female president or prime minister.

The findings from Table 5.1 also show that a country's executive
system influences whether a woman takes the family path to office
despite expectations that this political institutional factor only influences the use of the political career path. In fact, the results indicate
that women in countries with semi-presidential executive systems are
less likely to become executives via the family path than those in
countries with presidential or parliamentary[19] executive systems. To
be exact, 12.9 percent and 7.4 percent less likely, respectively. However, there is no difference between the use of this path in parliamentary and presidential executive systems.

Interesting findings also result from the control variables. As Table 5.1 shows, women in the Global South are not more likely to take the family path at a rate that is statistically different than those in the Global North. When comparing the use of this path among interim, appointed, and elected female executives, the results indicate that (1) there is no statistically significant difference between appointed and elected or interim and appointed[20] women executives, but (2) interim presidents and prime ministers are 0.48 percent less likely to take the family path to office than their elected counterparts.

Political Activist Path

With 11 percent of women taking the political activist path to executive office throughout the time period of 1990–2015, it is the least popular route for becoming president or prime minister. As the results from Table 5.1 show, relatively few variables achieve statistical significance and explain why a woman takes this route to executive power. In particular, the results do not indicate that women in undemocratic countries or those with low levels of human development are more likely to take the political activist path to executive power (rejects H1 and H2). Nor does it appear that higher numbers of women in the nation's legislature mean that political activists have launched political careers to further their cause and will eventually reach the presidency or premiership (rejects H5). Also in contrast to expectations, following in the footsteps of another female executive does not facilitate women taking the political activist path to become president or prime minister (rejects H6).

Similar to the family path, the findings from Table 5.1 show that a country's executive system influences whether a woman takes the political activist path to office despite expectations that this political institutional factor only influences the use of the political career path. Specifically, women are less likely to utilize the political activist path in countries with semi-presidential and parliamentary systems than in presidential systems. To be exact, 23.4 percent and 23.6 percent, respectively, less likely. As these likelihoods show, there is no statistically significant difference between the use of the political activist path in semi-presidential and parliamentary systems.[21]

Again, interesting relationships emerge from the impact of the control variables on whether a woman reaches an executive position via the political activist path. The most striking result in Table 5.1 is

that women from the Global South are 0.4 percent less likely to utilize the political activist path.[22] When comparing the types of executives that use the political activist path, as previously mentioned,
interim executives are excluded from the model because none of
them took this route to the presidency or premiership. As far as
appointed and elected female executives, neither is more likely to use
the political activist path than the other.[23]

Political Career Path

Roughly 70 percent of women who became presidents and prime
ministers beginning in 1990 through 2015 utilized the political career
path. As the results from Table 5.1 show, relatively few variables
achieve statistical significance and explain why a woman takes this
route to executive power. In contrast to expectations, it does not
appear that women in countries with high levels of human development or in those with high levels of democratic institutionalism, multiparty systems, or numerous female legislators are more likely to
become presidents and prime ministers via the political career path
(rejects H1, H2, H4, and H5). However, following in the footsteps of
a previous female executive decreases the likelihood that a woman
takes the political career path to the presidency or premiership
(rejects H6). This relationship is statistically significant: women who
break the glass ceiling have a 96.2 percent likelihood of taking the
political career path to power, which decreases to 85.2 percent for
subsequent female executives. These substantive results suggest it is
nearly a prerequisite to use the political career path in order to
become a country's first female president or prime minister, but it
does not necessarily constrain future women executives from using
other paths. For example, Zinaida Greceanîi became prime minister
of Moldova via the political career path in 2008, and Natalia Gherman later took the family path to the same position in 2015.

Some of the results are as expected, where women are more
likely to take the political career path to office in semi-presidential
and parliamentary systems (supports H3). In presidential systems,
women have a 25.4 percent likelihood of taking the political career
path to executive power, which increases to roughly 86 percent in
parliamentary systems and 96 percent in semi-presidential systems.
Furthermore, this difference between parliamentary systems and
semi-presidential systems is also statistically significant.[24]

As far as the control variables, women are just as likely to take the political career path to executive office in the Global North and the Global South. Examining how women in elected, appointed, or interim executive positions use the political career path reveals that interim executives are more likely to utilize this path than their elected and appointed counterparts.[25] More specifically, interim executives have a 99.6 percent likelihood of reaching executive positions via the political career path, which decreases to 96.7 percent and 96.2 percent, respectively, for appointed and elected executives. As these latter likelihoods show, there is no statistical difference between the use of the political career path among appointed and elected executives.

Discussion

There are two bodies of literature on women presidents and prime ministers: the paths women take to office and the factors that help females reach executive posts. This analysis united these two areas of research in an effort to explain which factors lead women to take the three different paths to executive office: family, political activist, and political career. Overall, there are three key findings from this analysis regarding the paths women take to executive power: (1) the independent variables have relatively little explanatory power; (2) few patterns emerge based on region; and (3) the type of executive position seems to matter. In this section we will discuss these findings in turn and their implications for understanding how women overcome various types of sexism (voter, institutional, and cultural) to become presidents and prime ministers.

Explaining the Paths Women Take to Executive Office

The first key finding is that relatively few independent variables explain why a woman takes each path to executive office. Starting with the family path, there is mixed support for existing research. In accordance with prior work, women do tend to take this route to power in undemocratic countries; however, in contrast to these studies, women do not use this path more often in countries with low levels of human development, some of which could be characterized as patriarchal (Baturo and Gray 2018; Hodson 1997; Jalalzai 2013;

Jalalzai and Rincker 2018; Richter 1991). For the political activist path, none of the hypothesized relationships were supported. In other words, a woman's use of this path does not appear to depend on her country's level of democracy, human development, or female representation in government as suggested by prior research (e.g., Beckwith 2000; Jalalzai 2013). These results are likely because the use of both paths is dependent upon being from a dynastic family or taking up a cause and advocating for it, neither of which may relate to low levels of democracy or human development—for example, prime minister of Iceland Jóhanna Sigurðardóttir's activism in trade unions.

Findings regarding the political career path are also mixed. In contrast to expectations, the path is not common in democratic countries or those with high levels of human development, multiparty systems, or numerous female legislators. Additionally, women are actually less likely to take this route to power if they are following in the footsteps of a former female president or prime minister, although the substantive results show that the likelihood of using this path is still over 80 percent. However, the results showing that women are more likely to take this path in semi-presidential and parliamentary systems support previous studies, suggesting that appointment-based executive systems help women bypass sexist voters and attain executive positions that are well-suited to feminine leadership styles revolving around consensus-building and collaboration (e.g., Duerst-Lahti 1997; Hodson 1997; Jalalzai 2013, 2016a; Whicker and Isaacs 1999).

Interestingly, a country's executive system can also help women on the family and political activist paths reach the presidency or premiership. Women are more likely to take the family path in presidential and parliamentary systems than semi-presidential systems, whereas women in presidential systems are more likely to become executives via the political activist path. Although unexpected, these results collectively suggest and confirm observations that these paths help women overcome gender stereotypes via their family name and by already having voters mobilized on their behalf to reach powerful executive positions (e.g., Baturo and Gray 2018; Jalalzai 2013, 2016a; Jalalzai and Rincker 2018). For example, President Chandrika Kumaratunga of Sri Lanka started her political career by following in the footsteps of her parents, Prime Ministers Solomon West Ridgeway Dias Bandaranaike and Sirimavo Bandaranaike, as the chief minister of the Western Province and a member of the Sri Lanka Parliament for Gampaha.

The Impact of Executive Position and Region

The second key finding is that the type of executive position appears to impact the path a woman takes to executive office. As expected, interim executives assume power via the political career path because they are selected from individuals currently holding other government positions who likely have had an extensive political career. Consequently, this is likely the reason why interim presidents and prime ministers are (1) less likely to take the family path than their elected counterparts, and (2) not using the political activist path. This speculation is confirmed by examining the women presidents and prime ministers included in this data set in which all but one interim female executive took the political career path to office.[26] Across each of the three paths, there is no difference among elected and appointed executives.

The third key finding is that relatively few patterns emerge regarding the use of each path in different regions of the world. In contrast to prior research, women in the Global South are not more likely to take the family path or political activist path to power (e.g., Jalalzai 2013). In fact, women are actually less likely, albeit by only 0.4 percent, to take the political activist path to the presidency or premiership in the Global South. As a result, these findings refute prior work that found both paths are common in Latin America and Asia with the political activist path also being prevalent in Africa (e.g., Jalalzai 2013). However, these results do support research that observed the use of the political activist path in Eastern Europe (e.g., Jalalzai 2013). Also, in support of the women executives literature is the finding that there is no variation in the use of the political career path in the Global North or Global South. More specifically, this shows how the path is frequently used in Europe and Africa (e.g., Jalalzai 2013). Taken collectively, there are two likely reasons for the errant results. First, previous work codes women as taking multiple paths to executive office rather than focusing on which route launched them toward the presidency or premiership. Second, women in the Global South are not restricted to the family or political activist paths. In particular, thirty-six women in the Global South used the political career path to obtain executive power, such as President Laura Chinchilla of Costa Rica.

Broader Implications

Gaining a better understanding of the political and institutional factors that influence the path a woman takes to executive office advances the literature by providing insight into not only each path but also how women overcome various types of sexism (i.e., voter, institutional, and cultural) to become presidents and prime ministers. Taken collectively, it appears that the use of each path depends on the country's political and institutional characteristics, especially its executive system, and the executive position itself. Election-based systems facilitate women taking the family and political activist paths to power, whereas women who take the family and political career paths tend to reach executive office in parliamentary and semi-presidential appointment-based systems, respectively. Similarly, interim executives tend to use the political career path while elected executives take the political activist path.

In addition to showing the political and institutional factors— especially executive system and the nature of the position—that ensure each path leads to an executive position, these results speak to how women overcome voter, institutional, and cultural sexism on their way to becoming president or prime minister. In particular, (1) women using the family path can rely on their family name to over- come gender stereotypes that men are better suited for executive posi- tions to secure powerful appointed and elected executive positions in parliamentary and presidential systems; (2) women taking the politi- cal activist path to power can rely on the fact that voters are already mobilized on their behalf in order to reach executive positions in pres- idential, election-based systems; and (3) women who reach executive posts via the political career path do so in semi-presidential systems or on an interim basis because they can rely on their political experi- ence to overcome stereotypes that disproportionately lead to men becoming presidents or prime ministers. Overall, the findings from this chapter provide greater insight into both the paths women take to executive office and how they are able to prevail despite voter, insti- tutional, and cultural sexism.

Conclusion

Thus far, we have focused on providing a better understanding of the dynamics surrounding the paths women take to reach executive posts around the world and the implications this has on women navigating sexism to become presidents and prime ministers. However, two questions remain: (1) Does the path a woman takes to office help or hinder future women from becoming presidents or prime ministers via the same or a different path? (2) Does the path a woman takes to executive office or various political and institutional factors dictate how long she stays in office? In order to begin answering these questions and advancing the literature, in the next chapter we examine the institutional and political factors that predict whether a country has a female executive, especially one who took each path to office, and how a female executive's path to office impacts her successors. In doing so, the chapter continues to provide insight into how women overcome voter, institutional, and cultural sexism to become executives around the world.

Notes

1. In particular, 1990 and 2015 are the first and last years in which yearly estimates are available for the Human Development Index, which is used to measure the level of human development in a country.

2. These women are President Ameenah Gurib-Fakim of Mauritius and Prime Minister Chang Sang of South Korea. President Gurib-Fakim's background was in academia as a professor of organic chemistry at the University of Mauritius and managing director of the Centre for Phytotherapy Research prior to being selected as a presidential candidate by the Alliance LePep (BBC 2015). Prime Minister Chang Sang's background is also in academia. She received a PhD from Princeton Theological Seminary and was the president of Ewha Women's University prior to becoming prime minister (Christensen 2011).

3. Freedom House scores were not calculated for East Germany in 1990, so President Sabine Bergmann-Pohl is excluded from the analysis.

4. President Sabine Bergmann-Pohl of East Germany and President Atifete Jahjaga of Kosovo are excluded from the analysis because HDI scores are not calculated for these countries. Prime Minister Radmila Šekerinska, who took office in 2004, is also omitted from the analysis because HDI scores for Macedonia are not available until 2005.

5. In an effort to avoid multicollinearity and for the sake of parsimony and data availability, this study does not include a separate measure of gender inequality. Although the Gender Development Index was introduced in 1995 to measure gender inequality, it is calculated as the ratio of the gaps between men and women on the factors included in the calculation of the HDI, so including it in the model would lead to multicollinearity. Additionally, limiting the time frame to 1995 eliminates another 13.5 percent of all female presidents and prime ministers, which would mean excluding 28 percent of all cases from this analysis.

6. For example, Jamaica has a parliamentary system, so Prime Minister Portia Simpson-Miller is coded as 1 on *Executive System—Parliamentary* and 0 on *Executive System—Presidential* and *Executive System—Semi-Presidential*.

7. This approach improves upon Jalalzai's (2013) measure that codes multiparty systems as those with more than two "competitive" parties in general

elections. Since the threshold for competitiveness is not specified, this approach cannot be replicated systematically.

8. When the party system of a country cannot be delineated easily and/or data are available for relatively few general elections, a variety of outside sources, such as the International Foundation for Electoral Systems Election Guide and the International Institute for Democracy and Electoral Assistance, are consulted to verify the typical number of effective parties and/or whether there has been a change in the country's party system (e.g., a one-party system becoming a multi-party system or vice versa).

9. President Sabine Bergmann-Pohl of East Germany, Prime Minister Ertha Pascal-Trouillot of Haiti, Prime Minister Sylvie Kinigi of Burundi, and President Catherine Samba-Panza of the Central African Republic are excluded from the analysis because data are not available for the years each woman took office. Another woman omitted from this study is President Atifete Jahjaga because data are not collected for Kosovo. The final woman executive excluded from this analysis is Prime Minister Kazimira Danutė Prunskienė, who took office in 1990, because data for Lithuania are not available until 1991.

10. The family path has not been utilized in Africa, the Middle East, North America, Oceania, or the Caribbean; women do not ascend to power via the political activist path in the Middle East, North America, Oceania, or the Caribbean; and women only take the political career path to power in the Middle East, North America, Oceania, and the Caribbean.

11. Global South and Global North are terms used to categorize countries based on their level of economic development, in which those in the Northern Hemisphere tend to be more developed than those in the Southern Hemisphere (e.g., Green and Luehrmann 2017). Classifying countries as in the Global North or Global South is challenging because geography is an imprecise guide and not all developing countries are alike; for example, emerging economies (e.g., South Korea and Brazil) and low-income countries (e.g., Malawi) are all considered developing (e.g., Green and Luehrmann 2017).

12. Countries in Africa, Asia, the Caribbean, the Middle East (with the exception of Israel), and Latin America are coded as in the Global South. Turkey and Georgia are also coded as in the Global South. Israel along with all other countries in North America, Oceania, and Europe are coded as in the Global North. President Sabine Bergmann-Pohl of East Germany and President Atifete Jahjaga of Kosovo are excluded from the analysis because these countries are not categorized by the United Nations Statistics Division.

13. Coding each woman executive reveals that interim executives have not taken the political activist path to power. Consequently, the statistical model analyzing the political activist path only includes the *Appointed Executive* variable because a set of dummy variables cannot be used when the interim variable is omitted from the model for predicting failure perfectly. Theoretically, this is not problematic because women are expected to reach executive positions easier via appointments than elections.

14. The tolerance levels for all the independent variables are above the recommended cutoff of .2 (Menard 1995).

15. It is important to note that this relationship is significant at the .1 level. There is debate as to whether coefficients significant at the .1 level should be reported as statistically significant because the conventional cutoff in the social sciences is .05. However, coefficients with p values between .05 and .1 can be

considered "approaching" significance (e.g., Samprit, Hadi, and Prince 2000) and are increasingly being reported as statistically significant results in political science research (e.g., Goldstein 2010). Presenting such results as substantively meaningful can be supported for reasons relating to research design (usually the size of the data set), theoretical considerations, and/or the results of prior research (e.g., Lewis-Beck 1995; Noymer 2008). Since the data set is relatively small ($N = 100$) and the finding accords with the extant literature, it is worth discussing the substantive results of this relationship. This is also the case for the other variables that are statistically significant at the .1 level in this analysis that will be discussed later.

16. Predicted percent likelihoods are calculated using SPost in Stata 14 (Long and Freese 2005). Throughout this analysis, for variables in the model not of interest, continuous variables are set at the mean and all dichotomous and categorical variables are set at the mode (see Table 5.2 for these values).

17. None of the countries in the data set received a score of 7.

18. None of the countries in the data set received a score of 7.

19. This result was determined by running the model and omitting the *Parliamentary Executive* system variable. The relationship is statistically significant at the .05 level.

20. This result was determined by running the model and omitting the *Appointed Executive* variable.

21. This result was obtained by omitting the *Parliamentary Executive* system variable.

22. See note 15 above for a discussion of why it is worth reporting the results of variables statistically significant at the .1 level.

23. This result was partially obtained by substituting the *Appointed Executive* variable with the *Elected Executive* variable in the model and observing that the coefficient does not achieve conventional levels of statistical significance.

24. This result was determined by running the model and omitting the *Parliamentary Executive* system variable. The relationship is statistically significant at the .05 level.

25. This result was partially determined by running the model and omitting the *Appointed Executive* variable.

26. The one exception is Prime Minister Natalia Gherman of Moldova, who launched a political career by following in the footsteps of her father, President Mircea Snegur.

6

The Impact of Previous Women Leaders

As mentioned at the end of Chapter 5, in this chapter we explore the conditions under which a country has a female executive in general and one who assumed power via the family, political activist, or political career path. In doing so, we address how the path a woman executive takes to office is impacted by the route(s) taken by her predecessor(s). Again, as was discussed extensively in Chapter 1 and at the beginning of Chapter 5, this analysis continues to unite the two areas of literature on women executives and enhance it. In the remainder of this chapter we will develop hypotheses, describe the data and methods for the statistical analysis, explain the results, and discuss the implications of the findings, especially with respect to how women overcome voter, institutional, and cultural sexism.

Explaining the Presence of Female Executives

Democratic Stability and Development

Politically unstable countries often have women presidents and prime ministers for a couple of reasons. First, women from dynastic political families can inherit or obtain power through undemocratic means after coups and/or the imprisonment or assassination of the current executive (Hodson 1997; Jalalzai 2013). Second, women who are active in democratization or social movements often launch political careers to pursue change within formal political institutions and eventually become the president or prime minister (Jalalzai 2013). These women can overcome gender stereotypes that men are better suited for executive positions that deal with "masculine" issue areas, such as national defense, because of their family name and/or views that women are best able to promote peace and build consensus after periods of political turmoil (Baturo and Gray 2018; Fox and Oxley 2003; Geske and Bourque 2001; Huddy and Terkildsen 1993; Jalalzai 2008, 2013; Jalalzai and Rincker 2018; Katzenstein 1978; Saint-Germain 1993; Salo 2010; Sczesny et al. 2004). This prior research suggests the following hypothesis:

> *H1: Democratically unstable countries are more likely to have women presidents and prime ministers, especially those who take the family and political activist paths to power.*

In addition to democratic stability, the women-executives literature has also focused on the pervasiveness of patriarchy in a country and its level of economic development. Studies suggest that women in patriarchal societies, especially those where women have recently gained suffrage, must capitalize on their family name or activist background as a caretaker and peacebuilder during politically tumultuous times to overcome gender-based perceptions that men should be presidents and prime ministers (Baturo and Gray 2018; Beckwith 2000; Geske and Bourque 2001; Jalalzai 2013; Jalalzai and Rincker 2018; Salo 2010). In economically developed countries, women struggle to break the executive glass ceiling because men are perceived as best able to run these nations that are global leaders in "masculine" policy areas, such as the world economy and foreign affairs (Jalalzai 2013). Women on the political career path are best positioned to overcome this obstacle to executive power, because they are able to gain experience with these issues while serving in the cabinet or parliament. Given that a country's level of economic development and patriarchy impact its level of human development—or its economic growth in conjunction with the degree in which citizens have freedom of opportunity and chances to improve their well-being—the following hypothesis can be derived from the extant literature:

H2: Countries with low levels of human development are more likely to have a female executive who took the family or political activist path to power, whereas countries with high levels of human development are more likely to have a woman president or prime minister who assumed power via the political career path.

Political Institutions

Previous work has identified two factors directly related to political institutions that influence whether a country has a female president or prime minister: the executive and party systems. With respect to how the executive office is structured, it is easier for women to assume executive power in semi-presidential and parliamentary systems for a couple of reasons. First, women can be appointed, which allows them to avoid voters with gender stereotypes about executives that favor men in presidential, election-based systems (Duerst-Lahti 1997; Hodson 1997; Jalalzai 2013, 2016a; Whicker and Isaacs 1999). Second, "feminine" governing styles focused on collaborating and building consensus are considered well-suited for the office of prime minister because it is important to unify parties within the legislature to work toward common policy goals (Duerst-Lahti 1997). Although the literature indicates that appointment-based systems produce more female executives in general, it is probable that most assume power via the political career path because women who are active within the party and hold elected office or other government positions are more apt to be considered and selected for an executive position. These expectations are summarized in the following hypothesis:

H3: Countries with semi-presidential and parliamentary executive systems are more likely to have a female executive, especially one who took the political career path to office.

A country's party system is the second political institutions–related factor that is directly associated with whether a country has a female president or prime minister. Previous work suggests that women are best able to assume power in multiparty systems because this is the common party structure in countries with parliamentary executive structures: those that seek prime ministers with stereotypical "female" governing styles focused on collaboration and consensus-building to lead the coalition government (Jalalzai 2013). Despite multiparty systems' ability to propel all women to office, it is likely those on the political career path benefit the most because prime ministers are usually legislators, party leaders, and/or former cabinet members.

> *H4: Countries with multiparty systems are more likely to have a woman president or prime minister, especially one who assumed power via the political career path.*

Female Political Advancement

The literature has observed that it is easier for females to become presidents and prime ministers when they are from countries that have multiple women in parliament and/or former women executives (e.g., Jalalzai 2013; Reynolds 1999). This is due to parties and voters (1) overcoming gender stereotypes and electing women to the national legislature and/or an executive post and (2) having multiple women to nominate and/or elect to the presidency and/or premiership. Although all prospective women presidents and prime ministers can benefit from female representation in the legislature, women on the political career and political activist paths to executive office stand to gain the most. These women either started in politics or launched a political career, so they are among the group of potential female candidates for executive office within parties and/or the government. Similarly, since the literature observes that women benefit from having the executive glass ceiling broken (e.g., Jalalzai 2013; Reynolds 1999), it is likely easier to follow in the footsteps of previous female executives by taking the same path to office. Overall, these expectations can be summarized as such:

> *H5: Countries with high numbers of female legislators are more likely to have a woman president or prime minister, especially one who took the political activist path or political career path to power.*

> *H6: Countries that have had a woman president or prime minister are more likely to have additional female executives, particularly those who take the same path to office as their predecessor(s).*

Data and Methods

The aforementioned hypotheses will be tested for the time period of 1990–2015 due to data availability.[1] Consequently, the terms of 79 percent of all women executives are analyzed; however, this still enhances the research on women executives because most studies are often restricted to relatively short time periods, a few regions, or select cases (e.g., Genovese 1993b; Jalalzai 2013; Liswood 2007; Montecinos 2017a; Opfell 1993; Richter 1991). The data set consists of country-level panel data for 187 countries. Each country is included in the data set each year it was in existence[2] and/or when data for each variable are available,[3] for a total of 4,057 observations or 85 percent of the entire population. The rest of this section contains variable measurement and the methods used in this analysis.

Dependent Variables

The dependent variables in this analysis are whether a country has a female president or prime minister and, if so, the path she took to reach that executive office: family, political activist, or political career. The first dichotomous dependent variable, *Female Executive*, is coded as 1 if one or more women served as president and/or prime minister at any point that year and 0 otherwise. The remaining dependent variables, *Female Executive—Family Path, Female Executive—Political Activist Path*, and *Female Executive—Political Career Path*, are a set of dichotomous indicators that code countries with one or more female executives in any given year as 1 on the variable(s) corresponding to the path each took to office and 0 otherwise (see discussion in Chapter 5 of how we determined which path a woman executive took to office). Countries without female executives are coded as 0 on each of these three variables.

Independent Variables

The independent variables correspond to the aforementioned hypotheses regarding political and institutional factors that should impact whether a country has a female executive and the path she took to office. Since this analysis uses the same data sources as in Chapter 5, in this section we will focus on the coding of each variable (see discussion in Chapter 5 of our rationale behind the use of each data source). Starting with variables measuring democratic and human development, *Democratic Institutionalism* is coded as the country's yearly Freedom House political rights score, which can range from 1, or most free, to 7, or least free. *Human Development* is coded as the country's yearly HDI score, which can range from 0 (low human development) to 1 (high human development).[4]

The next variables measure the type of political institutions present in each country. Beginning with a country's executive system, only countries with semi-presidential, parliamentary, and presidential systems—not other systems (i.e., monarchies and authoritarian regimes)—have had women presidents and/or prime ministers. This means that a set of dummy variables cannot be used because certain variables would be omitted from the model for predicting failure or success perfectly. Consequently, the *Appointment-Based Executive System* dichotomous variable is constructed. For each year, countries with parliamentary and semi-presidential systems are coded as 1 and presidential, election-based systems and other systems are coded as 0.[5] This is because the literature focuses on how appointment-based systems facilitate women reaching executive office more so than election-based systems (e.g., Jalalzai 2013). *Multiparty System* is another dichotomous variable in which, for each year, countries with multiparty systems are coded as 1 and all other countries as zero.[6]

The remaining independent variables measure the level of female political advancement in each country. *Female Representation in Government* is coded as the yearly percentage of women in each country's parliament.[7] *Previous Female Executive* is a dichotomous indicator in which countries that have had a woman president or prime minister prior to each year included in the data set are coded as 1 and all others as 0. Additional dichotomous variables are created that measure the path(s) that one or more previous female executives took to office: *Previous Female Executive—Family Path*, *Previous Female Executive—Political Activist Path*, and/or *Previous Female Executive—Political Career Path*. Countries that have had one or more previous female executives in any given year are coded as 1 on the variable(s) that correspond to the path these presidents or prime ministers took to office and 0 on the others (see discussion in Chapter 5 of how we determined which path a woman executive took to office). Countries that have not had a female executive are coded as 0 on each variable.

Control Variables

As was the case with the independent variables, this section will focus on the coding of each variable because this analysis uses the same control variables as Chapter 5 (see Chapter 5 for a discussion of the rationale behind the inclusion of each variable and the use of each data source). Starting with region, the *Global South* dummy variable is constructed by coding countries listed as developing regions by the United Nations Statistics Division as 1 and those considered developed regions, or in the Global North, as 0. For the models examining whether each country has had a female executive who took each of the three paths to power, dichotomous variables are created to designate whether the country has had one or more of the three types of woman executives (*Previous Female Executive— Elected*, *Previous Female Executive—Appointed*, and *Previous Female Executive—Interim*) prior to each year included in the data set. Countries are coded as 1 on the variable(s) that correspond to the type of female executive(s) the country has had and 0 on the others. If a country has not had a woman president or prime minister, these variables are coded as 0.[8]

Methods

The dependent variables are dichotomous indicators of whether a country has a female president and/or prime minister and, if so, what path she took to executive office (see Table 6.2 for descriptive statistics). Consequently, logistic regression analysis is needed to test the aforementioned hypotheses (Menard 1995).[9] Diagnostic tests did not reveal substantial issues with multicollinearity.[10] The chi-square statistics in Table 6.1 achieve standard levels of statistical significance and indicate that the independent variables accurately explain whether a country has a female president or prime minister each year and the path she took to office: family, political activist, or political career. With respect to explanatory power, the models are relatively weak, according to the Nagelkerke (1991) *r*-square statistics, and the models underestimate whether a country has a female executive and the path she took to office. Regardless, in the next section we discuss the effect that various factors have on whether a country has a female president or prime minister and the path she took to office.

Table 6.1 Logistic Regression Results on Women Executives and Paths to Power

Variable	Women Executives		Family Path		Political Activist Path		Political Career Path	
	Coefficient (robust SE)	z score	Coefficient (robust SE)	z score	Coefficient (robust SE)	z score	Coefficient (robust SE)	z score
Democratic Institutionalism	-0.37** (.07)	-5.08	-0.25 (.20)	-1.27	-0.57** (.18)	-3.09	-0.34** (0.09)	-3.86
Human Development	-0.34 (1.37)	-0.25	0.53 (2.59)	0.21	-4.49 (3.46)	-1.30	-0.50 (1.57)	-0.32
Appointment-Based Executive System	0.39 (0.38)	1.02	0.37 (0.83)	0.44	-2.06** (0.53)	-3.86	1.81** (0.58)	3.13
Multiparty System	.92** (0.36)	2.59	1.59* (0.71)	2.25	0.70 (0.87)	0.81	0.38 (0.41)	0.91
Female Representation in Government	0.03* (0.01)	2.52	-0.03 (0.03)	-1.20	0.05* (0.02)	2.05	0.04* (0.02)	2.35
Previous Female Executive	0.85** (0.27)	3.12						
Previous Female Executive–Family Path			4.11** (1.46)	2.81			-0.67 (0.79)	-0.80
Previous Female Executive–Political Activist Path			2.16* (0.90)	2.40	2.73† (1.45)	1.88	-1.32† (0.79)	-1.66
Previous Female Executive–Political Career Path			-0.69 (0.92)	-0.75	-0.48 (1.13)	-0.42	0.47 (0.73)	0.64
Previous Female Executive–Appointed			0.61 (0.91)	0.66	-0.04 (0.96)	-0.04	-0.24 (0.84)	-0.29
Previous Female Executive–Elected			-1.46 (1.40)	-1.04	-1.61 (1.26)	-1.28	1.21* (0.59)	2.05

continues

Table 6.1 Continued

Variable	Women Executives Coefficient (robust SE)	z score	Family Path Coefficient (robust SE)	z score	Political Activist Path Coefficient (robust SE)	z score	Political Career Path Coefficient (robust SE)	z score
Previous Female Executive—Interim			-1.03 (1.12)	-0.92	-2.95 (2.38)	0.19	-0.22 (0.87)	-0.25
Global South	0.79† (0.43)	1.81	3.01** (0.91)	3.32	-0.85 (1.00)	-1.24	0.29 (0.56)	0.52
Constant	-3.41 (1.29)	-2.65	-7.99 (2.24)	-3.57	0.55 (2.82)	0.19	-4.63 (1.59)	-2.91
N	4,057		4,057		4,057		4,057	
Model chi-square	80.39**		94.73**		60.00**		93.73**	
Reduction in error	0.00%		-13.70%		-1.85%		3.50%	
Nagelkerke r-square	0.15		0.38		0.16		0.23	

Note: †$p < .1$, *$p < .05$, **$p < .01$ (two-tailed tests).

Table 6.2 Summary Statistics

Variable	Mean	Standard Deviation	Minimum–Maximum	Mode
Dependent Variables				
Female Executive	.08	.27	0–1	0
Female Executive—Family Path	.02	.13	0–1	0
Female Executive—Political Activist Path	.01	.11	0–1	0
Female Executive—Political Career Path	.05	.22	0–1	1
Independent Variables				
Democratic Institutionalism	3.29	2.09	1–7	1
Human Development	.65	.16	.19–.95	
Appointment-Based Executive System	.66	.47	0–1	1
Multiparty System	.57	.50	0–1	1
Female Representation in Government	14.64	10.64	0–63.8	
Previous Female Executive	.22	.41	0–1	0
Previous Female Executive— Family Path	.04	.21	0–1	0
Previous Female Executive— Political Activist Path	.05	.22	0–1	0
Previous Female Executive— Political Career Path	.13	.33	0–1	1
Control Variables				
Previous Female Executive— Appointed	.08	.27	0–1	0
Previous Female Executive—Elected	.10	.30	0–1	1
Previous Female Executive—Interim	.06	.24	0–1	0
Global South	.72	.45	0–1	1
N	4,057			

Results

Countries with Women Executives

The results of the statistical analyses analyzing the factors that determine whether a country has a female president or prime minister and the path she took to executive office are shown in Table 6.1. Beginning with the model examining whether a country has a woman executive, the results reveal that there is support for most of the hypothesized relationships. As shown in Table 6.1, unstable, undemocratic countries are not more likely to have a woman president or prime minister (rejects H1).

In fact, Figure 6.1 shows the exact opposite: countries with high levels of democratic institutionalism (i.e., a Freedom House political rights score of 1) have a roughly 19 percent likelihood of having a female executive.[11] This likelihood drops to roughly 14 percent and 10 percent for countries with moderate levels of democratic institutionalism, or Freedom House political rights scores of 2 and 3, respectively. Countries with low levels of democratic institutionalism (i.e., Freedom House political rights scores of 4 through 7) have a less than 10 percent chance of having a woman executive in any given year. These findings are likely because women in undemocratic, politically tumultuous countries have to rely on familial ties to power or an activist background in order to overcome gender stereotypes and assume power (e.g., Beckwith 2000; Geske and Bourque 2001; Jalalzai 2013; Hodson 1997; Salo 2010; Whicker and Isaacs 1999). Furthermore, the political and institutional factors, such as multiparty systems and female representation in government, that tend to produce women executives are most common in democratic environments.

Figure 6.1 Having a Female Executive:
The Impact of Democratic Institutionalism

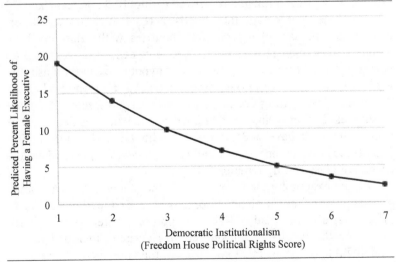

Although stable, democratic countries are more likely to have women presidents and prime ministers, this is not because of certain institutional structures, such as appointment-based executive systems. As Table 6.1 shows, countries with semi-presidential and parliamentary systems are not more likely to have female executives (rejects H3). These findings are likely due to the fact that women can and do reach executive positions in presidential systems. In the time frame under analysis (1990–2015) five presidents assumed office in the 1990s (e.g., president of Guyana Janet Jagan in 1997), six in the 2000s (e.g., president of Indonesia Megawati Sukarnoputri in 2001), and four in the 2010s (e.g., president of Malawi Joyce Banda in 2012).

Regardless of the errant results thus far, Table 6.1 shows that the remaining hypotheses are supported in that countries are more likely to have female executives if they have a multiparty system, numerous women in parliament, and/or a previous woman executive (supports H4, H5, and H6). In terms of substantive results, countries with multiparty systems have a roughly 19 percent likelihood of having a female president or prime minister. This decreases by half to 8.5 percent in countries with two-party or one-party systems. The substantive results for women in parliament are shown in Figure 6.2. When a country has relatively low levels of women in parliament, the likelihood of having a female executive is less than 20 percent. For countries that have moderate levels of women in parliament, or between 20 percent and 30 percent, the likelihood of having a woman president or prime minister is between roughly 22 percent and 27 percent. These percentage likelihoods increase to as low as 34 percent to as high as 49 percent for countries with relatively high amounts of women in parliament (i.e., between 40 percent and 60 percent). The last statistically significant hypothesized relationship in Table 6.1 shows that countries where women have already broken the executive glass ceiling are more likely to have subsequent female executives. In fact, countries that have had female presidents and/or prime ministers have a 35 percent likelihood of having another female executive compared to roughly 19 percent for those where the executive glass ceiling remains firmly intact.

Before examining the results for whether a country has a woman president or prime minister who took one of the three paths to office—family, political activist, or political career—it is worth reviewing the results of the one control variable included in this model. Table 6.1 shows that countries in the Global South are more

Figure 6.2 Having a Female Executive:
The Impact of Women in Parliament

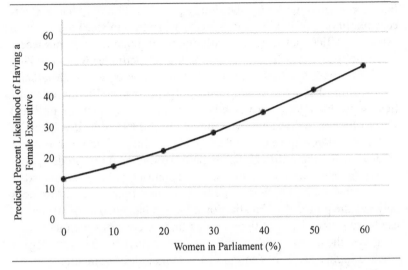

likely to have women presidents and prime ministers.[12] In fact, countries in the Global South have a roughly 19 percent likelihood of having a female president or prime minister compared to a roughly 10 percent likelihood for those in the Global North.

Family Path

The results regarding whether a country has a female executive who took the family path to office can also be found in Table 6.1. As can be seen, relatively few of the hypothesized relationships are supported in that neither unstable, undemocratic, nor lesser developed countries are more likely to have a female president or prime minister who took the family path to office (rejects H1 and H2). These results are likely because the family path is dependent upon whether a woman has a family member to follow to executive office. Various political conditions can be present that facilitate the use of the path, but it may not be seen due to the lack of a dynastic family.

However, as predicted, countries are more likely to have a woman executive who took the family path to office if her predecessor also reached executive office via this path (supports H6). In fact, countries that have had a female executive take the family path to the presidency or premiership have a 68 percent likelihood of having another woman executive take this path. Conversely, a country that has not had a female executive who took the family path to office only has a 3 percent likelihood of having a president or prime minister who reached executive office that way. Interestingly, having one or more predecessors who took the political activist path also facilitates women taking the family path to office, but the likelihood decreases to 23 percent. This finding shows the overlap among the factors the literature identifies as producing executives who took the family path or political activist path to office, namely, political instability and/or low levels of human development (e.g., Jalalzai 2013). A similar relationship is not evidenced for the political career path, so one or more predecessors taking this path to office does not lead countries to have female executives who took the family path. This highlights the differences between the political and institutional factors that encourage women to use these two paths. Additionally, this finding confirms the qualitative results on the decline of the family path in Latin America as the region reached higher levels of economic and human development.

The results regarding the other independent variables in the model indicate that multiparty systems make it more likely that a country will have a female executive who reached an executive spot via the family path. However, the substantive results reveal that the difference between multiparty systems and two- or one-party systems is relatively slight, and neither facilitates women overwhelmingly taking the family path to office. In particular, countries with multiparty systems have a 3 percent chance of having a female executive who took the family path to office, whereas one- and two-party systems have less than a 1 percent, or .69 percent to be exact, chance of having a president or prime minister take this path. Although unexpected, this finding is likely because many women from dynastic families launch political careers. In other words, they hold lower political offices before obtaining an executive post and benefit from factors that tend to best help women on the political career path. For instance, multiparty systems allow women to use gender stereotypes to their advantage to reach executive posts by demonstrating their skills as collaborative consensus-builders who are needed in a coalition government (e.g., Jalalzai 2013).

In terms of the control variables, whether a country has had an appointed, elected, or interim president or prime minister does not appear to impact whether it has a female executive who took the family path in any given year. However, countries in the Global South are more likely to have a female executive who took the family path to office, but the difference is modest at best. Countries in the Global South have a 3 percent likelihood of having a female president or prime minister who reached executive office via the family path compared to a .17 percent likelihood in the Global North.

Political Activist Path

The results in Table 6.1 for whether a country has a female executive who took the political activist path to power are mixed when it comes to supporting the hypothesized relationships. First, unstable, undemocratic countries or those with lower levels of human development are not more likely to have women who took the political activist path to the presidency or premiership (rejects H1 and H2). In fact, the results show that stable, democratic countries are actually more likely to have female presidents and/or prime ministers who reached executive office via the political activist path.

Figure 6.3 shows the substantive results of this relationship and reveals that the impact is relatively small. Specifically, the likelihood

Figure 6.3 Having a Political-Activist Female Executive: The Impact of Democratic Institutionalism

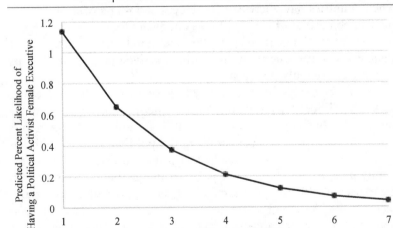

that a country with high levels of democratic institutionalism, or a Freedom House political rights score of 1, has a female executive who reached the presidency or premiership via the political activist path is just over 1 percent, which decreases to less than 1 percent for less democratic countries. This is likely because, first, political activism spans more than fighting for democratization to include social movements and work focused on advancing women's rights. Consequently, political activism can occur regardless of whether a country is stable and democratic although the literature tends to highlight political activists in the Global South who engaged in democratization movements, particularly in Africa, Asia, and Latin America (e.g., Jalalzai 2013). Such a focus misses women like former president of Iceland Vigdís Finnbogadóttir, who participated extensively in rallies protesting the presence of the US military in Iceland during the 1960s and 1970s. Second, use of the political activist path is dependent upon whether a country has or is going through democratization and/or social movements.

Second, countries are more likely to have a female executive who took the political activist path to power if they have higher percentages of women in parliament (supports H5). As Figure 6.4 shows, countries with relatively low percentages of women in parliament (i.e., 0–20 percent) have a less than 2 percent likelihood of having a female president or prime minister who took the political activist path to office. This increases to as high as almost 4 percent when countries have between 30 percent and 40 percent of the parliament comprised of women. However, even when women hold half or more of the legislative seats, the likelihood that a country has a female executive who took the political activist path to office only increases to roughly 9 percent.

Third, countries are more likely to have a woman executive who took the political activist path to office if her predecessor(s) used the same path, but not the family or political career paths (supports H6).[13] In fact, first, no woman using the political activist path has ever been preceded by a president or prime minister who took the family path. Although the same political and institutional factors that are expected to facilitate women taking the family path to office also increase the likelihood of women taking the political activist path— namely, political instability, a lack of democratic institutionalism, and low levels of human development—this finding is likely due to the lack of women who have the opportunity to use the family path

Figure 6.4   Having a Political-Activist Female Executive:
The Impact of Women in Parliament

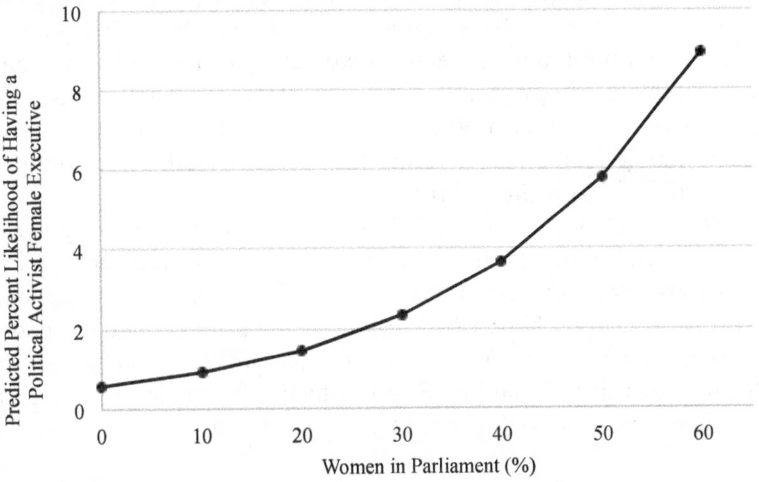

prior to the political activist woman rising to power (e.g., Jalalzai 2013). This is further supported by the findings reported previously that a predecessor who took the political activist path to office does facilitate a future executive taking the family path to the presidency or premiership. Second, countries that have had a female executive take the political activist path to office have a roughly 15 percent likelihood of having another woman reach the presidency or premiership via the same path. Conversely, a country that has not had a political-activist female executive has only a 1 percent likelihood of having a woman take that path to office.

As far as the other independent variables in the model that are not expected to directly influence whether a country has a female president or prime minister who took the political activist path to office, one interesting result emerges from Table 6.1. In particular, appointment-based systems make it less likely that a country will have a female executive who reached office via the political activist path. The substantive results show that countries with appointment-based systems have a roughly 1 percent likelihood of having a female executive who used the political activist path, but that likelihood increases to 8 percent in election-based systems. This is probably due to political activists having a preexisting constituency that can help them (1) launch a political career in order to realize additional change and (2) continue advancing to higher office (e.g., Jalalzai 2013). Thus, these women benefit from the same political and institutional structures that typically help women take the political career path. Furthermore, political activist women can triumph by drawing on the female stereotypes that women are caretakers and peacebuilders to justify their political involvement, especially following and/or during democratization movements (e.g., Geske and Bourque 2001; Jalalzai 2013; Salo 2010).

When it comes to the control variables, first, it does not appear that whether a country has had an appointed, elected, or interim female executive impacts the likelihood of having a female president or prime minister who reached office via the political activist path. Second, a country's location in the Global North or Global South also does not impact the likelihood of having a female executive in any given year who took the political activist path.

Political Career Path

Similar to the political activist path, the results in Table 6.1 are mixed when it comes to the factors that are expected to predict whether a country has a female president or prime minister who took the political career path to office. Starting with the hypotheses that are not supported in Table 6.1, countries with high levels of human development or multiparty systems are not more likely to have women presidents and prime ministers who took the political career path to office (rejects H2 and H4). The results relating to level of human development are probably due to the fact that the political career path can be used across the globe. In particular, the political career path is common in both Europe and Africa (e.g., Jalalzai 2013), which tend to differ when it comes to levels of human development. As far as the multiparty system findings, these are likely because women taking the family and political activist paths to office often launch political careers and can benefit from political and institutional factors that appear to help women on the political career path the most (e.g., Jalalzai 2013).

Additionally, previous female executives' reaching office via the political career path does not restrict future women to this path (rejects H6). Having a predecessor take the family path also does not impact whether future presidents or prime ministers take the political career path. However, women are actually less likely to take the political career path to power if their predecessor(s) reached executive office via the political activist path.[14] Specifically, a country has a 2.7 percent likelihood of having a female executive who came to power via the political career path if her predecessor(s) took the political activist path. This likelihood increases to 9.4 percent if the predecessor(s) reached the presidency or premiership via one of the other paths. These findings are likely because a country must have a democratization or social movement for women to participate in before they can take the political activist path to office. Thus, countries that have had a woman reach executive office via the political activist path likely spurred additional women to get involved in politics fighting for the same or similar causes who would become subsequent political-activist female executives. Conversely, countries with a glass-ceiling-breaking-political-career executive likely encouraged other women to launch political careers but not for the reasons relating to democratization or social movements. All in all, this shows how it is less likely that women would have started political careers and reached executive posts after a glass-ceiling-breaking-political-activist executive because many democratization and social movements can last for years.

Some of the hypothesized relationships are supported in that, first, countries with high levels of democracy are more likely to have a female executive who took the political career path to office (supports H1). Figure 6.5 shows the results of the effect that democratic institutionalism has on whether a country has a female executive who took the political career path to office. Countries with high levels of democratic institutionalism, or a Freedom House political rights score of 1, have a 9.5 percent likelihood of having a female president or prime minister who took the political career path to office. Countries with moderate levels of democratic institutionalism (i.e., Freedom House political rights scores of 2 and 3) have between a 5 percent and roughly 7 percent likelihood of having a female executive who took the political career path to office. This likelihood decreases to 3.6 percent and 2.6 percent for countries with lower levels of democratic institutionalism, or Freedom House political rights scores of 4 and 5, respectively. Countries with low levels of democratic institutionalism (i.e., Freedom House Political Rights scores of 6 and 7) have a less than 2 percent likelihood of having a woman president or prime minister who reached her position via the political career path.

Figure 6.5 Having a Political-Career Female Executive:
The Impact of Democratic Institutionalism

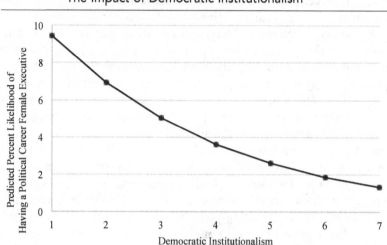

Second, countries with appointment-based systems tend to have women presidents and prime ministers who used the political career path (supports H3). In particular, the likelihood that a country has a female executive who took the political career path to office in an appointment-based system (i.e., semi-presidential or parliamentary system) is roughly 9.5 percent compared to 1.7 percent in election-based systems. Third, having more women in parliament also increases a country's likelihood of having a female executive who took the political career path to the presidency or premiership (supports H5).

Figure 6.6 shows this relationship in which countries with low levels of women in parliament (i.e., 0–10 percent) have a less than 10 percent likelihood of having a female executive who reached the presidency or premiership via the political career path. This likelihood increases to over 10 percent and 15 percent for countries with parliaments composed of 20 percent and 30 percent women, respectively. These likelihoods continue to increase to between 22 percent and roughly 30 percent as countries reach relatively high percentages of women in parliament (i.e., 40–50 percent). Countries with more than half of their parliaments composed of women have over a 30 percent likelihood that a woman president or prime minister will reach an executive post via the political career path.

Figure 6.6 Having a Political-Career Female Executive:
The Impact of Women in Parliament

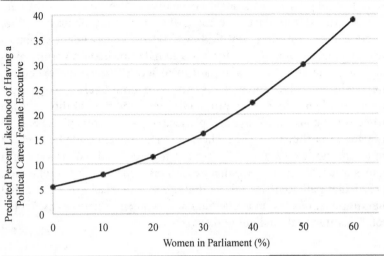

As far as the control variables, there are few statistically significant relationships. First, countries in the Global South and the Global North are just as likely to have women presidents and prime ministers who rose to power using the political career path. Second, having a woman executive who took the political career path does not appear to be influenced by whether a previous female president or prime minister was appointed or served in an interim capacity. However, if countries have elected one or more female executive(s), it increases the likelihood of having a woman president or prime minister who took the political career path. In fact, countries that have had one or more elected female executives have a 26 percent likelihood of having a woman reach the presidency or premiership via the political career path. This likelihood decreases to roughly 9.5 percent for countries that have not elected a female executive.

Discussion

In this chapter we united the two bodies of research on women executives: the paths women take to office and the conditions under which a country has a female president or prime minister. In doing so, we explain (1) whether a country has a woman executive in general and one who took each path to office, and (2) how the path(s) that one or more female predecessors take to executive office influences the path that additional women use to reach the presidency or premiership. Overall, there are three key findings: (1) the independent variables best explain whether a country has a female president or prime minister, not one who took each path to office; (2) once the executive glass ceiling has been broken, countries are more likely to have additional female presidents and prime ministers, and their ability to reach office is not constrained by their predecessor(s) in terms of the path(s) they took to office or whether they were elected, appointed, or served on an interim basis; and (3) there are few regional patterns when it comes to countries with women executives, especially ones who took a particular path to office. These findings will be discussed in turn and their implications for understanding how women executives overcome voter, institutional, and cultural sexism.

Explaining Countries with Women Executives and Their Paths to Office

The first key finding is that the political and institutional factors from the women-executives literature best explain whether a country has a female president or prime minister, not the path she took to office. Yet even in the model explaining whether a country has a female executive, the findings only provide mixed support for the hypothesized relationships and the previous literature. In particular, countries are more likely to have women presidents and prime ministers if a multiparty system is in place, there are multiple women parliamentarians, and a woman has already broken the executive glass ceiling. However, in contrast to expectations and the existing literature, unstable, undemocratic countries or those that have semi-presidential or parliamentary executive systems are not more likely to have a female executive (e.g., Hodson 1997; Jalalzai 2008, 2013, 2016a). Overall, these results are not entirely unexpected because the two areas of literature on women presidents and prime ministers have developed separately. This means that certain factors, such as executive system, best explain the path a woman takes to office, not whether a country has a female president or prime minister.

In the models explaining whether a country had a female executive who took each path to office, a few patterns emerged when explaining the errant results. First, even if political and institutional conditions are present that facilitate the use of the path, it must be available to the woman. For example, a woman cannot take the family or political activist paths to executive office if they are not part of a dynastic family or there are no active political and/or social movements in their country, respectively. Second, various factors hypothesized to help women on the political career path also aided those on the other two paths. For instance, women who took the family and political activist paths to office often launched political careers, so multiparty systems and appointment-based systems, respectively, can also facilitate their reaching executive office. Third, the three paths are not nearly as constrained to certain political and institutional contexts as suggested by the literature. For example, many political activists focused on advancing women's rights in stable, democratic countries although the focus is usually on women who participate in democratization movements in unstable, undemocratic contexts. Furthermore, the political career path is used in areas that tend to have both higher and lesser amounts of human development, such as Europe and Africa (e.g., Jalalzai 2013).

Broken Glass Ceilings and the Resulting Constraints on Future Female Executives

The second key finding of this analysis is that countries are more likely to have additional female presidents and/or prime ministers once the executive glass ceiling has been broken, but women are not substantially constrained by (1) the path(s) their predecessor(s) took or (2) whether their predecessor(s) were appointed, elected, or interim executives. The primary explanation for women not being restricted to the path used by their predecessor is that not all paths are available to all women, and the country's political environment and institutional characteristics may differ. As previously noted, the use of the family or political activist path is dependent upon a woman being from a dynastic family or being in a country with active democratization or social movements. In terms of the political and institutional factors present in any given country, political stability and level of human development tend to dictate a successor's path to executive office. For example, the family path can be used by a successor if her predecessor took the family or political activist path—paths the literature observes as being used most often in politically unstable and/or lesser developed countries (e.g., Jalalzai 2013). Similarly, having a predecessor who used the political activist path decreases the successor's likelihood of using the political career path—the route to power the literature sees as being used most often in politically stable countries and/or those with higher levels of human development (e.g., Jalalzai 2013).

Women are also relatively unconstrained by whether their predecessor(s) were appointed, elected, or served in an interim capacity. Countries are just as likely to have women take the family and political activist paths to power if their predecessor(s) were appointed, elected, or served on an interim basis. Similar results were found when examining the political career path with the exception that a country is more likely to have a woman who reached an executive position using that path if she was preceded by a female president or prime minister who was elected. This is likely because these elected women were able to gain experience in "masculine" policy areas, such as national security, and exhibit "masculine" traits of being strong, quick decisionmakers who demand respect on a global stage. In other words, these women were able to overcome gender stereotypes that cause voters to prefer male candidates. As such, because these women broke the glass ceiling, it is likely easier for future women to gain similar experiences and/or benefit from the weakening of gender stereotypes held by voters. For example, in Switzerland, President Micheline Calmy-Rey served as the head of the Federal Department of Foreign Affairs prior to being elected president in 2007 and was succeeded by President Doris Leuthard in 2010, who served as the head of the Federal Department of Economic Affairs prior to her election.

Regional Patterns

The third and final key finding of this analysis is that few regional patterns emerge. The results suggest that countries in the Global South are more likely to have women presidents and prime ministers. This accords with the results of previous studies that find that with the exception of Europe, most female executives hail from Africa, Asia, Latin America, and the Caribbean (e.g., Jalalzai 2013). An examination of whether countries have a woman executive who took each path to executive office reveals that the Global South is only more likely to have a female president or prime minister who took the family path, as women are just as likely to take the political activist and political career paths across the globe. These findings support the previous literature that suggests that the family path is prevalent in Latin America and Asia while the political activist and political career paths are common in Africa and Europe (e.g., Hodson 1997; Jalalzai 2004, 2008, 2013).

Broader Implications

In this chapter we provide specific insight into how women rise to executive power in certain contexts by gaining a better understanding of (1) the factors that determine whether a country has a female president or prime minister, especially one who took each path to office, and (2) how a female predecessor's path to office and whether she was appointed, elected, or served on an interim basis impacts her successors. However, analyses like these also speak to how women executives overcome various types of sexism: voter, institutional, and cultural. Taken collectively, it appears that, first, whether a country has a female executive depends on a variety of political and institutional factors, which differ depending on the path she took to office. Second, countries will likely have additional female presidents and prime ministers once the glass ceiling has been broken.

First, although a variety of political and institutional factors impact whether a country has a female executive, if and to what extent each factor determines the path she took office differ. The most striking finding is that no one factor consistently predicts whether a country has a woman executive who took each path to office. As was the case in Chapter 5, this continues to show that women take the path that is available to them and allows them to leverage political and institutional factors that are conducive for navigating sexism and rising to executive power.

In particular, women from dynastic families will use the family path, women participating in democratization or social movements will use the political activist path, and women with previous political experience will use the political career path. Furthermore, across each of the three paths, women benefit from institutional characteristics that allow them to overcome sexism by demonstrating that they have the necessary political experience, electoral support, and/or leadership style that is best suited for a country's executive position.

Specifically, first, countries with high levels of democratization and females in parliament tend to have women executives who reached the presidency or premiership via the political activist or political career paths. These political factors enable women to gain the necessary political experience, especially in "masculine" policy areas, that lead voters to prefer male candidates over female ones. Second, countries with multiparty systems tend to have women who took the family path to office, whereas countries with appointment-based systems tend to have women who reached executive office using the political career path. Both of these institutional characteristics allow women to bypass sexist voters who prefer male executives with masculine qualities and highlight their leadership style that focuses on collaborating and building consensus. Lastly, countries that elect their executive tend to have women who took the political activist path to power, which shows that these women are better able to overcome sexist voters who prefer male candidates because they already have voters mobilized on their behalf due to their involvement in democratization or social movements.

Second, countries are more likely to have female executives once the glass ceiling has been broken, and future women are relatively unconstrained by the path their predecessor took to office or the type of executive position (i.e., elected, appointed, or interim) she held. This shows how the ability to successfully navigate and overcome voter, institutional, and cultural sexism is imperative and more difficult for glass ceiling–breaking women than for their successors. The fact that glass ceiling–breaking presidents and prime ministers pave the way for future women executives without constraining them to the same path or executive position demonstrates the impact that a woman executive can have on realizing gender parity and decreasing voter, institutional, and cultural sexism. In particular, glass ceiling–breaking women can show how female executives may have the masculine leadership qualities and policy experience rewarded by voters, institutions, and society and/or a more feminine approach and policy credentials that are just as effective.

Conclusion

In this chapter we continue to unite the two bodies of literature on women presidents and prime ministers that examine the paths taken to executive office and the factors that facilitate a country having a female executive. In particular, in this chapter we addressed the unanswered questions of (1) under what conditions a country has a woman executive who took each path to office, and (2) whether a woman's path to office limits or enables additional female executives. In addition to answering these questions, we discussed the implications the findings have on a woman's ability to navigate and overcome voter, institutional, and cultural sexism to become president or prime minister. Despite gaining a better understanding of the dynamics surrounding whether a country has a female executive who took each path to office, especially the impact of her predecessor's path, one question remains: How does the path a woman takes to executive office or various political and institutional factors dictate how long she stays in office? The extant literature has largely ignored this question with the exception of Jalalzai (2008, 2013), who found that male and female executives spend relatively the same amounts of time in office. In order to fill this gap in the literature, in the next chapter we explore how the path a woman takes to office and the factors that are conducive to a country having a woman president or prime minister impact how long she stays in office. In doing so, we continue to provide insight into how voter, institutional, and cultural sexism impacts women executives.

Notes

1. In particular, 1990 and 2015 are the first and last years in which yearly estimates are available for the Human Development Index, which is used to measure the level of human development in a country.

2. For example, the USSR ceased to exist after 1991 so it is only included in the data set for the year 1990, whereas South Sudan did not gain independence from Sudan until 2011, so it only appears in the data set from 2011 to 2015.

3. Most countries are excluded due to missing data on the HDI and the percentage of women in parliament used to measure human development and female representation in government, respectively.

4. The United Nations Development Program relies on a variety of data sources in order to calculate a country's yearly HDI score. Consequently, any missing data will lead to missing HDI scores. Due to missing data, 462 cases are eliminated from this analysis, or roughly 10 percent of all cases.

5. Although countries tend to have relatively stable executive systems, Elgie's blog denotes any changes and the year in which they occurred so countries can be coded on a yearly basis. For example, Angola went from having a presidential system to a semi-presidential system in 1992 and did not switch back until 2010.

6. The party system of a country is usually relatively stable. In the event that there has been a change in the country's party system, such as a one-party system becoming a multiparty system or vice versa, the coding of this variable reflects that change. For example, the Democratic Republic of Congo went from having a one-party system to a multiparty system in 2006.

7. This variable is another source of missing data and leads to the exclusion of 285 observations, or roughly 6 percent of the cases. However, 50 of those cases were already excluded due to missing HDI scores so only 235 or roughly 5 percent of the observations are eliminated due to this variable.

8. Coding each country reveals that women who took the political activist path to executive office have never had a predecessor who took the family path to office. Consequently, that variable is eliminated from the model for predicting failure perfectly.

9. Although this analysis uses time-series panel data, neither a fixed nor random effects model is appropriate. Fixed effects models are used to explain the causes of change within an individual or entity based on time-variant, not time-invariant, factors; however, most of the variables in this model do not vary over time (e.g., Kohler and Kreuter 2009). Conversely, random effects models are used when the differences across entities are expected to influence values on the dependent variable (e.g., Greene 2008). A random effects model is also inappropriate because differences across countries are not expected to influence whether any given country has a female executive and the path she took to office.

10. The tolerance levels for nearly all of the independent variables are above the recommended cutoff of .2 (Menard 1995). The exception is the variable measuring whether a country with a woman president or prime minister was preceded at some point by a woman who took the political career path to executive office. The tolerance level for this variable is .1732, which is slightly below the .2 recommended cutoff. However, the variance inflation factor (VIF) score of 5.77 is well below the recommended cutoff of 10 (e.g., O'Brien 2007). It is not entirely surprising that a substantial amount of the variance in this variable is explained by others in the model. Whether a woman takes the political career path to office is influenced heavily by a country's institutional political structures and systems (e.g., Hodson 1997; Jalalzai 2013). Theoretically, it is important to keep the variable in the model in order to test fully whether the path a woman takes to executive office is dictated by that of her predecessor. For this reason, in conjunction with the diagnostics only identifying a slight, to no, issue with multicollinearity, the variable will remain in the model (see O'Brien [2007] for a discussion of [1] the dangers associated with adjusting models because of possible issues with multicollinearity gleaned from tolerance levels and VIF scores; [2] the importance of taking theoretical reasons into account when modifying models due to multicollinearity; and [3] how reliable results can be derived from models with multicollinearity issues). This choice is supported by the relatively small confidence intervals for this variable's regression coefficients in each model, which, according to O'Brien (2007), show whether conclusions can confidently be drawn from the results.

11. Predicted percent likelihoods are calculated using SPost in Stata 14 (Long and Freese 2005). Throughout this analysis, for variables in the model not of interest, continuous variables are set at the mean, and all dichotomous and categorical variables are set at the mode (see Table 6.2 for these values).

12. It is important to note that this relationship is significant at the .1 level. There is debate as to whether coefficients significant at the .1 level should be reported as statistically significant because the conventional cutoff in the social sciences is .05. However, coefficients with p values between .05 and .1 can be considered "approaching" significance (e.g., Samprit, Hadi, and Prince 2000) and are increasingly being reported as statistically significant results in political science research (e.g., Goldstein 2010). Presenting such results as substantively meaningful can be supported for reasons relating to research design (usually the size of the data set), theoretical considerations, and/or the results of prior research (e.g., Lewis-Beck 1995; Noymer 2008). Since the finding accords with the extant literature, it is worth discussing the substantive results of this relationship as statistically significant.

13. See note 12.

14. See note 12.

7

The Longevity Puzzle

The preceding chapters have been directed at unifying the two bodies of literature on women presidents and prime ministers: the paths that women take to office and the factors that make it likely that a country will have a female executive. However, as the literature review in Chapter 1 notes, a puzzle exists regarding how long women executives stay in office because existing work has said very little about this topic. Jalalzai (2008, 2013) does find that there is no difference in the tenures of male and female presidents and prime ministers, but we cannot speak to whether this is because both genders have similar experiences reaching their posts and/or serving in office. Consequently, work is needed on both genders separately. In this chapter we start to fill this gap in the literature and solve the longevity puzzle. We begin by developing and statistically testing hypotheses to uncover global patterns in how long a woman stays in office based on her path to the presidency or premiership and on various political and institutional factors. Next, descriptive analyses with case examples are utilized to provide additional insight based on the factors that are focused on in most studies of women executives: time, region, path to office, and type of executive (i.e., elected, appointed, or interim). We conclude by discussing the implications of the results—particularly on the women-executives literature and the ability of female presidents and prime ministers to overcome voter, institutional, and cultural sexism—and how unsuccessful female candidates remain under-studied but are essential to fully understanding how women reach executive office.

The Dynamics of the Duration of Women Executives in Office

Political, Economic, and Human Development

Politically unstable, undemocratic countries tend to have women executives because (1) women from dynastic families can inherit or acquire executive power through undemocratic processes after coups and/or the imprisonment or assassination of the existing executive (e.g., Hodson 1997; Jalalzai 2013), and/or (2) women who are active in democratization and social movements often pursue additional change by launching political careers that can culminate in executive positions (Jalalzai 2013). Due to their family name, women from dynastic families, especially if they reside in countries where women have recently gained suffrage, are able to bypass voter stereotypes that men are better suited for executive positions because of their perceived toughness and experience with policy areas such as national defense (Baturo and Gray 2018; Fox and Oxley 2003; Huddy and Terkildsen 1993; Jalalzai and Rincker 2018; Sczesny et al. 2004). Women who launched political careers after extensive participation in democratization and social movements can also overcome voter preferences for male executives by highlighting their feminine qual-ities—such as promoting cooperation, collaboration, and peacebuild-ing—that are needed after politically tumultuous times (Jalalzai 2008; Katzenstein 1978; Saint-Germain 1993). In light of these rea-sons that politically unstable, undemocratic countries have female executives, simply the presence of political turmoil suggests that these women presidents and prime ministers will remain in office for shorter periods of time than their counterparts in politically stable, democratic countries. This expectation is supported by Jalalzai's (2008, 2013) findings that executives, both male and female, in polit-ically tumultuous countries often face coup attempts or rise to power as an interim executive. Overall, this expectation is summarized in the following hypothesis:

> *H1: Female executives in politically unstable, undemocra-tic countries stay in office for shorter periods of time than*

their counterparts in countries that are not experiencing political turmoil.

Two other political factors often discussed by the women-executives literature are the persistence of patriarchy and a country's level of economic and human development. In order to become a president or prime minister in a patriarchal country, women must overcome gender stereotypes by using their family name or activist background to gain legitimacy and show that they can handle a position revolving around "masculine" policy areas, build consensus in a coalition government, and/or act as a caretaker following politically tumultuous periods in the nation's history (e.g., Baturo and Gray 2018; Beckwith 2000; Geske and Bourque 2001; Hodson 1997; Jalalzai 2004, 2013; Jalalzai and Rincker 2018; Richter 1991; Salo 2010). In economically developed countries, especially in nations that are perceived as world leaders, voters prefer male executives due to the focus on "masculine" policy areas like the world economy and foreign policy (e.g., Jalalzai 2013; Sczesny et al. 2004). Yet, women have been relatively successful at securing executive positions in economically developed countries because they are able to gain experience in these policy areas within the parliament or cabinet (Jalalzai 2013). Overall, the literature leads to two expectations. First, women will serve for shorter periods of time in countries with high levels of patriarchy because a female president or prime minister will be less readily accepted by the populace and elites. Second, women in economically developed countries will serve for longer periods of time because their prior political experience justifies their election or appointment. Since a country's level of economic development and patriarchy influence its level of human development—or economic growth coupled with whether citizens have freedom of opportunity and the ability to improve their well-being—the following hypothesis will be tested:

H2: Women executives in countries with low levels of human development stay in office for shorter periods of time, whereas women in countries with high levels of economic development stay in office for longer periods of time.

Political Institutions

The extant literature has focused on two aspects of a country's political institutions in order to determine whether a woman can reach the presidency or premiership: the executive and party systems. Findings from these studies suggest that women are more likely to become executives in semi-presidential and parliamentary systems because appointment-based systems (1) allow women to overcome gender stereotypes that lead voters to prefer male executives in presidential, election-based systems (Duerst-Lahti 1997; Hodson 1997; Jalalzai 2013; Whicker and Isaacs 1999), and (2) value "feminine" leadership qualities, such as collaboration and consensus-building, that are needed from prime ministers in order to unify parties in the legislature and pursue policy agenda items (Duerst-Lahti 1997). Although it is easier for women to reach executive posts in appointment-based systems, some do get elected (e.g., President Ellen Johnson Sirleaf of Liberia), and the literature provides little guidance on which system allows women to stay in office the longest. However, Jalalzai's (2008, 2013) finding that there are no differences between the tenure of male and female presidents or prime ministers suggests that it is not the gender of the position's holder that dictates length of tenure, but possibly the nature of the position itself. As such, the characteristics of both types of executive systems will be examined, particularly political durability and the presence of term limits, both of which provide some insight into which system should produce the longest-serving women executives.

As scholars often note, presidential systems are conventionally considered politically durable because elected executives receive a fixed term in office—for example, four years in the United States (e.g., Linz 1990, 1994; Maeda and Nishikawa 2006). Conversely, parliamentary and semi-presidential systems are usually viewed as more politically fragile by allowing for the dismissal of the prime minister and the dissolution of parliament (e.g., Linz 1990, 1994; Maeda and Nishikawa 2006). In parliamentary systems, the governing coalition within parliament can break down and result in a new prime minister and/or parliament can be dissolved (e.g., Linz 1990, 1994). In semi-presidential systems, the president selects the prime minister, but countries vary regarding who can dismiss the prime minister and dissolve parliament (e.g., Shugart and Carey 1992). In premier-presidential semi-presidential systems (e.g., France), parliament can dismiss the prime minister, and the president and/or cabinet, in consultation with the prime minister, can dissolve parliament (Shugart and Carey 1992). In president-parliamentary semi-presidential systems (e.g., Russia), the president or parliament can dismiss the prime minister, but only the president can dissolve parliament (Shugart and Carey 1992). Thus far, it appears as though women prime ministers in appointment-based systems would serve for shorter periods of time because they can be removed from office by the president, a vote of no confidence by parliament, a breakdown of the governing coalition, or the dissolution of parliament. However, this does not consider the role of term limits in presidential and appointment-based systems and that women can serve as presidents in these systems, such as President Pratibha Patil of India.

Presidential, election-based systems impose term limits on its executives, such as in the United States where presidents can serve two terms in office for a total of eight years (e.g., Linz 1990, 1994). Similarly, term limits are also imposed on presidents in parliamentary and semi-presidential systems; for example, France's president can serve two consecutive five-year terms. However, term limits are not imposed on prime ministers (e.g., Linz 1990, 1994). The lack of term limits on prime ministers can allow for relatively lengthy terms of service provided party control of government is relatively stable, as Maeda and Nishikawa (2006) show through an examination of Great Britain. From 1979 to 1997, the Conservative Party was the governing party and Great Britain had two prime ministers: Margaret Thatcher and John Major (Maeda and Nishikawa 2006). The Labour Party became the governing party in 1997, and Major was replaced by Tony Blair. Taking the presence, or lack thereof, of term limits into account for prime ministers, it appears that female prime ministers in appointment-based systems would serve for longer periods of time than their counterparts in presidential, election-based systems. Although female prime ministers can be removed from executive office in a variety of ways in appointment-based systems, the executive system is structured to allow them to retain power for substantial periods of time or regain power in the event that parliament is dissolved.

Up to this point, there are reasons to predict that female prime ministers stay in office for longer *and* shorter periods of time than their counterparts in presidential, election-based systems. However, this does not explain which system produces the longest-serving executives. In other words, how do appointment-based parliamentary and semi-presidential systems featuring both presidents with term limits and prime ministers without term limits compare to presidential, election-based systems in terms of the length of time executives are in office? This is of interest for this study because women can serve as both presidents and prime ministers in appointment-based systems. Despite the lack of guidance from the characteristics of executive systems, the mere presence of an executive position without term limits (i.e., premierships) suggests that women executives in appointment-based systems stay in office longer than their counterparts in election-based systems. This is further bolstered by the fact that women are best able to obtain and thrive in appointed positions because sexist voters can be avoided and female leadership skills are valued (e.g., Jalalzai 2013). This expectation is summarized in the following hypothesis:

H3: Women executives in countries with semi-presidential and parliamentary executive systems serve for longer periods of time than those in presidential executive systems.

The second political institutions–based factor that impacts whether a country has a female president or prime minister is the party system that is in place. Existing research suggests that countries with multiparty systems are more likely to have a woman executive, particularly a prime minister. This is the common party structure in countries with parliamentary and semi-presidential executive systems that prefer women with stereotypical "female" leadership styles focused on collaboration and consensus-building to lead a coalition government (Jalalzai 2013). This, in conjunction with the finding that male and female presidents and prime ministers serve for roughly the same amount of time (Jalalzai 2008, 2013), and the fact that prime ministers do not have term limits (see above), suggests that women in multiparty systems should stay in office for lengthy periods of time. Much longer than their counterparts in two-party or one-party systems common in presidential, election-based systems and authoritarian regimes, respectively. In sum, this expectation can be summarized as follows:

H4: Women executives in multiparty systems stay in office longer than their counterparts in two-party or one-party systems.

Female Political Advancement

Previous work suggests that women often reach executive posts in countries that have substantial numbers of women in parliament and/or have had a female president or prime minister (e.g., Jalalzai 2013, 2016a; Reynolds 1999). Having higher numbers of women in parliament and one or more female executives indicates that parties and voters have overcome gender stereotypes and are now more willing to elect women to political office (e.g., Jalalzai 2008, 2013, 2016a). Furthermore, as women gain a larger presence in parliament, the chances of a country having a female executive increases as there are now multiple qualified women to nominate and/or elect as president and/or prime minister (e.g., Jalalzai 2008, 2013, 2016a; Reynolds 1999). Outside of results suggesting that there are no gender differences in the tenure of male and female presidents and prime ministers (Jalalzai 2008, 2013), the women-executives literature provides little insight into how long a woman stays in office outside of factors relating to political instability. However, having a large number of women in parliament and a previous woman executive facilitates women launching political careers, which is common in countries that are politically stable and democratic with less executive turnover (Jalalzai 2013). Thus, it is probable that women in countries with high levels of women in parliament and a female predecessor serve in office longer than their counterparts in countries with lower levels of female representation in government. Furthermore, a lack of female representation in government shows that voters and parties have not overcome gender stereotypes to consistently elect or reelect women to political office, which may make it difficult for a woman who has reached executive office to be reelected as president or reselected as prime minister. Overall, the predictions made in this section can be summarized in the following hypotheses:

H5: *Women presidents and prime ministers serve for longer periods of time in countries with high numbers of female legislators.*

H6: *Having one or more female predecessors increases the length of time a female president or prime minister serves in office.*

Path to Executive Office

Another important factor in determining how long a woman stays in executive office is the path she used to reach the presidency or premiership. The path a woman takes to office provides insight into the political climate within the country, especially in terms of political stability and gender equality, that can impact her ability to remain in office. As such, women who take the political career path to office likely spend long periods of time as presidents and prime ministers. This is because the political career path is common in countries that can be characterized as one or more of the following: politically stable, democratic, economically developed, meritocratic, and/or with high numbers of women who hold political office (e.g., Jalalzai 2013). Although the presence of more women in government suggests that voters and parties have overcome gender stereotypes that favor men for executive positions, women can still struggle to obtain these positions, the exception being if they have experience in "masculine" policy areas, such as foreign affairs or national defense (e.g., Jalalzai 2013; King 2002; Thompson and Lennartz 2006). Even if women struggle to be elected president, many countries have institutional frameworks, such as appointment-based executive systems and multiparty systems, that still allow women to obtain these positions. These systems help women bypass sexist voters and highlight their "feminine" leadership qualities of promoting collaboration and consensus-building that are needed in coalition governments. The predisposition for women to be prime ministers and the lack of term limits in these appointment-based systems also make it likely that these women stay in office for long periods of time. Furthermore, since this path is frequently used in countries with lower levels of patriarchy, women who are elected president or appointed as prime minister have a better chance of being reelected or reappointed after their term ends or the dissolution of parliament.

Women who took the political activist and family paths to office likely serve for shorter periods of time than those who reached an executive post via the political career path. Both paths are common in countries that are unstable, undemocratic, less economically developed, and/or patriarchal (e.g., Hodson 1997; Jalalzai 2013). Women who took the political activist path to power started out participating in democratization or social movements and, in order to realize additional change, ran for political office (e.g., Beckwith 2000; Jalalzai 2013). These women have to justify their political involvement due to widespread gender stereotypes that favor male politicians by showing how the country needs a caretaker or peacebuilder after a politically tumultuous time (e.g., Geske and Bourque 2001; Jalalzai

2013; Salo 2010). Despite these obstacles, these women can thrive in election-based systems because they already have a constituency built up from their time as a political activist. Conversely, women who take the family path to executive office usually do so after the assassination or imprisonment of a male family member, such as a father, husband, or brother (Hodson 1997; Jalalzai 2013). Although the presence of a dynastic family and of stereotypes that women promote peace and unity (e.g., Jalalzai 2008; Katzenstein 1978; Saint-Germain 1993) implies that these women could stay in power for lengthy periods of time, the unstable political environment makes it more plausible that this is not the case. Taken collectively, the literature suggests that women who take the political activist path will still have moderately long tenures in office because the presence of democratization and/or social movements indicates the country is shifting toward having more political stability and/or gender equality. Since the woman is pursuing this change, she will likely stay in power unless the will of the people shifts and/or the status quo persists within her country. Conversely, the presence of political instability in countries where women reach executive office via the family path should make her time in office relatively short. These predictions can be summarized as the following hypothesis:

> H7: *Taking the political career path to office increases a female executive's time in office, as does reaching executive office via the political activist path; however, becoming a president or prime minister via the family path decreases a woman executive's time in office.*

Data and Methods

The hypotheses above will be tested using the same data set as in Chapter 5 that includes all women who assumed office as president or prime minister at any point throughout the time period of 1990–2015.[1] Consequently, 79 percent of all women presidents and prime ministers are examined in this study.[2] Regardless, this improves upon previous studies that covered relatively short time periods, one or a few regions, and/or select cases (e.g., Genovese 1993b; Jalalzai 2013; Liswood 2007; Montecinos 2017a; Opfell 1993; Richter 1991). As mentioned in Chapter 5, each woman president and prime minister is included in the data set once unless she served nonconsecutive terms or changed positions, in which case she is included multiple times. We proceed by discussing the data and methods used in this study.

Dependent Variable

The dependent variable measures the length of time a woman held executive office in days.[3] Days are the appropriate level of analysis because many women presidents and prime ministers are temporary executives put in place by legislatures, presidents, temporary ruling coalitions, or constitutional provisions stating succession (Jalalzai 2008, 2013).[4] Women who served as presidents and prime ministers at some point during 1990–2015 were in office as few as one day, such as President Ivy Matsepe-Casaburri of South Africa, and as long as 5,113 days, like president of Ireland Mary McAleese, who held her executive post for fourteen years from November 11, 1997, to November 10, 2011. Despite these extremes, the average length of time in office is 958 days or over two and a half years.

Independent Variables

The independent variables correspond to the aforementioned hypotheses that predict how long a woman stays in executive office. Since this analysis uses the same variables as in Chapter 5, in this section we will briefly review how each variable is coded before discussing the methods used in the analysis (see discussion in Chapter 5 of the rationale behind the use of each data source and our approach to coding each variable). Starting with variables measuring political, economic, and human development, *Democratic Institutionalism* is coded as the country's Freedom House political rights score the year each woman executive took office, which can range from 1 (most free) to 7 (least free). *Human Development* is coded as a country's HDI score, which can range from 0 (low human development) to 1 (high human development) the year each woman executive took office.

The next set of variables measures a country's political structures and level of female political advancement expected to influence the length of time a woman executive spends in office. First, three dummy variables are constructed to represent the executive system in each woman president or prime minister's country: *Executive System—Presidential, Executive System—Parliamentary,* and

Executive System—Semi-Presidential. Female executives are coded as 1 on the variable that represents the executive system that was in place the year she took office and 0 on the others. Second, *Multiparty System* is a dichotomous variable in which female presidents and prime ministers from countries with multiparty systems are coded as 1 and all others are coded as 0. Third, *Female Representation in Government* is measured as the percentage of women in parliament the year each woman executive took office. Lastly, *Previous Female Executive* is a dichotomous variable in which women presidents and prime ministers who have one or more female predecessors are coded as 1 and women who broke the executive glass ceiling in their country are coded as 0.

The last set of independent variables denotes the path the woman executive took to office: family, political activist, or political career. For each path, a dichotomous variable is constructed that codes women as 1 on the variable corresponding to the path they took to office and 0 on all others. If a woman did not take any of the three dominant paths to power, she is coded as 0 on all three variables.

Control Variables

This analysis also uses the same control variables that were included in Chapter 5: region and type of executive. Since the data sources used are the same, in this section we will discuss why the control variable is still needed and briefly review how each variable was coded in the analysis. It is important to control for region because (1) the literature on women presidents and prime ministers suggests that certain paths are common in certain regions due to the presence or lack thereof of political instability (e.g., Jalalzai 2013), and (2) the path to office and political stability are both hypothesized to influence a woman executive's length of time in office. In particular, the family path, which is common in countries with high levels of political instability, tends to be used most often in Latin America and Asia (e.g., Jalalzai 2013). Similarly, the political activist path is also used frequently in politically unstable countries located in Latin America and Asia, but also Africa (e.g., Jalalzai 2013). Conversely, the political career path is seen most often in Europe, which is characterized as a region with higher levels of political stability (e.g., Jalalzai 2013). Taken collectively, women executives in politically unstable countries and/or taking the family or political activist path should stay in office for shorter periods of time, whereas women presidents or prime ministers in countries with high levels of political stability and/or those taking the political career path should stay in office for relatively long periods of time. In order to control for region, the dichotomous *Global South* variable is created that codes women executives from countries in developing regions as 1 and female presidents and prime ministers from the Global North, or developed regions, as coded as 0.

It is also important to control for whether a woman executive was elected, appointed, or served on an interim basis because this likely impacts how long she stays in office. Given that interim executives come to power when the country is experiencing a political transition, such as a shift toward democratization or the removal, resignation, or death of a president or prime minister (Jalalzai 2013), these women should serve for relatively short periods of time because they are only placeholders, or meant to serve on a temporary basis. Appointed and elected female executives should serve for much longer periods of time since they were selected originally for their positions. As previously mentioned when discussing a country's type of executive system, the absence of term limits can result in appointed prime ministers remaining in office for long periods of time because the position is institutionally structured to allow for longer reigns and the ability to regain power after the dissolution of parliament (Linz 1994; Maeda and Nishikawa 2006). Conversely, the imposition of term limits in presidential systems shortens time in office in general; also, female presidents must run for reelection, which can be difficult depending on the prevalence of patriarchy, especially gender stereotypes held by voters that give preference to male presidents with experience in "masculine" policy areas, such as national defense (e.g., Jalalzai 2013). In light of these possibilities, a set of dummy variables is created for each type of executive: *Elected Executive, Appointed Executive,* and *Interim Executive.* Each woman executive is coded as 1 on the variable that corresponds to the type of executive she is and 0 on the others.

Methods

Since the dependent variable is the number of days a woman executive served as president or prime minister, a count model is required to test the aforementioned hypothesized relationships. The standard count model is the Poisson regression model (PRM) (Cameron and Trivedi 1998); however, the likelihood-ratio test indicates that the data are overdispersed, which is to be expected as most women spent three years or less in office but some served for much longer, such as President Mary McAleese of Ireland, who held her executive post for fourteen years. Since the data are overdispersed, the negative binomial regression model is preferred to the PRM (see Table 7.1) (Cameron and Trivedi 1998). Diagnostic tests did not reveal an excessive amount of overlap between any of the variables.[5]

The model's chi-square statistic (see Table 7.1) is statistically significant at the .05 level and shows that the independent variables accurately explain how long a woman remains in her executive post. In terms of explanatory power, the model is relatively strong with a Nagelkerke (1991) r-square statistic of .63. In the next section we discuss the effect that the path a woman takes to office and various political and institutional factors have on how long female presidents and prime ministers stay in office.

Results

The results of the statistical analysis of the factors that determine how long a female executive remains in office are shown in Table 7.1. As the results show, none of the hypothesized relationships are supported. More specifically, women do not stay in office longer in countries that are politically stable or in those that have higher levels of human development, appointment-based executive systems, or multiparty systems (rejects H1, H2, H3, and H4).[6] Furthermore, women presidents and prime ministers who hail from countries that have had a female executive and/or high levels of women in parliament do not stay in office longer than their counterparts from countries with little female participation in government (rejects H5 and H6). The path that a woman takes to office also does not impact how long she stays in office (rejects H7).[7]

Despite the unexpected findings up to this point, it is still important to mention the results for the control variables. As shown in Table 7.1, women executives in the Global South serve for shorter periods of time than their counterparts in the Global North. In particular, women executives in the Global South spend 1,480 fewer days in office than female presidents and prime ministers in the

Table 7.1 Negative Binomial Regression Results on the
          Length of Time in Office for Women Executives

Variable	Coefficient	Standard Error	z score
Democratic Institutionalism	0.067	0.101	0.67
Human Development	−1.223	0.843	−1.45
Executive System—Semi-Presidential	−0.014	0.403	−0.03
Executive System—Parliamentary	−0.325	0.371	−0.88
Multiparty System	−0.247	0.254	−0.97
Female Representation in Government	−0.003	0.009	−0.30
Previous Female Executive	−0.226	0.197	−1.15
Family Path	0.442	0.308	1.43
Political Activist Path	0.094	0.365	0.26
Global South	−0.790*	0.334	−2.37
Appointed Executive	−1.417**	0.245	−5.77
Interim Executive	−3.414**	0.281	−12.15
Constant	9.008	0.969	9.30
N	100		
Overdispersion	$\chi^2[1] = 4.8e+04$		
Model chi-square	99.66**		
Nagelkerke r-square	0.63		

Notes: Omitted categories: Executive System—Presidential; Political Career Path; Elected Executive. $†p < .1$, $*p < .05$, $**p < .01$ (two-tailed tests).

Global North.[8] As far as the type of executive position held by the woman, in contrast to expectations, women executives who are elected serve for longer periods of time than their appointed counterparts. However, as expected, women who are elected and appointed do stay in office longer than those women who are serving as executives on an interim basis.[9] More specifically, elected female executives serve roughly 931 days and 1,189 days longer than those who were appointed and served on an interim basis, respectively. Women who are appointed stay in office for 258 days longer than interim female executives.

Given the relative lack of support for the hypothesized relationships, in the next section we will present descriptive analyses with case examples of factors prominently focused on by the women-executives literature. These analyses seek to uncover more nuanced patterns regarding how long a woman spends in executive office. In particular, we will pay special attention to patterns based on region, path to office, executive type, and time. The time frame of the study will also be expanded to cover 1960–2015.

The Length of Time Women Spend in Executive Office: A Qualitative Perspective

Region

Looking at the cases from a qualitative perspective, there is a high frequency of women executives in the Global South from countries marked by political instability and violence. But what is more striking is the long tenure of those women presidents and prime ministers considering such political instability. For example, prime minister of Bangladesh Sheikh Hasina served five years from 1996 to 2001, took office again in 2009, and started her fourth term in 2019 despite substantial political unrest and controversy surrounding the fairness of elections. Similarly, President Violeta Chamorro of Nicaragua served for a little over six and a half years from April 1990 to early January 1997 despite winning office during a civil war and enduring a constitutional crisis. However, the Global North, which is typically marked by more political stability, also has had long-serving executives. For example, Prime Minister Margaret Thatcher of Great Britain served ten and a half years from May 1979 to November 1990, and prime minister of New Zealand Helen Clark served for almost nine years from December 1999 to November 2008. Overall, when comparing whether women from the Global South or the Global North serve longest, they both tend to serve roughly three years.

Path to Office

Family path. Isolating the women executives who came to office through the family path yields seventeen cases. One striking aspect is the high frequency of their reelection or reappointment to executive office. Due to their famous family names, these women enjoy large political networks, name recognition, and greater access to the media. Once in power, these women executives enjoy extended tenures in office. On average, they stay for four and a half years, which corresponds to more than one term in most cases. In fact, the seventeen women executives who took the family path served for a combined thirty terms in office (see Table 2.1). For example, Prime Minister Indira Gandhi of India and Prime Minister Sirimavo Bandaranaike of Sri Lanka each served three terms for more than fifteen and seventeen years, respectively. The longevity of these women's tenures also demonstrates the efficacy of this particular path to power.

Political activist path. On average the seventeen women executives who came to power through the political activist path also stayed in power for four and a half years. Although the use of this path sometimes denotes the presence of political conflict, it is important to note that women who were able to reach an executive seat tended to remain in office for an extended period of time. In this category, many were elected to office and served lengthy terms. For example, President Vigdís Finnbogadóttir served four terms for a total of sixteen years in Iceland, and with this tenure, she remains the longest-serving-elected woman executive in Europe. Similarly, Prime Minister Eugenia Charles of Dominica served for fifteen years, and President Ellen Johnson Sirleaf of Liberia, who was the first elected woman executive in Africa, served two terms for a total of twelve years. In short, the political activist path includes some pioneering women, and quite a few of them had exceptionally long executive tenures.

Political career path. The political career path is by far the most popular route to executive power with seventy-four women reaching the presidency or premiership this way. On average, these women stay in power for two years. However, since interim executives most often use this path, it is important to expound upon this finding a bit more. Average time in office increases to three years for the fifty-five women who were elected or appointed to office, for example, Prime Minister Julia Gillard of Australia, who served for three years from 2010 to 2013 until she resigned after losing a leadership vote. Conversely, the nineteen women who served as president or prime minister on an interim basis tended to hold their executive positions for three and a half months, for example, Rose Francine Rogombé, who served as president of Gabon for four months from June to October 2009. Overall, these findings underscore how this path is common for women who serve as executives on an interim basis and as appointed prime ministers, as they can be pressured to resign or be removed from office via various mechanisms, such as votes of no confidence.

Executive Type

When comparing the length of time a woman spends in office based on whether she was elected, appointed, or selected to serve on an interim basis, the most expected finding is confirmed in which interim executives serve the least amount of time: three and a half months. Elected executives serve the longest amount of time at five years, and appointed executives serve less at almost two years. As mentioned previously, it appears that elected executives serve the longest because they are shielded more from pressures to resign or efforts to remove them from office via mechanisms such as votes of no confidence. Women who serve as examples of these three findings are prime minister of Dominica Eugenia Charles, who was elected and served for almost fifteen years from July 1980 to June 1995; Prime Minister Jadranka Kosor of Croatia, who was appointed and served for two years and five months from July 2009 to December 2011; and Prime Minister Reneta Indzhova of Bulgaria, who served on an interim basis from October 1994 to January 1995.

Time

On average, women executives who took office throughout 1960–2015 served three years. Although more women became presidents and prime ministers over this period of time, women assuming office in most of the decades included in this data set served three to almost four years: in the 1970s, 1990s, and 2000s. Interestingly, the female executives who served longer on average were some of the very first who took office in the 1960s and those in the 1980s. Conversely, the shortest serving executives took office in the 2010s.

Beginning with the longest-serving female executives, these women assumed power in the 1960s and, on average, served for seven years. Sri Lankan prime minister Sirimavo Bandaranaike was the first female executive appointed in July 1960. She would serve until March 1965 for a tenure of four years and eight months. She would later serve as prime minister again from May 1970 to July 1977 and November 1994 to August 2000. Prime Minister Indira Gandhi became the second woman executive when she was elected in January 1966. She would serve until March 1977 for a total of eleven years and two months. Gandhi would again be elected prime minister in January 1980 and serve until October 1984. Prime minister of Israel

Golda Meir would become the third female executive, assuming office in March 1969 and serving until June 1974 for a total of five years and three months.

In the cases of Bandaranaike and Gandhi, their longevity can largely be explained by having taken the family path to office, which, as previously discussed, provided them with the political connections, name recognition, and media access needed to secure and remain in an executive position. Meir, on the other hand, took the political career path to office, which often requires women to leverage their political experience and stereotypical female leadership styles to their advantage to reach the presidency or premiership, and in the case of Meir, remain in executive office. For Meir, reaching office was accomplished by focusing on collaboration. In particular, she built good relations with foreign countries throughout her diplomatic and ministerial career, for example, with the Soviet Union as minister plenipotentiary to Moscow and with newly independent African countries as foreign minister (Burkett 2008; Meir 1975). While in office, Meir continued to seek collaboration but also consensus by, for example, leading and maintaining the national unity government formed after the Six-Day War and the 1969 general election and collaborating with foreign nations to work on promoting peace in the Middle East (Burkett 2008; Meir 1975).

During the 1980s, all but two of the nine women who took executive office served for less than four years: President Carmen Pereira of Guinea-Bissau (three days) and Prime Minister Benazir Bhutto of Pakistan (one year, eight months). Five of the remaining women served between four and six years: Prime Minister Milka Planinc of Yugoslavia (four years), Prime Minister Gro Harlem Brundtland of Norway (four years, two months combined: eight months in 1981 and three years, six months from May 1986 to October 1989), Prime Minister Indira Gandhi of India (four years, ten months), President Agatha Barbara of Malta (five years), and President Corazon Aquino of the Philippines (six years, four months). The two remaining female executives are two of the longest-serving female executives: Prime Minister Eugenia Charles of Dominica (fifteen years) and President Vigdís Finnbogadóttir of Iceland (sixteen years). Nearly all of the women serving four years or more took the family or political activist path to office. The exceptions are Prime Minister Gro Harlem Brundtland of Norway and Prime Minister Milka Planinc of Yugoslavia, who took the political career path. Consequently, these findings continue to underscore how the family path and political activist paths provide women unique opportunities and political resources to help them reach and remain in executive office. As previously noted, the family path provides women a political network, media access, and name recognition, whereas the political activist path provides women with mobilized voters and the opportunity to capitalize on the gender stereotypes of women as caretakers and peacebuilders, especially during democratization movements, to help them reach and remain in executive power. For example, prime minister of Dominica Eugenia Charles became politically active by speaking out against restrictions on the press, helped found the Dominica Freedom Party composed of a variety of opposition groups, and became the first prime minister after Dominica gained independence from Great Britain in 1978 (Jalalzai 2013).

The female executives serving for the shortest periods of time are those assuming office in the 2010s. On average, these women served as presidents and prime ministers for about one and a half years. Although it may seem as if women are serving for shorter periods of time, this is likely because the data set only extends through 2015 and many women are still in office. Thus, full lengths of tenure will not be known until 2020 or later. For example, Prime Minister Erna Solberg of Norway assumed office in October 2013 and was still in office on December 31, 2015. Another example would be President Bidhya Devi Bhandari of Nepal, who took office in October 2015 and was still serving at the conclusion of 2015.

Discussion

The literature on women executives around the globe has focused on explaining (1) what factors dictate whether a country has a female president or prime minister and (2) which path a woman takes to executive office. Our analysis united these two bodies of work in an effort to explain how long women presidents and prime ministers stay in power. Outside of Jalalzai's (2008, 2013) observations that women remain in office for similar amounts of time as men, how long a woman stays in power has been overlooked by studies thus far. Work on both genders separately is needed to determine whether the reason for Jalalzai's (2013) finding is because men and women have similar experiences reaching executive office and/or serving as president or prime minister. Our analysis begins to address this gap in the literature, and through quantitative and qualitative analyses, there are two takeaways: (1) relatively few factors systematically explain how long a woman president or prime minister stays in office, and (2) there are more nuanced patterns that are interesting over time and based on region, path to office, and executive type (i.e., elected, appointed, or served on an interim basis). This section will discuss each in turn and conclude by explaining the broader implications for women trying to overcome sexism (voter, institutional, and cultural) to become presidents and prime ministers.

Systematically Predicting Time in Office

The primary finding of the quantitative analysis is that relatively few factors explain how long a woman president or prime minister stays in office. This is somewhat expected since the literature on women presidents and prime ministers provides relatively little guidance on this matter. Additionally, studies on the institutional structure of different executive systems have indicated that women executives in appointment-based systems could serve both longer and shorter periods of time in office than elected women executives. This is because the absence of term limits also coincides with institutional arrangements that allow for parliament to be dissolved or for presidential dismissal of the prime minister (e.g., Linz 1994; Shugart and Carey 1992).

Of the political and institutional factors included in the model, the most unexpected null findings are that neither political stability nor path to office impacts a woman executive's time in office. It was expected that women executives in undemocratic, politically unstable countries would serve for shorter periods of time; however, it is possible that once they are in power, they are able to remain in office for relatively similar amounts of time as their counterparts around the world. For example, president of Nicaragua Violeta Chamorro served for seven years (April 25, 1990–January 10, 1997) despite multiple attempts by Sandinista rebels to take over the government (Jalalzai 2013).

It was also unexpected that the path a woman takes to office has no impact on how long she stays in office. However, the prediction that women taking the family and political activist paths to executive power would stay in office for shorter periods of time was based on the literature's observation that these paths are used frequently in unstable, undemocratic countries. Since this factor was not found to impact time in office, it is possible that once reaching an executive post, women are able to stay in power for substantial amounts of time regardless of the political conditions *and* the path she took to office. For example, Prime Minister Benazir Bhutto of Pakistan, who took the family path to office, was able to serve for roughly two years before the government was ousted and again for another three years until her assassination (Jalalzai 2013). Furthermore, this speculation is supported by the results of the qualitative analysis that shows that women taking the family and political activist paths to power can remain in their positions for lengthy periods of time.

Interestingly, the control variables were able to systematically predict how long women executives stay in office. Women from the Global North serve for longer periods of time than those in the Global South, and elected female presidents and prime ministers stay in power the longest, followed by those who are appointed and served on an interim basis. Although it was expected that women executives in the Global South serve for the shortest periods of time, this was based on how regions in the Global South (i.e., Africa, Asia, and Latin America) tend to have higher levels of political instability and lower levels of democratic institutionalism, which make it more difficult for women to reach executive office and force them to use the family or political activist paths. As such, only mixed support can be provided to the rationale behind this expectation.

In terms of elected women executives staying in power longer than those who are appointed, this suggests that the absence of term limits for prime ministers is not enough to lead to longer tenures in office. It appears that because presidents have set terms and are harder to remove from office, they serve for longer than prime ministers, who can lose their posts by being removed by the president or after the dissolution of parliament. However, there was no difference in the time women executives served in office between election-based and appointment-based executive systems, thus, again, only providing mixed support for the rationale behind this result. Regardless, the results do support the observations of previous studies (e.g., Jalalzai 2013) and conventional wisdom that elected and appointed executives serve for longer periods of time than those who serve as presidents and prime ministers on an interim basis.

Uncovering Nuanced Patterns of Time in Office

The key takeaway from the qualitative analysis is that there are quite a few nuanced patterns regarding the length of time in office for female executives over time and based on region, path to office, and type of executive position: elected, appointed, and interim. In particular, there is no difference based on region and very few over time, with the exception of the first few women who assumed executive positions in the 1960s and those in the 1980s who had lengthy tenures. However, the findings do suggest that women taking the family and activist paths to office serve longer than their counterparts using the political career path, and elected executives serve longer than appointed or interim executives. Only the findings related to the type of executive position a woman held were revealed by the quantitative analysis, thus showing the nuance of these patterns in which the differences are relatively slight or likely impacted by the type of executive position a woman is holding: elected, appointed, or interim. Regardless, this chapter has been able to provide greater insight into the length of time a woman spends in executive office. As more women become presidents and prime ministers, more will be able to be learned about the dynamics of how long they stay in office.

Broader Implications

Gaining a better understanding of how long a woman executive stays in office given various political and institutional factors and the path she takes to office not only advances the literature on women executives, but also (1) serves as a foundation for studies on the gender differences in executive tenure and (2) offers insight into how women overcome voter, institutional, and cultural sexism. Taken collectively, it appears that the biggest obstacle for women is assuming, not retaining, power. This is highlighted by women, such as prime minister of Pakistan Benazir Bhutto and president of Nicaragua Violeta Chamorro, who served for multiple years in office despite experiencing political instability and using paths that are associated with political and institutional factors that should reduce an executive's tenure: family and political activist. A similar study on whether this is the case for males would allow for a richer understanding of Jalalzai's (2013) findings that there are no gender differences in executive tenure length and facilitate additional work comparing the length of time males and females serve in executive positions. Regardless, it appears that the need to overcome sexism is most apparent in order to reach executive office, not to get reelected or reappointed.

Each of the three paths allows women to overcome sexism. First, women taking the family path to office can use their household name to overcome voter, institutional, and cultural sexism that results in a preference for a male executive (e.g., Jalalzai and Rincker 2018; Sczesny et al. 2004). Second, females using the political activist path can overcome voter sexism because many already have a base of support from their time participating in democratization or social movements (Jalalzai 2013). Third, women on the political career path to office can use their political experience, especially in masculine policy areas like foreign affairs and defense, in order to overcome voter, institutional, and cultural sexism (e.g., Jalalzai 2013; Thompson and Lennartz 2006).

Across each of these three paths, women can also successfully navigate sexism present in their country by highlighting their feminine leadership qualities focused on collaboration and consensus-building. For women taking the family and political activist paths, this is beneficial because these paths are common in politically turbulent countries with frequent executive turnover; consequently, executives who can exhibit feminine qualities and serve as caretakers and promote peace are desired (e.g., Geske and Bourque 2001; Jalalzai 2008, 2013; Katzenstein 1978; Saint-Germain 1993; Salo 2010). Although also the case for these two paths, women using the political career path can best achieve prime minister appointments due to their feminine leadership and policymaking style that is perceived to be needed for the leader of a coalition government (e.g., Duerst-Lahti 1997). Although it appears that the need to overcome voter, institutional, and cultural sexism is most apparent in reaching, not remaining in, executive office, the results from this chapter have provided more insight into how long women executives stay in office and how they navigate various types of sexism.

Conclusion

Thus far, our results have been couched in terms of better understanding the dynamics surrounding how women reach executive posts around the world and how long they stay in office. Although important, such research must also be able to speak to why women in countries with political and institutional conditions that are favorable to women rising to executive power fail to have female presidents and prime ministers. Only then can studies entirely show the obstacles facing female candidates for executive office. In the next chapter we do just that by examining the failed presidential candidacies of Hillary Clinton of the United States in 2008 and 2016 and Marine Le Pen of France in 2012 and 2017. Despite the global scope of the book, these two women from Western countries were chosen because they are the most prominent unsuccessful female candidates for executive office during the time period covered by this book, 1960–2020; both of their two failed campaigns received extensive global media coverage; and many scholars and political pundits sought to explain their losses. In the next chapter we will summarize their runs for office, discuss the reasons put forth by both the academic literature and the news media for their losses, and explain their failed attempts to become president using the results of our book.

Notes

1. The analysis is restricted to this time period because variables are coded based on the year the woman assumed office, and 1990 and 2015 are the first and last years in which all of the data are available for each of the variables, specifically, yearly estimates for the Human Development Index, which is used to measure the level of human development in a country.

2. The time frame for this study means that 85 percent of all women who reached executive posts could be included; however, additional data availability issues discussed in Chapter 5 decreased this to 79 percent.

3. For women who were still in office at the end of 2015, such as President Ellen Johnson Sirleaf of Liberia, the dependent variable is the number of days in office up to December 31, 2015. An alternative approach would be to exclude these women from the analysis. This would eliminate another fifteen female executives and drop the percentage of women included in the analysis over 10 percentage points from 79 percent to 67 percent. Since the results are substantively similar, the model with these women is presented below.

4. For example, in 1997, Vice President Rosalía Arteaga of Ecuador assumed the presidency after Abdalá Bucaram was impeached for mental incompetence. She was only in power for three days because the constitution was amended to alter the line of succession so the president of Congress would be first in line in the event of a presidential vacancy (Schemo 1997).

5. Multicollinearity is not an issue because the tolerance level for each independent variable is over the recommended cutoff of .2 (Menard 1995). See Table 5.2 for descriptive statistics.

6. It is also worth noting that there is no statistically significant difference between how long women executives remain in office in semi-presidential systems or parliamentary systems. This result was determined by omitting the semi-presidential system variable from the model instead of the presidential system variable.

7. In order to determine whether there is a difference in how long a woman who took the family path to power stays in office compared to one who utilized the political activist path, the political activist path variable was omitted from the model instead of the political career path variable. The results reveal that there is no difference in the length of time spent in office for women who took the family path and the political activist path.

8. The predicted number of days in office is calculated using SPost in Stata 14 (Long and Freese 2005). For variables in the model not of interest, continuous variables are set at the mean and all dichotomous variables are set at the mode. See Table 5.2 for these values.

9. Whether there is a difference in tenure length for appointed and interim female executives was determined by excluding the appointed executive variable from the model instead of the elected executive variable.

8

Why Not Clinton or Le Pen?

In the preceding chapters, we seek to provide a richer view of how women become presidents and prime ministers around the world by addressing three questions: (1) What factors lead women to take each path to power: family, political activist, or political career? (2) Does a woman's path to power constrain or enable her successors from reaching executive office via the same or a different path? (3) Does the path a woman takes to power or the factors that facilitate women reaching executive posts influence how long she stays in office? While answering these questions is important in order to merge the two bodies of research on women presidents and prime ministers— which focus on the paths taken to office and the factors that lead countries to have female executives—and advance the literature overall, a complete understanding of the dynamics surrounding women executives requires an examination of women who have failed to reach an executive post. These failed attempts better show the obstacles facing female candidates for executive office.

This chapter is directed at providing a thorough picture of why women can or cannot reach the presidency or premiership by examining two recent unsuccessful presidential candidacies: Hillary Clinton of the United States in 2008 and 2016 and Marine Le Pen of France in 2012 and 2017. Despite the global scope of this book, these two women from globally powerful Western nations were chosen for a couple of reasons. First, Clinton and Le Pen are globally renowned female politicians who recently failed twice to reach an executive position during the time frame covered by our book: 1960–2020. Second, global media outlets covered both women's failed campaigns extensively, and both journalists and scholars attempted to explain their losses. We add to these explanations by proceeding in a manner similar to other case studies in the women-executives literature (see Jalalzai 2013): we will summarize the campaigns of both women, discuss reasons put forth by the academic literature and global news media outlets[1] for their losses, and offer an alternative explanation as to why neither woman was able to become president of her respective country, using the results of our book. In doing so, we advance the literature, because none of the existing explanations for either candidate's losses focus on their paths to executive office. We will conclude the chapter by discussing the implications of the findings.

Hillary Clinton's Bids for the US Presidency in 2008 and 2016

In 2008 and 2016, Hillary Clinton attempted to secure the Democratic nomination for president and shatter the glass ceiling of the US presidency but came up short both times. Hillary Clinton's bid for the Democratic nomination in 2008, which she ultimately lost to eventual two-term president Barack Obama, was historic as she came the closest of any female to capturing a major party's presidential nomination (e.g., Jalalzai 2013). As the 2016 election primary season got under way, Clinton was considered the frontrunner, and she remained the favorite once securing the Democratic Party's nomination since her opponent and the eventual president, Donald Trump, was considered politically inexperienced and anti-establishment (e.g., Bevan 2017; Cohen 2016; Peck 2017; Robbins 2017). We will proceed by summarizing Clinton's campaigns in 2008 and 2016, present reasons offered by the academic literature and the media for her losses, and offer an alternative explanation for her inability to shatter the US presidency's glass ceiling, using the results of this book.

Vying for the Democratic Nomination in 2008

Hillary Clinton was considered a viable candidate for the Democratic Party's presidential nomination in 2008 as she had become a fixture in

US politics. Despite receiving a law degree from Yale University and having practiced law, Clinton was best known for being the first lady of Arkansas and the first lady of the United States while her husband, Bill Clinton, served as the governor of Arkansas and president of the United States. As first lady of the United States, Clinton tackled health-care issues (Jalalzai 2013). Her political career took off once her husband finished his second presidential term in office. Clinton went on to represent the state of New York in the US Senate in 2000 and was reelected in 2006. As a US senator, Clinton served on the Health, Education, Labor, and Pensions Committee and the Armed Services Committee. With the 2008 election looming, the media speculated whether Clinton would run, and in January 2007, she launched an exploratory committee (Duerst-Lahti 2006; Jalalzai 2013). She quickly became a frontrunner due to her name recognition, close relationships with Democratic Party insiders (built while her husband had served as president), ability to fundraise, and access to experienced campaign staff (Jalalzai 2013; Nelson 2009). Clinton received extensive media coverage as she was the first serious female presidential candidate (Jalalzai 2013).

Clinton's historic campaign was quickly overshadowed by Senator Barack Obama's bid for the Democratic nomination (Jalalzai 2013). Obama was a first-term senator from Illinois, so despite his lack of national political experience, his campaign elicited attention and enthusiasm among voters as he was the most competitive African American Democratic Party candidate in US history (Jalalzai 2013). After former US senator John Edwards of North Carolina dropped out of the race, it was essentially Clinton and Obama left vying for the Democratic Party's nomination. In June 2008, Obama secured the nomination having won 2,201 delegates to Clinton's 1,896 delegates (CNN 2008). Despite running a close race, enjoying name recognition, and having sufficient campaign funds, Clinton came up short, which led academics and the news media to ask why. In the next section we will discuss the dominant reasons offered for why Clinton was unable to secure the Democratic Party's nomination for president in 2008: excessive media attention about her gender, a lack of overwhelming support from the Democratic Party, prevalence of sexism and gender stereotypes within the electorate, and the presence of Obama.

Gender-related media attention. Although being the first serious female contender for a major party's presidential nomination helped Clinton launch her campaign and gain attention, this media frame may have later become a detriment (Falk 2008). Because the media continued to talk about Clinton's historic campaign, it reinforced how women are "out of place" and "unnatural" in presidential politics, which likely had "longer lasting . . . political consequences" (Falk 2008, 37). Regardless of the possible long-term damage this media frame did to Clinton's campaign, she was hampered by the media's repeated questioning of her political qualifications (Carlin and Winfrey 2009; Jalalzai 2013). The media was quick to point out how as first lady she did not have security clearance or receive daily briefings; furthermore, her health-care policy reform failed (Healy 2007a). The media also struggled to find that Clinton had any significant accomplishments during her time as a US senator from New York (e.g., Healy 2007a). Clinton's frontrunner status quickly became justified primarily by her marriage to former president Bill Clinton (Jalalzai 2013). According to Murray (2010, 15), women are penalized for following in their husbands' footsteps because they are subjected to the "wife of" frame that diminishes their qualifications.

Media coverage of Clinton's campaign was gendered in that she received more negative and trivial coverage than her male counterparts (Carlin and Winfrey 2009; Lawrence and Rose 2010; Miller, Peake, and Boulton 2010). For example, the media focused on Clinton's wardrobe, criticized her laugh, depicted her in political cartoons as a cold and calculating politician, and even referred to her as a bitch (Brady 2008; Carroll 2009; Givhan 2007a, 2007b; Goldberg 2008; Healy 2007b; Lawless 2009; Matthews 2008; Simon 2008). When media attention was not directed at Clinton, it shifted to her husband, Bill. Journalists watched for Bill's missteps, speculated about what his equivalent role to first lady would be in the White House, and pondered whether Hillary would have full control over her presidency (Burden 2009; Jalalzai 2013; Nelson 2009; Murray 2010).

Democratic Party support or lack thereof. Clinton's connection to Democratic Party insiders substantially helped her launch her campaign, fundraise, and hire adept campaign staff; however, the party did not overwhelmingly support her bid for the presidency (e.g., Burden 2009; Jalalzai 2013). It is unclear whether Clinton's gender had anything to do with the party's failure to coalesce around her campaign (Jalalzai 2013). However, studies have found that Clinton did not suffer from a lack of funds, like other female candidates for president (e.g., Burden 2009). According to Burden (2009), the party-related factor that played the most integral role in Clinton's defeat was the nomination process; in particular, four changes to the nomination process influenced the results: (1) more states used primaries instead of caucuses; (2) states awarded delegates on a proportional rather than a winner-take-all basis; (3) superdelegates were used; and (4) states changed their primary election schedules.

Clinton tended to perform better than Obama in primaries, whereas he won the caucuses, which were usually held in smaller, conservative states (Burden 2009). Despite Clinton's success in primaries, especially in large states, delegates were awarded on a proportional basis, which hampered her ability to secure the nomination in February (Burden 2009). Clinton's bid for the nomination was also hurt by Michigan and Florida moving their primaries to January despite national Democratic Party opposition. The party decided only half of the delegates from these two states, which she won, would count (Burden 2009). Controversy surrounding the use of superdelegates also ended up impairing Clinton's campaign. Clinton started out having the most support among superdelegates but could not maintain it after voters became outraged at the undemocratic possibility that Obama may not receive the nomination despite having won the most pledged delegates (Burden 2009).

Gender stereotypes and sexism within the US electorate. Whether sexism played a role in Clinton's inability to secure the Democratic Party's presidential nomination was investigated by a variety of scholars. For example, Huddy and Carey (2009) did not find evidence of gender discrimination against Clinton in state exit polls of voters. Voters who did mention that gender played a role in their vote choice typically supported Clinton, and despite receiving a majority of votes cast by women, Huddy and Carey (2009) contend that this was due more to impressions of Clinton's stances on issues than preferences based solely on gender.

The absence of voter gender-based discrimination against Clinton was underscored by her ability to gain widespread appeal in a variety of large and diverse states, such as California, Massachusetts, and Ohio (Jalalzai 2013). However, scholars, like Jalalzai (2013), argue that these findings and observations do not suggest that gender did not impact Clinton's campaign. In fact, others noticed that Clinton often tried to ward off gender stereotypes by being more hawkish on national defense and foreign policy issues while still showing her feminine side (e.g., Carroll 2009; Lawrence and Rose 2010; McDonagh 2009). For example, Clinton advocated for withdrawing troops from Iraq and discussed the importance of her being a role model for young women (Goldberg 2008). Clinton's gender-balancing tactics appeared to work in that poll respondents viewed her as a stronger leader in "masculine" policy issues, such as defense, foreign policy, and economics, than hypothetical female candidates garnered in polls administered in prior years (Bystrom 2010; Jalalzai 2013).

Barack Obama. Having been a US senator from Illinois for only four years, Barack Obama was a relative newcomer with little connection to the Democratic Party establishment when he launched his campaign to secure the party's nomination for president (Jalalzai 2013). Not appearing as a Washington or party insider and using social media benefited his campaign as he was able to build a base of supporters, which included young voters, and rely on small campaign contributions (Jalalzai 2013). Obama was further aided by a simple and consistent campaign message focused on the idea of change (Jalalzai 2013).

Obama's campaign garnered media attention as this was the most competitive an African American Democratic Party presidential candidate had been in US history (Jalalzai 2013). Interestingly, Obama distanced himself from the issue of race and instead focused on the issues important to the African American community, such as health care, affirmative action, and poverty (Jalalzai 2013). Not being willing to risk any sort of negative political ramifications, his opponents also avoided discussing race (Lawrence and Rose 2010; Nelson 2009). There were questions regarding whether Obama could secure support from white voters, but winning Iowa erased those doubts (Jalalzai 2013; Nelson 2009). Gaining support from white voters helped Obama make strides with African American voters, especially those within the South and/or in conservative states (Nelson 2009). As Obama came to find, African Americans are a loyal constituency, which ensured him success in the Democratic primary and the general election (Abramson, Aldrich, and Rohde 2010; Jalalzai 2013). In the end, Clinton's historic candidacy was no match for Obama's and his ability to attract a loyal base of supporters, especially among African Americans and young voters. Although Clinton could appeal to female voters, women were not as loyal a constituency as Obama experienced with African Americans (Jalalzai 2013).

Trying to Break the US Presidency's Glass Ceiling in 2016

Despite Clinton losing the Democratic Party's nomination for president in 2008, President Obama appointed her as his secretary of state upon taking office in 2009. Resigning from the Senate and serving as secretary of state provided Clinton with another opportunity to strengthen her credentials before another attempt to capture the Oval Office. The beginning of her tenure as secretary of state was spent developing diplomatic relationships to help advance President Obama's foreign policy agenda and ensuring diplomatic missions abroad achieved specific objectives (Allen and Parnes 2014; Richter 2009). The first half of her time as secretary of state was spent dealing with the war in Afghanistan and attempting to repair ties with Russia and Pakistan (Allen and Parnes 2014; Baker 2014; Klein 2009; Landler 2016). The second half of her tenure as secretary of state was marked by instability throughout the Middle East—particularly the protests in Egypt and civil wars in Libya and Syria—and the raid in Pakistan that killed Osama bin Laden (Allen and Parnes 2014; Bowden 2012; Calabresi 2011; Cooper and Myers 2011; Ghattas 2013; Thrush 2011). The most notable event during Clinton's time as secretary of state occurred near the end of her tenure in 2012. On September 11, 2012, the US diplomatic mission in Benghazi, Libya, was attacked, which resulted in the deaths of a US ambassador and three other Americans (Labott 2012). Although Clinton took responsibility for the security lapses, she testified in multiple congressional hearings, most of which were conducted by the House Select Committee on Benghazi (Labott 2012; Singer 2016). Regardless of the controversy surrounding Benghazi, Clinton was already set to leave office at the end of Obama's first term. Once her successor, Senator John Kerry, was confirmed, Clinton left office in January 2013 to join the Clinton Foundation (Allen and Parnes 2014).

Clinton announced her candidacy for the Democratic Party's nomination for president in April 2015 (Chozick 2015). She was able to quickly relaunch her 2008 campaign and regain her frontrunner status (Chozick 2015; Von Drehle 2014). However, she faced stronger opposition than expected from Senator Bernie Sanders of Vermont, whose dissatisfaction with the undue influence of the wealthy and corporations on US politics resonated with citizens concerned about income inequality and Clinton's ties to Wall Street (Confessore and

Horowitz 2016; Pace 2016). Despite narrow wins in Iowa and a loss in New Hampshire, Clinton won Nevada and South Carolina and seven of the eleven primaries on Super Tuesday (Collison 2016; Healy and Chozick 2016; Hepker 2016; Thrush and Karni 2016). Clinton went on to take a commanding lead in pledged delegates and garnered significant support among superdelegates (Chozick and Healy 2016). Clinton became the first woman to be nominated for president by a major US political party after securing 2,219 pledged delegates and 594 superdelegates compared to Sanders's 1,832 and 47, respectively (CNN 2016a; Rappeport, Alcindor, and Martin 2016).

Clinton, who named Senator Tim Kaine as her running mate, went on to run against the Republican Party candidate and well-known businessman, Donald Trump (Keneally and Struyk 2016). Clinton initially enjoyed a substantial lead over Trump in the polls; however, Trump closed the gap once the FBI concluded its investigation into Clinton's use of a private email account during her time as secretary of state and determined that she had been "extremely careless" when it came to classified government information (Barro 2016; Chozick and Thee-Brennan 2016). Trump led Clinton in the polls after the Republican National Convention, but Clinton regained her lead after the Democratic National Convention (Lauter 2016). As the election drew near, Clinton was predicted to win the White House (e.g., Long 2016). Yet, despite winning the popular vote by 2.9 million votes, Trump bested Clinton with electoral votes by a 304–227 margin (with a record seven electors voting for someone besides their party's nominee) (Federal Election Commission 2017).

In addition to having name recognition and sufficient campaign funds, Clinton improved upon her run from 2008 by garnering more support from the Democratic Party and being acknowledged as the most qualified candidate; however, yet again, she was unable to break the executive glass ceiling of the US presidency (Caldwell 2013; Sachar and Cusack 2014). Going into Election Day as the frontrunner led many academics and the news media to speculate why Clinton ultimately lost. In the next section we will discuss the most common reasons: gendered media coverage, sexism and gender stereotypes among voters, involvement in political controversies, campaign strategy missteps, and the presence of Trump.

Gendered media coverage. As was the case in 2008, Clinton received gendered media coverage in 2016. The media initially expressed an interest in how the United States could have its first female president (Jalalzai 2018). However, the focus quickly turned to how she was the wife of former president Bill Clinton and her personal characteristics (e.g., Jalalzai 2018). Clinton was criticized for launching her political career after serving as first lady and using "wife of" President Bill Clinton to her advantage (Murray 2010). Consequently, the media and the public perceived Clinton as power hungry, calculating, and disingenuous (Jalalzai 2018; Paquette 2016; Patterson 2016b). The perception that the Clintons were constantly embroiled in scandals led to perceptions that Hillary was corrupt, dishonest, and unethical (McCarthy 2016; Patterson 2016a, 2016b, 2016d). Since the public tends to prefer honest and trustworthy female politicians, Clinton appeared to be punished much more so for her alleged transgressions than Trump was for his (Barnes and Beaulieu 2014; Esarey and Schwindt-Bayer 2017; Jalalzai 2018).

Journalists also commented on how little she smiled, the shape of her mouth, her voice, her appearance, and the importance that she appear feminine (Cauterucci 2016; Satlin 2016; Noonan 2016). For example, Geraldo Rivera described her voice as "unpleasant," "unrelaxed," and "bitter," whereas *Wall Street Journal* columnist Peggy Noonan (2016) wrote that Clinton reminds her of a "landlady" yelling (Satlin 2016). These observations are supported by Patterson's (2016b, 2016c) studies of the media during the 2016 election in which news coverage of Clinton's personal life and character was eleven-to-one negative.

Voter sexism and gender stereotypes. Despite the gendered media coverage Clinton received, the role of voter sexism and gender stereotypes appeared to be subtle at best as was the case in 2008 (e.g., Huddy and Carey 2009; Jalalzai 2013, 2018). The reasons for this stem from relatively little change in voter perceptions of male and female candidates, the gender gap, and the status of feminism within the United States. According to Lawless and Fox (2018), media coverage on Clinton's personal characteristics had more to do with the fact that voters disliked her for a variety of reasons, not because she was a woman. However, the media's excessive coverage of her physical appearance and demeanor and the possibility of voter sexism at the polls tended to reinforce the myth that women struggle to get elected (Lawless and Fox 2018). A Pew Research Center poll conducted in 2014 found that over half of the respondents noted that more women do not hold political office because many Americans are not ready to elect women, voters hold female candidates to higher standards, women get less support from party leaders, and women have too many family responsibilities. Yet research conducted by Lawless and Fox (2010) demonstrates that women are not systematically discriminated against by voters, but media coverage, especially that which was seen in 2016, does little to dispel the myth that Americans are unwilling to vote for a woman. In reality, the obstacles that women can face during a campaign have little to do with the outcome of an election but more with the willingness of women to run for office in the first place (Lawless and Fox 2018). Additionally, the fact that Clinton won the popular vote shows that Americans are willing to vote for a woman and ready for a female president.

A second reason that voter sexism appeared to play very little role in the results of the 2016 election is the persistence of the gender gap—women identify with and vote for Democrats and men do the same for Republicans. In the 2016 election, Clinton received 13 percent more support from women whereas Trump had an eleven-point advantage among male voters (Center for American Women and Politics [CAWP] 2017). The gender gap (which is generally measured as the difference between the percentage of women and the percentage of men voting for the winning candidate) of eleven points in 2016 tied with the 1996 presidential election as the largest gender gap since 1980 (CAWP 2017). However, it was not drastically different from the average gap of eight points (CAWP 2017; Lawless and Fox 2018). Thus, had voters, especially female voters, been sexist against Clinton, the gap would have differed quite a bit from the typical average. Delving into the gender gap that did persist shows that Trump's sexist comments and Clinton's ability to tout her historic run to break the executive glass ceiling did very little to move the gender gap (Lawless and Fox 2018). Exit-poll data suggest that income, social welfare issues, and Trump's sexist comments accounted most for the gender gap (Lawless and Fox 2018; Hartig, Lapinski, and Psyllos 2016). Specifically, Americans, especially women, who made less than $50,000, supported Obamacare and criminal justice reform, and viewed Donald Trump unfavorably were more likely to vote for Clinton (Lawless and Fox 2018; Hartig, Lapinski, and Psyllos 2016).

A final reason voter sexism and gender stereotypes had little impact on Clinton's loss in 2016 is the status of feminism in the United States. According to Lawless and Fox (2018), Trump voters overlooked his sexist comments as exit polls (e.g., CNN 2016b) show that many who voted for him recognized that he lacked the temperament needed to be president and had a questionable track record with women. This is not entirely surprising because Americans are relatively ambivalent toward the women's movement and feminism and unwilling to label themselves feminists yet support feminist policies, such as equal pay for equal work (Lawless and Fox 2018). Thus, this disconnect between feminism and support for women's policies in conjunction with voters being forgiving of candidates with questionable pasts likely contributed to Trump's success in 2016 because voters had to balance competing priorities (Lawless and Fox 2018). For example, Trump was also touting typical Republican platforms, especially economic policy promises in Rust Belt states to voters disillusioned by the economic recovery promised by Obama and the Democrats (Lawless and Fox 2018).

Political scandals and controversies. One of the reasons that Clinton was perceived as dishonest and untrustworthy and considered unlikable was because of her association and/or involvement in political scandals during her husband's time as governor of Arkansas and president of the United States and her tenure as secretary of state (Newport 2016). The scandals that seemed to impact Clinton's campaign the most were her husband's infidelity and sexual misconduct, the attack on Benghazi, her use of a private email account during her time as secretary of state, and Wikileaks. Allegations of sexual assault filed by Paula Jones and affairs with Gennifer Flowers and Monica Lewinsky entered into Trump's attacks on Clinton (e.g., Stokols 2016). For example, before even declaring his candidacy, Trump retweeted a supporter's view of Clinton: "If Hillary Clinton can't satisfy her husband, what makes her think she can satisfy America?" (Lawless and Fox 2018). Regardless of Trump's sexist remarks and the media's response to them, Clinton's personal life, both Bill's transgressions and her decision to remain married to him, detracted from her likability as a candidate (Goldberg 2016; Jalalzai 2018; Long 2016).

The attack on the US diplomatic mission in Benghazi during Clinton's tenure as secretary of state was frequently used as evidence by Trump that she was unfit to serve as president (Bixby and McCarthy 2016). For example, at a campaign rally in Anaheim, California, Trump said, "Now, if you look at the war in Iraq, if you look at Libya, which is a total catastrophe, and by the way, with Benghazi and with our ambassador—remember? That's all Hillary Clinton, folks" (Bixby and McCarthy 2016). Furthermore, Trump went on to attack Clinton for one of her 2008 Democratic primary campaign promises that she would be able to take 3 a.m. emergency calls by saying, "They called! They kept calling! Hundreds and hundreds of emails and calling, and she was sleeping, folks. She was sleeping!" (Bixby and McCarthy 2016). Although Clinton took responsibility for the security lapse in Benghazi and was praised for her performance before the House Select Committee on Benghazi, being involved in scandals hurt her campaign (e.g., Goldberg 2016; Jalalzai 2018; Patterson 2016a, 2016d; Reyes 2015).

Hillary Clinton's use of a private email account while serving as secretary of state, or what came to be known as Emailgate, also negatively impacted her campaign (Faris et al. 2017; Jalalzai 2018; Long 2016; Patterson 2016a, 2016d). The primary concern about Clinton's use of a personal email account related to the security of classified information (Leonnig, Helderman, and Gearan 2015). A number of emails on Clinton's server were determined to contain classified, secret, top-secret, and/or confidential information (Dinan 2016; Gerstein and Bade 2016; Myers 2016; Myers and Davis 2016). Clinton contended that the classified emails were not marked as such when she initially received them; however, the terms of her security clearance stipulated that she treat sensitive information as classified (Dilanian 2016). An FBI probe was launched in response to the allegations that Clinton mishandled emails (Cox 2015; Dilanian 2016; Kessler 2016; Shane and Schmidt 2015). The results of the probe were announced on July 5, 2016, and did not include a recommendation that Clinton be charged by the Justice Department for mishandling the emails (Zapotosky and Helderman 2016). However, FBI director James Comey informed Congress on October 28, just eleven days before the election, that the FBI was analyzing additional emails (Perez and Brown 2016a, 2016b). Comey notified Congress on November 6 that this investigation did not change the FBI's original conclusion (Alba, Thorp, and McCausland 2016). Although being surrounded by controversy substantially hurt Clinton's campaign (Jalalzai 2018; Long 2016), Clinton felt that Comey's actions just prior to Election Day contributed to her loss (Debenedetti 2016).

Another scandal that led voters to dislike Clinton and view her as untrustworthy stemmed from emails released by Wikileaks (e.g.,

Jalalzai 2018). During the Democratic National Convention, Wikileaks released emails showing that (1) the Clinton campaign had tried to reschedule the Illinois presidential primary one month later so the Republican candidate would not get a boost in the polls after Super Tuesday, and (2) CNN contributor, Donna Brazile, who later went on to chair the Democratic National Committee, provided Clinton with one of the debate questions beforehand (BBC 2016). Upon taking over the Democratic National Committee, Brazile later said that she found unethical agreements between the Clinton campaign and the party that implied favoritism; however, she never found evidence that the Democratic primaries had been rigged in Clinton's favor (Lima 2017; Rucker 2017). Regardless, additional controversy surrounding Clinton only stood to hurt, not help, Clinton's campaign and chance to break the executive glass ceiling.

Campaign strategy missteps. Clinton's loss has also been attributed to a variety of campaign missteps, primarily saying Trump supporters belong in a "basket of deplorables," choosing not to campaign in Michigan and Wisconsin, and underestimating Trump. Clinton's frustration with Trump's sexist and racist comments led her to say, "you could put half of Trump's supporters into what I call the basket of deplorables. They're racist, sexist, homophobic, xenophobic, Islamophobic—you name it" at a fundraiser held on September 9 (Flegenheimer 2016; Montanaro 2016). The remark failed to have the impact Clinton intended as she was criticized by Trump and the media alike for insulting his supporters, and Trump supporters adopted the "Deplorables" nickname proudly (Blake 2016; Chozick 2016; Cummings 2016; Hagen 2016; Montanaro 2016).

Another misstep by the Clinton campaign was choosing to campaign very little in Michigan and Wisconsin after losing both states in the primary to Senator Bernie Sanders (Hayden 2016). At the outset, it appeared as if Clinton would win these states handily as Trump had a 21.1 percent likelihood of winning Michigan and an even slimmer 16.5 percent chance of taking Wisconsin (Hayden 2016). Clinton's absence in Michigan and Wisconsin allowed Trump to gain ground and generate enthusiasm (Hayden 2016). Although deemed fruitless at the time, Trump included Michigan in his final day of campaigning, which in retrospect showed his ability to gain support from working-class voters (Hayden 2016). Consequently, Trump was able to overcome the odds and win both Michigan and Wisconsin.

In addition to underestimating Trump's ability to appeal to voters in Michigan and Wisconsin, Clinton discounted Trump's ability to win the election period. Clinton seemed to be of the opinion that her political experience and frontrunner status would win out and nobody would seriously vote for Trump (Cillizza 2016; Hayden 2016). Trump was dismissed early on because his campaign was viewed as a way to promote his business interests and brand (Lawless and Fox 2018). Furthermore, he lacked political experience, had a history of making sexist comments, and led a tabloid-worthy personal life (Lawless and Fox 2018). Yet, the Clinton campaign discounted his appeal as an anti-establishment candidate who spoke his mind and touted Republican policy platforms that appealed to voters who were disillusioned by the economic recovery the Democrats promised but were unable to deliver (Lawless and Fox 2018). Clinton also underestimated how American voters have a history of forgiving candidates with questionable pasts because Trump seemed beyond repudiation. This was even confirmed in a 1999 interview with Chris Matthews on *Hardball* where Trump stated, "Can you imagine how controversial I'd be? How about me with the women? Can you imagine?" (Lawless and Fox 2018; Orin 1999). Overall, discounting Trump is just one of many reasons Clinton was unable to break the US presidency's glass ceiling.

Donald Trump. The remaining reason that Clinton was unable to win the 2016 election is the fact that she was running against Donald Trump. As was the case in 2008 with Barack Obama, Clinton's run to break the glass ceiling of the US presidency competed with another prominent story line in the media. This time it was that her competitor was an anti-establishment candidate with no political experience best known for being a real estate tycoon and reality television star (e.g., Lawless and Fox 2018). Trump's candidacy was initially considered a publicity stunt meant to promote his business interests and the Trump brand (e.g., Lawless and Fox 2018). Although he gained some traction with voters, he was still written off as unpresidential due to his lack of experience and simplistically blunt public speaking skills (e.g., Lawless and Fox 2018). For example, he boasted that he "beats China all the time" and would "build a great, great wall on our southern border" because the Mexicans and other Latin Americans who are crossing the border are "bringing drugs. They're bringing crime. They're rapists" (*Time* 2016; Lawless and Fox 2018, 12). Trump was also dismissed for his personal life that was often tabloid-worthy news and his long-standing record of making sexist and crude comments about women (e.g., Lawless and Fox 2018). Overall, a man with no political experience, multiple marriages, a history of extramarital affairs, and a record of misogynist comments, like "a person who is very flat-chested is very hard to be a 10," was chalked up to be unfit and relatively unlikely to win the 2016 election (Fieldstadt 2016; Lawless and Fox 2018, 13).

However, Trump did go on to win the 2016 election. Primarily because of his ability to tout Republican policy platforms, appeal to voters who were disillusioned by the inability of the Democrats to deliver on their promised economic recovery, and the willingness of voters to forgive candidates with questionable pasts (Lawless and Fox 2018). Voters were also forgiving of comments that came to light or were made by Trump during his campaign (Lawless and Fox 2018). For example, unaired footage from *Access Hollywood* in 2005 was released where Trump is heard talking off-camera about how he grabbed and kissed women whenever and wherever he felt like it (Lawless and Fox 2018). Although Trump did not apologize for statements he made about Hillary Clinton during the campaign, Trump did deny touching women inappropriately and apologized for the "locker room talk" (Lawless and Fox 2018).

The willingness of voters to forgive Trump is best exemplified in exit polls that found one-third of his voters did not believe that he had the temperament to be president and were bothered by his treatment of women (CNN 2016b; Lawless and Fox 2018). However, others were not bothered whatsoever by his comments, those related to women or otherwise. For example, voters said they thought, "he will offend everyone equally," that his words were being taken "out of context," and his honesty was refreshing and genuine (Bassett and Cohn 2016; Lawless and Fox 2018, 16). Overall, sexist and unpresidential comments did not appear to hurt Trump's bid for the White House (Lawless and Fox 2018). In fact, according to Lawless and Fox (2018), the political climate was well-suited for an anti-establishment candidate with Republican, albeit slightly unconventional, policy proposals after the Democrats failed to deliver an economic recovery. In the end, underestimating Trump proved disastrous for Clinton as her political experience and historic run to the White House were not enough to overcome the aforementioned factors that also contributed to her loss and Trump's ability to connect with and be forgiven by voters.

Why Not Clinton?

Numerous reasons have been posited by the academic literature and the news media for why Hillary Clinton was unable to capture the US presidency in 2008 and 2016, such as gendered media coverage, gender stereotypes and sexism among voters, political scandals and controversies, campaign missteps, and her opponents. However, none of these possibilities engage with the academic literature on the paths women take to executive office. In order to fill this gap in the literature, in this section we examine Clinton's inability to become president using the results from previous chapters and offer an alternative explanation for her losses.

For the purposes of this study, Clinton can be classified as attempting to take the family path to power as she launched her political career by following in the footsteps of her husband, former president Bill Clinton. Consequently, it is important to refer back to the results of this book on the factors that facilitate a woman rising to the presidency or premiership via the family path. First, women executives take the family path in politically unstable, undemocratic countries. Second, the family path is commonly used by women presidents and prime ministers who are not serving on an interim basis or as the first female executive in their country. Lastly, women are less likely to take the family path to power in semi-presidential systems than in executive and parliamentary systems.

According to these results, the only factors working in Clinton's favor were that she was running for a full term, and women in executive and parliamentary executive systems are more likely to take the family path to power than their counterparts in semi-presidential systems. This speaks to the fact that women from political families are able to launch political careers successfully due to their name recognition. By following in her husband's footsteps, Clinton had the name recognition and the access to resources needed to successfully run for and secure political office, such as close relationships with party officials and experienced campaign staff (Jalalzai 2013; Nelson 2009). Yet this didn't seem to be enough to help Clinton capture the White House and break the executive glass ceiling in the United States. The other results from this book begin to show why.

Women in undemocratic, politically unstable countries are more likely to reach the presidency or premiership via the family path, especially if they are following in the footsteps of another female executive, neither of which describes the United States or the politics surrounding Clinton's run for office. Women in democratically institutionalized countries, like the United States, with a Freedom House political rights score of 1, have less than a 1 percent chance of taking the family path to power. This chance is still under 5 percent when another woman has already broken the executive glass ceiling. Overall, this suggests that (1) the level of democracy and political stability in the United States impacted Clinton's ability to reach the Oval Office the most, and (2) taking the family path in a democratic, politically stable country impedes, rather than facilitates, a woman reaching executive office.

These conclusions suggest that voters in stable democracies prefer female executive candidates with political qualifications who are self-made rather than members of dynastic political families. Yet these same voters make the family path viable for women to reach other lower political positions, such as senator and secretary of state in Clinton's case. The reason for this is grounded in the academic literature on women executives. In particular, prior political experience based entirely on merit, not all or in part because of family name, is essential for women in democratic, politically stable countries, especially those that are also economically developed, because they and their executives have more influence over worldwide economic issues and foreign affairs (Jalalzai 2013). Consequently, prior political experience is key, especially for women within these "masculine" policy areas. Given that some stable democratic economically developed countries, like the United States, also have lower levels of patriarchy and tend to be meritocratic, voters seem to prefer self-made executives where it is undoubtedly their credentials, not their last name, that makes them a suitable president or prime minister. It appears that this preference for self-made executives is applied more stringently to women, at least in the United States, considering men have used the family path to reach executive office—for example, George W. Bush followed in the footsteps of his father, George H. W. Bush. In Clinton's case, however, her last name was not only a liability but it led to questions regarding her policy success and/or leadership abilities stemming from her time as first lady, senator, and secretary of state. Conversely, such concerns are not at the forefront when voters or government officials are selecting candidates for lower political positions. Yet Clinton did win the popular vote, so the question becomes whether the family path was in fact her downfall.

It still likely was because absent these doubts about Clinton's credentials due to her last name, it is probable she would have secured the requisite votes needed to best Trump in the Electoral College. Overall, the literature demonstrates that it is the powerful and influential nature of an executive position that limits the use of the family path for women past lower political positions in stable, democratic countries with lower levels of patriarchy, like the United States.

In sum and thus far, our findings, in conjunction with the women-executives academic literature, have provided an alternative explanation for Hillary Clinton's failed attempts to break the US presidency's glass ceiling: that she tried to take the family path to a globally powerful executive post in a stable, democratic country with low levels of patriarchy. However, it is important to determine whether our results can speak to another instance of a woman failing to reach executive office. In the next section we examine Marine Le Pen's two failed attempts to become president of France.

Marine Le Pen's Presidential Campaigns in 2012 and 2017

In 2012 and 2017, Marine Le Pen attempted to become the first female president of France but was unable to do so both times. In 2012, she placed third behind François Hollande and Nicolas Sarkozy, but with 17.9 percent of the vote, she secured the highest percentage of votes for her party, the Front National, ever in a presidential election (Henley 2012). In 2017, she improved from 2012 by garnering 33.9 percent of the vote but came in second to eventual president Emmanuel Macron (Clarke and Holder 2017). In this section we will proceed by summarizing Le Pen's campaigns in 2012 and 2017, examining reasons offered by the academic literature and the media for her losses, and explaining her inability to become France's president using the results of this book.

Seeking the Presidency in 2012

Before running for president in 2012, Le Pen was well known in French politics as the youngest daughter of the Front National's founder, Jean-Marie Le Pen, who ran for president in 1974, 1988, 1995, 2002, and 2007 (Chrisafis 2017b). Although trained as a lawyer,

Le Pen eventually followed in her father's footsteps and joined the Front National in 1986 (Chrisafis 2017b). She was elected to various regional and municipal councilor posts until being elected as a member of the European Parliament in 2004 (Chrisafis 2017b). In 2011, Le Pen succeeded her father as the leader of the Front National having defeated Bruno Gollnisch with 67.65 percent of the vote (Erlanger 2010; Marquand 2010).

Le Pen launched her first presidential campaign in September 2011 and spent the bulk of her campaign publicizing her policy platforms across France, which included strengthening democracy, promoting reindustrialization, and reducing France's debt (e.g., Leroux 2011). In keeping with her mission to de-demonize the Front National, a party often characterized as far right or extreme right, she focused more on economic and social issues, like globalization and job creation, than immigration and law and order, which had been central themes of the Front National's politics (Chrisafis 2011). However, she still advocated for reducing legal immigration and reinstating the death penalty (Chrisafis 2011). In the first round of the presidential election in April 2012, Le Pen finished third behind François Hollande and Nicolas Sarkozy with 17.9 percent of the vote (Henley 2012). This was the highest vote share that the Front National had ever received in a presidential election; Le Pen's father, Jean-Marie, achieved 16.86 percent in the first round and 17.79 percent in the runoff in 2002 (Henley 2012; Wall 2014). The incumbent, Sarkozy, went on to lose in a runoff with Hollande in May 2012. Despite name recognition and setting presidential election vote records for the Front National, Le Pen was unable to advance to the second round. In general, her lack of success can be attributed to the relatively narrow appeal of her party, which is due to its categorization as far right or extreme right, and her father's legacy (e.g., Schofield 2012).

The Front National's lack of appeal. There are two primary reasons that the Front National does not appeal to voters: its categorization as a far-right party and its longtime party leader, Jean-Marie Le Pen. According to Crépon (as quoted in Schofield [2012]), the Front National appeals to two classes of voters. First are those who perceive themselves as victims of globalization: small business owners, low-paid workers, and the unemployed who are struggling due to economic crises and competition. Second are suburban and rural voters who have fled metropolitan cities due to the cost of living, an increase in immigrants, and rising crime. Overall, this accords well with the party's primary policy platforms that include opposing France's membership in the European Union, economic protectionism, a zero tolerance approach toward crime, and opposition to open immigration (Shields 2007). Although Le Pen worked toward the "de-demonization of the Front National" by recasting existing policy platforms, softening the party's stances against same-sex marriage and abortion, eventually abandoning the party's support of the death penalty, and focusing on economic issues rather than immigration and law and order during her campaign (Beardsley 2017), she failed to appeal to a large swath of voters. It appeared as if Le Pen struggled to overcome her party's reputation.

Le Pen's Le Pen problem. Le Pen's inability to change the Front National's reputation and distance herself from the party's controversial past is due mostly to her father and party founder, Jean-Marie Le Pen. Jean-Marie Le Pen founded the Front National in 1972 to unify a variety of French nationalist movements (Shields 2007). The party was initially anti-communist and anti-immigration and later advocated for economic protectionism, a zero tolerance approach to crime, and anti-immigration policies (Shields 2007). The party also supported the death penalty and opposed abortion and same-sex marriage (Shields 2007). Le Pen is very controversial as he frequently makes xenophobic, homophobic, and anti-Semitic remarks, such as denying the Holocaust (e.g., Taub 2017). Le Pen's controversial statements and far-right politics have led to his home being bombed in 1976 and numerous prosecutions and convictions for his Holocaust denial, homophobic, and anti-Muslim statements (Chrisafis 2016a; Walt 2017).

As the leader of the Front National and having run for president in 1974, 1988, 1995, 2002, and 2007 and served in the European Parliament, Le Pen was a fixture within French politics, and his controversial nature led to him being dubbed the "Devil of the Republic" (e.g., Britannica 2020; Nossiter 2018). The controversy surrounding Le Pen and his party's extreme-right politics made it difficult for him to attract voters in each of his bids for the presidency (Shields 2007). Despite capitalizing on the large number of leftist candidates and narrowly advancing to the second round in 2002 to face Jacques Chirac, he finished a distant second (Shields 2007). Overall, Le Pen's dominant and controversial presence within French politics was difficult for Marine to overcome. She appeared to inherit her father's inability to appeal to voters despite her efforts to soften the party's image (Beardsley 2017; Shields 2007).

Running Again in 2017

Before her second run for the French presidency, Marine Le Pen worked to build electoral coalitions to gain the Front National representation in parliamentary and local offices. Le Pen herself ran for parliament but was defeated in the second round (Samuel 2012, 2014a). She ended up winning a seat in the European Parliament (Samuel 2014a). Overall, these efforts show Le Pen's work to further de-demonize the Front National (Samuel 2014b).

In April 2015, Jean-Marie Le Pen described the use of gas chambers in concentration camps during the Holocaust as a "detail" of World War II history (Rubin and Breeden 2015). As party leader, Marine Le Pen organized a vote by the Front National executive office to expel him from the party (Vinocur 2015). Upon her father being ousted from the Front National, Le Pen ran unsuccessfully for the presidency of the regional council of Nord-Pas-de-Calais-Picardie (Bremmer 2015).

Despite the controversy surrounding her father and her electoral setbacks, Le Pen announced her candidacy for president in April 2016 and was considered a contender to advance to the second round for a few reasons (Pasha-Robinson 2016). First, as the most powerful member and leader of the Front National, Le Pen could capitalize electorally on her efforts to make the party more appealing to voters, which culminated in the expulsion of her father and other controversial members (Chrisafis 2016b). Second, the Syrian refugee crisis and terrorist attacks in France provided concrete examples of her anti-immigration policy stance (Chrisafis 2016b; Dearden 2017). Additionally, right-wing campaigns were becoming more common and proving successful in some instances. For example, Nicolas Sarkozy ran a right-wing campaign in the Les Républicains party primary, which he lost to François Fillon, and Donald Trump's conservative campaign landed him the Republican nomination for president and the White House (Chrisafis 2016b). Once the Republican and Socialist party primaries were over, Le Pen officially launched her presidential campaign in February 2017 (Henley 2017).

Le Pen's second campaign was marred with controversy. Le Pen first became embroiled in controversy when the European Parliament revoked her immunity from being prosecuted for tweeting the violent image of beheaded journalist James Foley in December 2015 (Nossiter 2017). Despite deleting the tweet, she was eventually charged in March of 2018 (Agence France-Presse 2018).[2] This was not the first time that Le Pen had been prosecuted for controversial statements. In December 2015, Le Pen was acquitted for "inciting hatred" after she compared public streets and squares being blocked for Muslim prayers with the Nazi occupation of France, during a speech to party members in December 2010 (Chrisafis 2015). The court found that her statements were protected under the freedom of expression (Chrisafis 2015). Additional controversy swirled around Le Pen as she was also facing prosecution for allegedly spending European Parliament funds on her own political party (Chrisafis 2017c). Le Pen was later ordered by the European Union's General Court to repay the $350,000 in misspent funds (Welle 2018).

Le Pen continued to make controversial statements while on the campaign trail. Shortly after an arson attempt at her campaign headquarters in April 2017, she mentioned how France as a nation was not responsible for the Vel' d'Hiv Roundup, where Paris police arrested Jewish citizens so they could be deported to Auschwitz, because the Vichy regime did not represent France; instead, Charles de Gaulle's Free France did (Masters and Deygas 2017). She made more controversial remarks later that month after a shooting of police officers was considered a suspected terrorist attack. In particular, Le Pen canceled a campaign event and called for all extremist mosques to be closed (Willsher 2017b). In light of the attack, US president Donald Trump tweeted support for Le Pen as the "strongest on borders and she's the strongest on what's been going on in France" (Quigley 2017).

During the first round of the election on April 23, 2017, Le Pen secured 21.3 percent of the vote, finishing second behind Emmanuel Macron to advance to the runoff to be held on May 7 (Clarke and Holder 2017). In between the two elections, Le Pen temporarily stepped down as the leader of the Front National in an effort to unite voters (Kroet 2017). While campaigning in the second round, Le Pen tried to garner support from voters for the far-left candidate, Jean-Luc Mélenchon, by criticizing globalization because her campaign committee believed that "the left-right divide is something of the past and the new divide is between the globalists and the patriots" (Melander 2017). Similarly, she touted anti-immigration to voters of conservative François Fillon and nationalist Nicolas Dupont-Aignan (Melander 2017). However, this strategy proved difficult as Fillon urged his supporters to vote for Macron to ensure France remains in the European Union (Amaro 2017).

Controversy continued to follow Le Pen during this portion of her campaign. In May 2017, she was accused of plagiarizing portions of a campaign speech from one given by François Fillon (Willsher 2017c). Le Pen's campaign manager denied the accusations of plagiarism by stating that the speech was a type of tribute to Fillon (Willsher 2017c). However, a former spokesman for Fillon said that Le Pen's speech was "blatant pillaging . . . and proof that the Front National has no backbone. François Fillon's voters are not fooled, they're not going to be bought just because someone copies their candidate's speech" (Willsher 2017c).

Despite Le Pen's efforts to garner support from voters across the ideological spectrum, initial polls favored Macron, and he went on to win the runoff with 66.1 percent of the vote (Clarke and Holder 2017; Embury-Dennis 2017). Le Pen's 33.9 percent of the vote was twice the number of votes her father garnered in 2002 and set the record for the highest percentage of votes obtained by the Front National in the second round of presidential elections (Bradley 2017). The primary reason put forth for Le Pen's inability to win is nearly identical to 2012: the Front National's lack of appeal to a wide swath of voters (e.g., Bradley 2017). Rather than repeat the reasons that the Front National fails to garner widespread support despite Le Pen's efforts to de-demonize the party, in the next section we will explain how Le Pen was able to advance to the runoff in light of this and the other two primary reasons for her loss: her challengers encouraging their supporters to vote for Macron and her poor performance in the debates.

Advancing to the runoff in 2017. Throughout the first round of campaigning, former prime minister François Fillon was polling relatively even with his conservative rival Le Pen (El Amraoui 2017). However, the centrist candidate, Emmanuel Macron, gained ground because of his ability to appeal to voters on the right and left (Serhan 2017). By finishing with 24.01 percent of the vote in the first round, it came down to Le Pen or Fillon to advance to the runoff to face Macron (Clarke and Holder 2017). In light of Macron's surge in the polls, which was later evidenced in the final election results, only

Fillon or Le Pen would advance to the runoff rather than both as polls originally indicated. With both candidates polling roughly even, it was unknown who would advance until Election Day. The level of support for both candidates and how voters reacted to scandals each was embroiled in ended up dictating who advanced to the runoff. Le Pen's support was fairly static, so she was relatively unaffected by her scandals (El Amraoui 2017). However, Fillon's support tended to fluctuate. At times he polled higher than Le Pen, but that ended after "Penelopegate" (El Amraoui 2017).

Penelopegate revolved around accusations that François Fillon had misused public parliamentary funds to pay his wife as a leg-islative staffer for over eight years without her ever actually work-ing (Chrisafis 2017a). Fillon denied the allegations and contended that his wife had in fact held the position and performed her duties (Chrisafis 2017a). Although Fillon promised to cooperate with investigators and provide evidence that his wife had served in her position, Penelope had made statements in the past that she had "never been involved in her husband's political life" (Chrisafis 2017a). Once the Penelopegate scandal broke, it was expected to slowly spoil Fillon's chances to become president (e.g., Chrisafis 2017a; Willsher 2017a; Vinocur 2017a).

Since Le Pen was also embroiled in a political financial scandal for allegedly paying party activists as parliamentary assistants in the European Parliament, some questioned why Le Pen's support remained static while Fillon's decreased drastically (e.g., El Amraoui 2017). According to Phillippe Marlière (as cited in El Amraoui 2017), Le Pen did not suffer because she did not stand to personally gain from her misuse of funds whereas that was not the case with Fillon funneling money to his wife. Fillon was also hurt because his campaign platform focused on promoting fiscal conser-vatism, reducing public spending, and eliminating waste and cor-ruption (El Amraoui 2017). Thus Penelopegate immediately dis-credited Fillon's campaign promises and helped Le Pen advance to the second round (El Amraoui 2017).

Anyone but Le Pen. One of the reasons for Le Pen's loss is that after the first round, only one candidate, Nicolas Dupont-Aignan, endorsed her, which led him to be named as her top choice for prime minister (Maxwell 2017). A right-wing candidate, Dupont-Aignan refuted claims that Le Pen and her party, the Front National, are extremist right wing (Maxwell 2017). The other candidates chose one of three options: endorsed neither candidate, condemned Le Pen, or encouraged supporters to vote for Macron (Evans and Ivaldi 2018). Candidates who refused to endorse either candidate were Jean-Luc Mélenchon, Philippe Poutou, Nathalie Arthaud, François Asselineau, and Jean Lassalle (Evans and Ivaldi 2018). Jacques Cheminade was extremely critical of Le Pen throughout the first round and was not considered her supporter (Samuel 2017), whereas François Fillon and Benoît Hamon called on supporters to vote for Macron (Evans and Ivaldi 2018). The inability of Le Pen to garner support from her eliminated opponents likely contributed to her inability to win against Macron in the second round.

Debate performance. Upon advancing to the second-round runoff election, Le Pen and Macron participated in a televised debate at the beginning of May. Macron characterized Le Pen as "an ill-informed, corrupt, dangerously nationalistic and 'hate-filled' liar who 'fed off France's misery' and would bring 'civil war' to France" (Chrisafis 2017d). In response, Le Pen referred to Macron as "an arrogant, spoilt, cold-eyed, 'smirking banker' who was colluding with Islamists, complacent on terrorism and intent on 'butchering France' in favor of 'big economic interests'" (Chrisafis 2017d). Both implied that the other assumed the French people were "imbeciles" (Chrisafis 2017d). Polls conducted after the debate indicated that Macron had been more "convincing," and the French media declared him the winner of a "dirty debate" (Chrisafis 2017d). The French media also found Le Pen "unconvincing" and criticized her for her "permanent aggression" (Chrisafis 2017d). Overall, Le Pen appeared to spend more time attacking Macron than explaining her policy proposals (Chrisafis 2017d). The general negative response that voters and the French media had to Le Pen after the debate is often cited as one reason that she was unable to emerge victorious over Macron on Election Day (e.g., Boutchie 2017; Vinocur 2017b).

Why Not Le Pen?

The academic literature and the news media have offered various explanations as to why Marine Le Pen could not become president of France in 2012 and 2017: namely, the Front National's inability to appeal to a wide array of voters as an extreme right-wing party, the controversy surrounding Le Pen's father Jean-Marie, and her debate performance. Despite these insights, none of these reasons are grounded in the literature on the paths that women take to become presidents or prime ministers. This chapter's next section fills that gap in the literature by examining Le Pen's inability to break the French presidency's glass ceiling and offers an alternative explanation for her losses using the results from previous chapters.

As was the case with Clinton, Le Pen can be classified as trying to take the family path to executive office since she pursued a political career by following in the footsteps of her father, Jean-Marie Le Pen, the founder and longtime leader of the Front National and five-time presidential candidate. Since Le Pen took the family path to power, it is important to review the results from this book about which factors facilitate a woman reaching executive power in this manner. First, women take the family path to become president or prime minister because their country is politically unstable and undemocratic, which requires them to assume power by inheriting it from a male family member who has been assassinated or imprisoned (e.g., Hodson 1997; Jalalzai 2013). Second, the family path is used prevalently among women who are not serving on an interim basis or as the country's first female executive. Third, and finally, women reach executive positions via the family path more in countries with executive and parliamentary systems than in semi-presidential systems.

These results suggest that Le Pen had numerous political and institutional factors working against her in her bid for president. The only factors working in her favor were that she was running for a full term and she would not have been France's first female executive, with Édith Cresson serving as prime minister for a period spanning 1991–1992. The fact that Le Pen was twice considered a viable presidential candidate in light of these obstacles shows how women from political families can rely on their name recognition to launch and pursue successful political careers. Although being the daughter of Jean-Marie Le Pen ended up being a liability for Marine in her presidential campaigns (Beardsley 2017; Shields 2007), her name recognition helped her get elected to various regional and municipal councilor posts and the European Parliament before succeeding her father as the leader of the Front National, thus making her a viable presidential candidate (Erlanger 2010; Chrisafis 2017b; Marquand 2010). Regardless, the fact that Le Pen had name recognition, was running for a full term, and would not have been France's first female executive did not end up being enough for her to emerge victorious over Macron on Election Day.

The primary finding from this book begins to show why Le Pen was unable to become the president of France via the family path: this route to power is common in undemocratic, politically unstable countries. These two characteristics fail to describe the political climate of France in general and during Le Pen's candidacies. There is a less than 1 percent chance that women taking the family path will reach executive office in democratic, politically institutionalized countries, such as France, with a Freedom House political rights score of 1. The chance of becoming an executive remains under 5 percent even when another woman has served as president or prime minister. Taken collectively, these results suggest that France's level of democratic institutionalism impeded Le Pen from reaching executive office via the family path.

As was the case with Clinton, it appears that French voters prefer female executive candidates with political qualifications who work to advance their careers without the help of ties to a dynastic family. Yet, also similar to Clinton and the United States, these same voters allow the family path to be a viable method for reaching lower political positions, such as party leader and a member of parliament in the case of Le Pen. Again, the same reason for why this was the case for Clinton can apply to Le Pen and arguably Ségolène Royal, who unsuccessfully ran for president of France in 2007 but was not the only prominent French politician in her family. Royal had built her political career alongside her domestic partner and future president of France, François Hollande.[3] In situations such as this, another example being the Kirchners in Argentina, the woman is still reliant on the male family member to secure her support from political networks and party factions (Baturo and Gray 2018).

The literature on the paths that women executives take to office suggests that prior political experience due to merit, not family name, is essential in democratically stable and economically developed countries with influence over the global economy and foreign affairs (Jalalzai 2013). This is especially the case for women who need to demonstrate adeptness at handling these "masculine" policy areas. Since some stable, democratic, economically developed countries have lower levels of patriarchy and tend to be meritocratic, such as France, voters shy away from women taking the family path to office because it is partially their last name, not their credentials, that makes them fit for executive office. Unlike Clinton, Le Pen never held positions within the executive branch; however, similar to Clinton, her last name was not considered a liability for the positions that she did hold. Overall, the case of Marine Le Pen continues to underscore how the use of the family path for women is limited to lower political posts in stable, democratic, economically developed countries with low levels of patriarchy, like France, because political experience is the primary selection criterion for executive positions that have substantial power and influence. In the next section we will focus on this more by discussing the implications of these two case studies.

Conclusion

In this chapter we examined the unsuccessful presidential campaigns of Hillary Clinton in the United States and Marine Le Pen in France in an effort to better understand how women become presidents and prime ministers around the world. Examining failed candidacies provides a more complete view of the dynamics surrounding a woman's rise to power and shows the obstacles facing female candidates that must be overcome in order to reach executive office. Following the losses of Clinton in 2008 and 2016 and Le Pen in 2012 and 2017, the academic literature and news media offered a variety of explanations as to why neither woman was able to become president of her country. However, none of these explanations engage with the literature on the paths that women take to the presidency or premiership. In this chapter we sought to fill that gap by taking the results presented thus far and applying them to these cases.

For the purposes of this study, both Clinton and Le Pen are coded as attempting to take the family path to office. In applying the results from the previous chapters to explain why neither woman was able to reach executive office via the family path, it became apparent that there were multiple similarities between these two failed presidential campaigns. First, very few factors were present that worked in their favor. Although both women were not being considered for interim executive positions, only Le Pen could have capitalized on the fact that women are better able to reach executive office via the family path if they are not the first female president or prime minister. However, Le Pen was further hampered by the fact that the family path is less likely to be used in countries with semi-presidential systems, like France, than those with presidential or parliamentary systems. Despite the family path being used more frequently to reach the presidency or premiership in presidential or parliamentary systems, this did not appear to substantially aid Clinton.

Second, the most apparent reason stemming from the results of this book that neither Clinton nor Le Pen was able to become president was because the family path is only useful in unstable, undemocratic countries where women benefit from being able to inherit or regain power from male family members who have been assassinated or imprisoned (e.g., Hodson 1997; Jalalzai 2013). The United States and France are democratic, politically institutionalized countries, which means that there is only a 1 percent chance of reaching executive power via the family path. Even when following in the footsteps of another female executive and not trying to break the executive glass ceiling, the likelihood is still under 5 percent.

Third, because so few factors were working in favor of Clinton and Le Pen, it shows how women from dynastic political families are able to use their name recognition to launch successful political careers regardless of the political and institutional climate of their countries. Yet, it appears that they are unable to reach an executive position because voters in democratically stable, economically developed countries with low levels of patriarchy, like the United States and France, prefer female executive candidates who gained political experience without the aid of their family name. This is due to the influence these countries have over foreign affairs and the global economy and the value placed on merit within society. Women seeking executive office cannot use the family path because they must demonstrate adeptness over these global "masculine" policy issues without relying on their last name.

Taken collectively, the key takeaway from this chapter is that the family path is not a viable path to executive office in stable, economically developed democratic countries with low levels of patriarchy, at least not globally powerful Western nations. This is because voters appear to prefer women with political experience not obtained using their family name in order to demonstrate an ability to handle the global economy and foreign affairs. This accords with prior findings presented in this book that the family path is only viable in undemocratic, unstable countries. Conversely, women are able to take the political activist and political career paths to executive office in countries with a wide range of levels of democracy and stability. Thus, even women in Western countries with less global power would likely struggle and be unable to reach executive office using the family path. It is by conducting these two case studies on Clinton and Le Pen that these results become more meaningful. Although this chapter added to the extant literature by using research on the paths that women take to executive office to explain the failed presidential campaigns of Hillary Clinton and Marine Le Pen and provided more insight into why women can or cannot reach executive office, there is still a need for more research. Consequently, in the next chapter we will summarize the findings of each chapter, explain the overall implications of the results, and discuss prospective topics for future research.

Notes

1. Global news media outlets (e.g., *New York Times, Washington Post,* BBC, *The Guardian,* and *Politico*) were selected because they report on international politics, are widely read online outside of their respective headquarter countries, and would have reported on both elections. This is in contrast to national news outlets that report primarily on US or French news, such as the *Chicago Tribune* or *Le Monde.*

2. The latest development in this case at time of publication is that Le Pen was ordered to stand trial (Baynes 2019).

3. See Jalalzai (2013) for an extensive discussion of Royal's unsuccessful run for office.

9

The Importance of the Paths to Power

The literature on women presidents and prime ministers can be classified as either examining the paths that women take to office—family, political activist, and political career—or exploring the factors that facilitate a country having a female president and prime minister. Consequently, there are numerous underexplored research questions: (1) Which paths are prevalent in different regions of the world? (2) What political and institutional conditions ensure that taking each path results in an executive position? (3) What factors increase the likelihood that a country has a female president or prime minister? (4) Does the path a woman takes to office impact the one taken by her successor(s)? (5) What circumstances dictate how long a woman remains in power? (6) Does the path a woman takes to power impact her length of time in office? We addressed these questions in an effort to advance the existing literature on women executives and unite these two bodies of work. While doing so, special attention was paid to changes that have occurred over time and differences among women executives who were elected, were appointed, or served on an interim basis.

Enhancing Prior Work on Women Executives

We also enhance the extant literature's approach to studying women executives. First, we expand the scope and coverage of prior work on female presidents and prime ministers. With the exception of Jalalzai's (2013) groundbreaking mixed methods research on women executives around the world, most other studies are descriptive analyses on only one or a few regions or cases (e.g., Genovese 1993b; Montecinos 2017a; Opfell 1993; Richter 1991). However, even more comprehensive studies, like Jalalzai's (2013), do not cover women executives who took office since 2010 and cover relatively short periods of time in statistical analyses (e.g., 2000–2010 in the case of Jalalzai [2013]). In response, the descriptive analyses in this book span from 1960—or when the first female executive, prime minister of Sri Lanka Sirimavo Bandaranaike, took office—until January 2020. This period covers more than 130 women executives and adds more than 50 new cases to the most comprehensive existing study by Jalalzai (2013). Due to data availability, the statistical analyses span 1990–2015; however, this is also substantially longer than Jalalzai's (2013) study that only spans ten years (2000–2010).

Second, we enhance previous studies that code women as taking multiple paths to executive office, exclude interim executives, include factors that directly and indirectly help women attain executive positions, and measure the same concept multiple times. An alternative approach would be beneficial because, first, when studies code women as taking multiple paths to executive office, it cannot be determined why certain paths are dominant in certain regions of the world but not in others with similar political and institutional conditions. Second, excluding interim presidents and prime ministers makes it unclear what the true dynamics are that lead to women rising to executive power. Third, studies that include factors that directly and indirectly help women attain executive positions usually do so while arguing that proportional representation systems, quotas, and leftist parties increase the number of women in parliament and the pool of possible female executives (Jalalzai 2013; Lovenduski 1993; Norris and Lovenduski 2010). Although parties nominate executive candidates and/or select presidents and prime ministers, the women being considered have already benefited from party efforts to advance female representation in government. Consequently, it is the party that put them in the pool of potential candidates, but that is not what helped them rise above the other women and become president or prime minister. Lastly, measuring the same phenomenon in multiple ways typically occurs by including variables for the length of female suffrage, the number of women in parliament, and the number of women in the cabinet to assess female representation in government (e.g., Jalalzai 2013). If the focus is to determine how female representation in government impacts whether a country has a female executive, one measure is sufficient.

In order to enhance the literature's approach to studying women executives, we first code women as taking one path to office. This was accomplished by the authors and two undergraduate research assistants, who read Jalalzai's (2013) biographies of women presidents and prime ministers to identify the path that launched each woman to an executive post. In particular, women hailing from dynastic political families are coded as taking the family path (e.g., Prime Minister Chandrika Kumaratunga of Sri Lanka). Although some of these women pursued political careers, it is likely their family name enabled them to do so successfully, especially in politically unstable and/or patriarchal countries where this path is common (e.g., Jalalzai 2013). Even in rare cases when women had simultaneous political careers along with their husbands, as in the case of the Kirchners in Argentina, research showed the critical support of the male family member in rallying political networks and party factions behind the female candidate (Baturo and Gray 2018). Similarly, women who participated in political or social movements prior to pursuing a political career are coded as taking the political activist path to power (e.g., President Ellen Johnson Sirleaf of Liberia, President Dilma Rousseff of Brazil). Again, these women were able to have successful political careers because they had already built up their reputation and constituency as activists that helped them get elected (e.g., Jalalzai 2013). A woman who held lower political offices and worked her way up before becoming president or prime minister is then coded as taking the political career path to office (e.g., Prime Minister Julia Gillard of Australia). Any coding disagreement was resolved by consulting the online biographical sources Jalalzai (2013) tended to use (e.g., *Encyclopedia Britannica* and the BBC). These same sources were consulted to code women who assumed executive office after 2010. Furthermore, we build on Jalalzai's (2013) data by including biographies for women who assumed office at any point from 2011 to 2020 in the appendix.

Additionally, we include interim women executives and focus on factors that directly relate to whether women attain executive positions, not those that increase female representation in government. Lastly, we measure female representation in government one way: as the percentage of women in parliament. In addition to highlighting the contributions of this book to the existing work on women presidents and prime ministers, it is also worth reviewing our findings, discussing their implications, and suggesting opportunities for future research.

Key Findings and Implications

Paths to Office

Family path. In Chapter 2 we qualitatively analyze the seventeen women executives who came to power through the family path. Aside from two outliers—Prime Minister Natalia Gherman of Moldova and President Eveline Widmer-Schlumpf of Switzerland—all of the women taking this path to office hail from Asia and Latin America, thus supporting the findings of prior research (e.g., Jalalzai 2013). Rather than using region to explain the prevalence of this path, a variety of socioeconomic factors were examined, in particular, level of development and modernization and the presence of political violence.

The results suggest that heightened levels of existential insecurity in a politically violent and/or less developed context contribute to greater discretion toward religion, tradition, and status quo institutions, such as the family. This also helps explain the progressively changing trends in Latin America. As the region became more democratic and developed, the reliance on tradition and family diminished and women executives began to emerge using the political activist or political career paths (e.g., President Dilma Rousseff of Brazil and President Laura Chinchilla of Costa Rica). Overall, these results support previous research identifying this path as common in Asia and Latin America. However, in this chapter we provide more context as to why this is the case and how the use of this path has evolved over time and become less common in Latin America.

Political activist path. Chapter 3 examines the eighteen women who took the political activist path to power and the conditions that encourage the use of this specific path. Unlike the family path, this path was utilized in a variety of geographic regions: Africa (e.g., President Ellen Johnson Sirleaf of Liberia and President Joyce Banda of Malawi), Europe (e.g., President Vigdís Finnbogadóttir of Iceland

and Prime Minister Yulia Tymoshenko of Ukraine), and Latin America (e.g., President Michelle Bachelet of Chile and President Dilma Rousseff of Brazil). In most cases, these women were active in political and social movements that revolved around human rights issues, anticorruption, and democratization.

The results indicate that women are best able to reach executive office via this path the longer they have been activists, particularly if they have extensive experience successfully mobilizing supporters (e.g., progressive political parties or social movements) or are in the right place at the right time (i.e., during transitional periods when the status quo is weakened). Even though this is a riskier path to power—often requiring serious confrontation with the political establishment or experiencing political persecution and/or exile—once in power, women who took this path to office are able to remain in power for lengthy periods of time. In sum, these results support existing work on regions where this path is common and how it can best be used to reach an executive position (e.g., Geske and Bourque 2001; Jalalzai 2013; Salo 2010). However, by coding women as only taking one path to power, we show that women who began their careers as activists are driving the results reported in the women-executives literature.

Political career path. The final path to executive power is the political career path. This path provided a steady stream of women to executive office all across the globe regardless of a country's level of economic and human development, which contrasts with the existing literature stating that the path is most common in Africa and Europe (e.g., Jalalzai 2013). Expanding the time frame of this study to January 2020 increased the women executives in this category to 101 and helped clarify some of the nebulous aspects in the existing literature. While most literature on women executives finds a strong connection between increased levels of female representation in parliament and the presence of a woman president or prime minister (e.g., Jalalzai 2013, 2016a), our results in Chapter 4 show that holding a cabinet position was a more common step for women prior to assuming executive power. More than 70 percent of women executives served as cabinet ministers prior to reaching the executive office while 52 percent of them served in the national legislature. Yet the findings in Chapter 4 were in line with the existing literature on the need to hold "masculine" cabinet posts (e.g., Jalalzai 2013; Thompson and Lennartz 2006). Most women executives served in more high-prestige, "masculine" posts, such as minister of justice or attorney general, minister of foreign affairs, or vice president or deputy prime minister. Very few women who served as minister of culture or communication or tourism, for example, reached an executive seat.

The Dynamics of a Woman's Path to Office and the Presence of Female Executives

In Chapters 5 and 6 we quantitatively test whether the factors that facilitate a country having a female executive impact (1) the path she takes to office and (2) if the path a woman uses to reach the presidency or premiership influences the path her successor(s) take to the same post. The results suggest that few factors explain why women take each path to office and women are not constrained by the paths of their predecessor(s).

Explaining a Woman's Path to Office

Our results in Chapter 5 indicate that the family path is prevalent in countries that are undemocratic, have presidential or parliamentary systems, and have never had a female executive. None of the factors that increase the likelihood of a country having a woman president or prime minister explain whether a female executive reaches her post by the political activist path. However, appointment-based executive systems lead to women taking the political career path to office. Women are also less likely to take this path to office if they are following in the footsteps of another female executive, but the likelihood of reaching executive power via this path is still 80 percent. The results reveal few regional patterns other than that the political activist path is uncommon in the Global South. The findings based on executive type suggest that only women who serve as interim presidents and prime ministers use the political career path. Overall, the results provide insight into the factors that lead a woman to take each path to office and, at best, provide mixed support for existing research (e.g., Jalalzai 2013, 2016a; Jalalzai and Rincker 2018), which shows how results are sensitive to the approach used to study female executives.

*Describing the presence of a female president or prime minis-
ter.* In Chapter 6 we looked at the factors that predict whether a country has (1) a female executive; (2) one that took each path to office;
and (3) whether a woman's path to office impacts the path her succes-
sor(s) use to reach an executive post. The results show that countries
with multiparty systems, high percentages of women in parliament,
and prior female executives are more likely to have a woman president or prime minister. The findings for each path show that, first,
women take the family path in multiparty systems and in countries in
the Global South. Second, democratic countries with election-based
systems tend to have female executives who reached their post via the
political activist path. Similarly, democratic countries and/or those with
appointment-based systems and/or high numbers of women in parliament tend to have women executives who took the political career path
to the presidency or premiership. Taken collectively, the findings provide mixed support for prior work (e.g., Jalalzai 2013) and suggest that
the factors identified by the extant literature as giving rise to women
executives do in fact best explain whether a country has a female president or prime minister, not one that took each path to office.

The results for whether a woman's path to office impacts her
successor(s) show that women are not constrained by their predecessor's path or whether they were appointed or elected or served on an
interim basis. Some interesting results do emerge, such as women are
more likely to take the family or political career paths to office if
their predecessor(s) took the family path. This finding confirms the
qualitative results on the decline of the family path in Latin America.
Women also take the political activist path if their predecessor(s) did
as well. None of the paths encourage women to take the political
career path to office; however, women are less likely to utilize this
path if their predecessors took the political activist path. Overall, this
analysis advances existing work by providing more insight into the
political and institutional characteristics that influence whether a
woman reaches executive office.

Understanding the Length of Time
Women Executives Stay in Office

In Chapter 7 we advance the women-executives literature by examining the length of time a woman spends in executive office based
on the path she takes to office or the factors that facilitate her

ascension to office. We begin Chapter 7 with a quantitative analysis that builds off of the models and findings from Chapters 5 and 6. These results suggest that few factors explain how long a female executive remains in office. The findings that do emerge suggest that female presidents and prime ministers in the Global North and those who were elected serve for the longest periods of time. Conversely, interim executives have the shortest tenures. The relatively few findings are not overly surprising since the existing literature on women presidents and prime ministers provides very little guidance on the matter. In order to provide more insight into these findings, we also provide a qualitative, descriptive analysis with case examples to uncover patterns using factors focused on in most research on women executives: time, region, path to office, and type of executive (i.e., elected, appointed, and interim).

The most striking findings emerged when examining women who took each path to power. Despite the family path being common in countries with low levels of democratic institutionalism, high levels of political instability, and/or patriarchy, the seventeen women who took this path to power stayed in office for nearly four and a half years on average and ruled for a combined thirty terms. Although it appears that the family path produces executive stability, the statistical results do not suggest that these women stay in office longer than those taking the other two paths to power. This is supported by the fact that women executives who take the political activist path also have relatively long tenures. In fact, many are repeatedly reelected, such as President Vigdís Finnbogadóttir of Iceland and president of Liberia Ellen Johnson Sirleaf. The most variation in tenure length was observed for women who took the political career path because this is the path used most frequently by interim executives.

Exploring Failed Executive Candidacies

In Chapter 8 we acknowledge how there is much to be gained from examining failed candidacies for president and prime minister. Such research best highlights the obstacles that women must overcome in order to break the executive glass ceiling in their country or follow in the footsteps of another female executive. In Chapter 8 we do just that by (1) summarizing the failed presidential candidacies of Hillary Clinton of the United States in 2008 and 2016 and Marine Le Pen of France in 2012 and 2017; (2) offering explanations for these losses from the news media and academic literature; and (3) explaining these failed attempts based on the results from our study.

Three main conclusions can be drawn from this chapter. First, since both women would be considered as taking the family path to office—with Clinton following in her husband Bill Clinton's footsteps and Le Pen having a politically prominent father, Jean-Marie Le Pen—various factors were working against them. Although neither was seeking office on an interim basis, only Le Pen could capitalize on the fact that women are better able to reach executive office via the family path if they are not their country's first female executive. Le Pen was further hampered by how the family path is less likely to be used in countries with semi-presidential systems, like France, than in those with parliamentary and presidential systems. Yet Clinton had this factor in her favor and it did not change her fate.

Second, the family path is not a viable route to executive power in stable, democratic countries, such as the United States and France. This is because women cannot inherit or regain power from male family members. Additionally, results from Chapter 5 suggest that such countries only have a 1 percent chance that a woman will reach an executive post via the family path. Third, women from dynastic political families are able to use their name recognition to launch successful political careers regardless of the political and institutional climates of their countries. However, it appears that women are impeded from reaching executive positions in democratically stable countries that are economically developed and have lower levels of patriarchy because voters prefer female candidates who gained political experience without relying on their family name. This is because these countries emphasize merit, albeit more so for female than male candidates, and have more global influence over international relations and the global economy. Consequently, women candidates must demonstrate experience with "masculine" policy areas, and that is best accomplished by not relying on the family path. Taken collectively, these two case studies provide more context to the results reported in the previous chapters and show the importance of explaining women's successful and unsuccessful attempts to reach executive positions.

Broader Implications

In addition to the implications of the specific results from each chapter, our work also has two broader implications for the literature on women executives: (1) the methodological approaches and choices used by researchers impact findings, and (2) the findings provide insight on how women overcome institutional, political, and cultural sexism. Throughout the book, most of the results provide mixed support for existing research. The reason for this is likely due to prior work coding women as taking multiple paths to office, examining only one or a few cases or regions, and/or restricting analyses to relatively short time periods (e.g., Genovese 1993b; Jalalzai 2013; Liswood 2007; Montecinos 2017a; Opfell 1993). This underscores the importance of examining the path that initially propelled a woman toward the executive branch and analyzing as many cases as possible. In our analyses, inclusion of the elected, appointed, and interim executives during the entire decade of the 2010s added more than fifty cases and nearly doubled the number of women presidents and prime ministers around the world. Furthermore, it is important to use mixed methods in order to (1) identify patterns based on the path a woman took to office, the type of executive position she secured (i.e., elected, appointed, or interim), and over time; and (2) determine which relationships are statistically significant.

It is also because of our findings that more is known about how women overcome institutional, political, and cultural sexism in order to reach executive positions. With respect to becoming a president or prime minister, women use the path that is available to them, each of which allows them to leverage political and institutional factors to overcome sexism. In particular, women from dynastic families take the family path, women who have taken up and advocated for a cause use the political activist path, and women with previous political experience use the political career path. However, there are many women on these paths who do not reach executive office. What also matters is the country's executive system and the nature of the open executive position. Women on the family and political activist paths capitalize on their ability to thrive in election-based systems due to their name recognition among voters and/or preexisting political support. Conversely, women on the political career path reach executive office most often in parliamentary and semi-presidential appointment-based systems because they can avoid sexist voters and use gender stereotypes that female governing styles valuing collaboration and consensus are needed in these positions. Similarly, women with political careers are also able to take advantage of sudden executive openings to become interim presidents or prime ministers while women who were activists often become elected executives because they already have mobilized supporters.

When examining whether a country has a female executive, our results continue to show the importance of political and institutional factors in a path leading to an executive position. Specifically, countries with high levels of democratization, increased numbers of women in parliament, and/or appointment-based systems have women who took the political career path to office because they are able to gain the political experience needed, especially in "masculine" policy areas, and have the leadership qualities focused on collaboration and consensus that are valued in appointed executive positions. Countries with high levels of women in parliament and/or an elected executive position also tend to have women who took the political activist path to office because voters are already mobilized on their behalf or supportive of women politicians. Lastly, multiparty systems tend to produce female executives who took the family path because many women who take this path to power launch political careers before becoming president or prime minister. Consequently, these women also benefit from factors that tend to help women on the political career path showcase their stereotypical female leadership qualities focused on collaboration and consensus-building.

Future Research

Despite enhancing and advancing the women-executives literature and providing additional insights into how female presidents and prime ministers overcome voter, institutional, and cultural sexism, there are still numerous opportunities for future research. Future research opportunities either pertain to our results or topics outside the scope of the questions addressed here. Each will be discussed in turn.

Enhancing and Advancing Our Findings

First, more work is needed on what factors lead a woman to take each path to executive office. Chapter 4 yielded surprising results about how cabinet positions are more favorable gateways to executive seats than the legislative branch. The results of Chapters 5 and 6 show that the literature is best able to predict whether a country has a woman executive, but not the path she used to reach that position even though many of the factors overlap between the two bodies of work. Similarly, while we focused more on the direct factors that impact whether a woman reaches executive office, more work is needed on those that are indirect—for example, parties, coalitions, candidate selection processes, and ideology. Turning to Chapter 7, additional research is needed on the factors that determine how long a woman remains in executive office. As the results indicate, the political and institutional factors that explain whether a country has a female executive and, to a certain extent, the path she takes to office provide few insights on the length of tenure. However, the chain of impeachments and imprisonments that targeted women executives around the world and caused them to prematurely leave office from Brazil to South Korea illustrates how tenure is a salient issue for women executives. We shed some light on this for certain paths, but more research is needed to explain how long women executives tend to serve as presidents or prime ministers. Such work can also serve as a foundation for studies on the gender differences in executive term length; for example, Jalalzai (2013) finds that male and female executives spend roughly the same amount of time in office, but it is unknown whether this is because they have similar or different experiences while serving as president or prime minister.

Our analysis in Chapter 8 of Hillary Clinton's and Marine Le Pen's failed candidacies provides multiple opportunities for future work. First, in terms of election results, why did Hillary Clinton perform worse than her husband, Bill Clinton, while Marine Le Pen did better than her father, Jean-Marie Le Pen? For example, it is possible that gender stereotypes interact with party ideology. Second, what are the differences between the media coverage of Le Pen's campaign by English-speaking and French-speaking news sources? Third, more research is needed on how men and women differ in their use of each path and whether it results in an executive position. For example, work should further explore the conclusions reached in this chapter regarding why the family path is a viable route to power for men, like George W. Bush, in stable democratic, economically developed countries with low levels of patriarchy, but not women, like Hillary Clinton. Lastly, the literature would benefit from the exploration of other failed candidacies. For example, this book focused on two women on the family path from globally powerful Western countries with multiple failed executive candidacies, but there is much to be learned from women who are trying to take other paths from similarly or less powerful countries or women who only ran once. The 2020 US Democratic primary is a prime opportunity for future research such as this because none of the women candidates could be competitive despite coming from large states and having substantial federal political experience. In fact, South Bend, Indiana, mayor Pete Buttigieg, with no federal political experience, could successfully compete against California senator Kamala Harris, Minnesota senator Amy Klobuchar, and Massachusetts senator Elizabeth Warren. Buttigieg won the Iowa caucus and placed second in the New Hampshire primary before dropping out just prior to Super Tuesday (Wagner, Willis, et al. 2020; Wagner, Alfonso, et al. 2020). The lackluster performance of women politicians in US presidential races needs to be further examined, particularly in a global context when more than 130 women executives have already reached executive office around the world.

Building the Women-Executives Literature

There are also a few promising avenues for future research that are worth discussing because they are outside the scope of our book. First, what are the similarities and differences between male and female executives? This can be with respect to their paths to office or behavior once in office. Does the family path impact male and female executives in the same way? For example, Carlin, Carreras, and Love (2019) compare the approval ratings of male and female presidents in Latin America, South Korea, and the Philippines and find that women executives are less popular and experience more extreme swings in their level of support, especially in light of security concerns and perceived corruption. Second, in addition to comparing male and female executives, it would be beneficial to examine female executives once they are in office. For example, what are the dynamics dictating their approval ratings and ability to advance "women's issues" and eliminate various types of inequality, such as paid family leave, the wage gap, and discrimination against the LGBTQ+ population? Does having women executives have any substantive impact on these issues? Relatedly, does the path a woman takes to office impact her leadership and ability to enact policy change in any way? The Covid-19 pandemic serves as a test for both male and female leaders. Less than a year into the crisis, most analysts agree that women leaders outperformed their male counterparts (Aldrich and Lotito 2020). Of these high-performing women leaders, all are from the political career path, except Prime Minister Katrín Jakobsdóttir of Iceland. Further research on paths and relative success could shed light on the performance of women leaders while in office. Lastly, it would be beneficial to examine female executives at lower levels of government, such as governors and mayors. Overall, there is still a substantial amount of research needed in order to better understand the dynamics surrounding women executives around the world at different levels of government.

Appendix:
Brief Biographical Notes
on Female Presidents and
Prime Ministers, 2010–2020

Áñez, Jeanine (August 13, 1967–)
President of Bolivia (November 12, 2019–)
Interim, Political Career Path
Áñez is an attorney who began her political career in 2006 by serving as a member of the Constituent Assembly where she worked on a variety of judicial-related endeavors, such as drafting a new constitutional charter. In 2010, she was elected to the Senate as a member of the Plan Progress for Bolivia–National Convergence Party where she represented the Department of Beni. She ran unsuccessfully for governor of Beni in 2012. In 2019, she was named the second vice president of the Senate. After the resignations of President Evo Morales, Vice President Álvaro García Linear, and President of the Senate Adriana Salvatierra Arriaza in November 2019 due to losing political support, Áñez named herself president of the Senate and acting president. Salvatierra later contended that her resignation had not been accepted by the Senate, which made her president of the Senate, but it was accepted by the Senate in November 2019. While president, Áñez has called for the police to restore order in light of protests against the interim government and has denounced foreign influence in the country.

Ardern, Jacinda (July 26, 1980–)
Prime Minister of New Zealand (October 26, 2017–)
Elected, Political Career Path
Ardern's political career began when she joined the Labor Party at age seventeen. She would go on to hold various positions within the Young Labor subsection of the party. She graduated from the University of Waikato in 2001 with a degree in politics and public relations. Her professional career in politics started by working as a researcher for Prime

Minister Helen Clark and a policy adviser to British Prime Minister Tony Blair. She became a list member of parliament in 2008 until she was elected in 2017. Subsequently, she became the deputy leader of the Labor Party and prime minister of New Zealand that same year. Taking office at age thirty-seven made her the youngest female head of government, and she is the second to give birth while in office. During her premiership, Ardern has focused on solving issues relating to housing, child poverty, and social inequality.

Aráoz, Mercedes (August 5, 1961–)
Prime Minister of Peru (September 17, 2017–April 2, 2018)
President of Peru (September 30, 2019–October 1, 2019 or– [ending
  date disputed])
Appointed; Interim, Political Career Path
Aráoz has degrees in economics from the University of the Pacific and the University of Miami. She began her political career by serving as the minister of foreign trade and tourism in 2006. In July 2009, she was named the minister of production, but five months later in December 2009 she would assume the position of minister of economy and finance. Aráoz is the first woman to hold this cabinet position in Peru. In 2011, she agreed to be the presidential candidate for the Peruvian Aprista Party but later withdrew her candidacy. In 2016 she ran for Congress as a candidate for the Peruvians for Change Party and as the running mate of Pedro Pablo Kuczynski. She was elected to Congress and as second vice president. In September 2017, she was sworn in as prime minister of Peru, an office she held until April 2018. In March 2018, President Kuczynski resigned over a corruption scandal, so First Vice President Martín Vizcarra assumed office on September 30, 2019. Vizcarra dissolved Congress and issued a decree for legislative elections to be held in January 2020. However, Congress suspended Vizcarra's presidency and named Aráoz acting president. There is disagreement over whether the suspension of Vizcarra's presidency is void as Congress had already been dissolved. Regardless, Aráoz resigned as interim president the day after on October 1, 2019. However, her resignation is not official because it has to be accepted by Congress, which is not holding meetings given the dissolution, and the Peruvian Armed Forces continue to recognize her as the president and head of the armed forces.

Banda, Joyce (April 12, 1950–)
President of Malawi (April 7, 2012–May 31, 2014)
Appointed, Political Activist Path
Joyce Banda has undergraduate and graduate degrees from Columbus University, Atlantic International University, and Royal Roads University. Banda's activism began in 1975 when she was inspired by the women's movement in Kenya to take her three children and leave an abusive marriage. She would go on to establish and manage various businesses that would allow her to help women achieve financial independence and break the cycles of poverty and abuse. Banda has also been involved in a variety

of grassroots projects focused on improving educational opportunities for women. Banda's political career began when she was elected to parliament in 1999. In 2009, she ran as a vice presidential candidate. After winning and becoming Malawi's first female vice president, she was fired by the party in December 2010, along with Second Vice President Khumbo Kachali, for antiparty activities. Banda remained as vice president because the position is constitutionally mandated despite calls from the party for her to resign. Since she was expelled from the Democratic Progressive Party, Banda founded the People's Party in 2011. She became the first female president of Malawi in April 2012 after the death of President Bingu wa Mutharika. Upon taking office, Banda called for national unity and was a staunch supporter of women's and LGBT rights. Her time in office was marred by the Capital Hill Cashgate scandal that led her to remove most of her cabinet members in 2013. She was defeated in the 2014 presidential election. A warrant for her arrest in connection with alleged corruption during her time as president was issued in July 2017. Banda denied any wrongdoing and said she would return to Malawi to face the charges as she had been living outside of the country. In 2016, she announced that she was willing to run as a presidential candidate.

Bhandari, Bidhya Devi (June 19, 1961–)
President of Nepal (October 29, 2015–)
Appointed, Political Career Path
Bhandari became active in politics at an early age as a member of the Youth League of the Communist Party–Unified Marxist/Leninist Party. She officially joined the party in 1980. She held various positions with the party and went on to be elected to parliament in 1994. In 2009, she served as Prime Minister Madhav Kumar Nepal's minister of defense. She was the first woman in Nepal to hold this post. Her party elected her to parliament in 2013, and, in 2015, she was elected as the first woman president of Nepal in a parliamentary vote. While in office she has been accused of taking partisan stances by delaying the formation of government after the 2017 election and holding onto the prime minister's nominations to the National Assembly.

Bierlein, Brigitte (June 25, 1949–)
Chancellor of Austria (June 3, 2019–)
Interim, Political Career Path
Bierlein received both her law degree and her doctorate from the University of Vienna. She served as a judge in several levels of the judicial branch, from district courts all the way to the Supreme Court. She was the vice president and then the president of the Constitutional Court before being appointed as the interim chancellor of Austria. She served as the chancellor until a new government was formed. Her interim nomination was accepted by all parties. While she is nominally independent and does not officially endorse any political party, she is known to be center-right leaning and conservative on moral issues.

Bellepeau, Monique Ohsan (Birth Date Unknown, 1942–)
President of Mauritius (March 31, 2012–July 21, 2012; May 29, 2015–June 5, 2015)
Interim, Political Career Path
Bellepeau began her career as a journalist and news announcer for Mauritius Broadcasting Corporation. Her political career began when she was elected to parliament as a member of the Mauritian Labor Party. She eventually became the party's president. In 2010, she was appointed vice president after the death of Vice President Angidi Chettiar. In 2012, President Anerood Jugnauth resigned because of a feud with the prime minister. Bellepeau served as president until the National Assembly elected Kailash Purryag as president. Purryag also went on to resign, once again leaving Bellepeau to serve as president on an interim basis until the selection of President Ameenah Gurib-Fakim in 2015.

Bratušek, Alenka (March 31, 1970–)
Prime Minister of Slovenia (March 20, 2013–September 18, 2014)
Appointed, Political Career Path
Bratušek has degrees from the University of Ljubljana. She began her professional political career as the head of the Directorate for the State Budget within the Ministry of Finance. In 2006, she was elected to the Kranj City Council as a member of the Liberal Democracy of Slovenia Party. She was reelected in 2010 after switching parties to Hermina Krt's List. In 2011, she was elected to parliament as part of the Positive Slovenia Party. While in parliament, she served as the chairwoman of the Committee on Budget Control. In 2013, she became the president of the Positive Slovenia Party and was elected prime minister by the parliament. She won a no confidence vote while attempting to avoid a financial bailout; however, she lost party leadership to Zoran Janković in April 2014. As a result, she resigned as prime minister, the first to do so in Slovenia. During her last days in office, Bratušek nominated herself to the position of vice president of the European Commission, but it was rejected by parliament due to her lack of experience. She would go on to form her own party, the Alliance of Alenka Bratušek, which won four seats in the National Assembly in 2014.

Brnabić, Ana (September 28, 1975–)
Prime Minister of Serbia (June 29, 2017–)
Appointed, Political Career Path
Brnabić is the first woman and first openly gay person to hold the office of prime minister in Serbia. She has an MBA from the University of Hull in the UK and worked in the nonprofit sector extensively before her appointment as the Minister of public administration and local self-government in 2016. She worked as a consultant on large, multimillion-dollar investment projects that promoted local development. Perceived more as a technocrat, she highlights transparency, social responsibility, and tolerance in her election campaigns. She is criticized by the LGBT community for not being more outspoken about LGBT rights in Serbia. She has refused to express her position on the legalization of same-sex marriage despite having a longtime partner and a child with her.

Bures, Doris (August 3, 1962–)
President of Austria (July 8, 2016–January 26, 2017)
Interim, Political Career Path
Bures started her professional career working with organizations on issues pertaining to unemployment and housing. She began her political career as a district councilor for Wien-Liesing in 1987. She went on to hold a variety of party leadership positions in Liesing for her party, the Sozialdemokratische Partei Österreichs. From 1990 to 2007, she served in the National Council of Austria. She served as the minister for women, media, and public service in 2007 before returning to the National Council. In 2008, she served as the minister of transport, innovation, and technology. Again, she would return to the National Council, and in 2014 she was elected one of its presidents. When President Heinz Fischer left office that same year, the role of acting president fell to the three presidents of the National Council: Bures, Norbert Hofer, and Karlheinz Kopt. Her time as one of the acting presidents ended with the election of Alexander Van der Bellen.

Čaputová, Zuzana (June 21, 1973–)
President of Slovakia (June 15, 2019–)
Elected, Political Activist Path
Čaputová was born in the town of Pezinok to working-class parents. She studied law in college and became involved in local government. She joined Greenpeace and other civic organizations in order to campaign against the toxic landfill in her hometown. She received several prizes for her success-ful environmental campaigns. She filed multiple complaints and appealed all the way to the European Union. She would come to be known as the Erin Brockovich of Slovakia, according to *Time* magazine. Her party never received any parliamentary seats, but she ran her election campaign as an outsider on an anticorruption platform and won the 2019 presidential elec-tion to become her country's first woman president.

Coleiro Preca, Marie-Louise (December 7, 1958–)
President of Malta (April 4, 2014–April 4, 2019)
Appointed, Political Career Path
Coleiro Preca has degrees in legal studies and international relations and served as a public notary before establishing her steady career in politics. She started her political career in the Labor Party and moved up the ranks to become the party's general secretary. She was first elected to parliament in 1998 and con-tinuously served in the legislative branch in various capacities until she was elected as the second woman president of Malta by the parliament in 2014. During her tenure, she prioritized civil society and supported organizations that addressed issues of social welfare, education, and cancer research.

Dăncilă, Viorica (December 16, 1963–)
Prime Minister of Romania (January 29, 2018–November 4, 2019)
Appointed, Political Career Path
Dăncilă received her college degree from the Institute of Petroleum and Gas and later earned a graduate degree in public administration. She served as an

engineer and teacher before starting her career in politics. She joined the Social Democratic Party and eventually became the first woman party leader. She served as a member of the European Parliament from 2009 to 2018 until her appointment as the first female prime minister by her party. Social Democrats were going through a period of instability when she was brought in as the prime minister. She faced a vote of no confidence while in office, and her term ended prematurely in less than two years.

Dejanović, Slavica Đukić (July 4, 1951–)
President of Serbia (April 5, 2012–May 31, 2012)
Interim, Political Career Path
Dejanović has medical degrees from the University of Belgrade School of Medicine. While pursuing a medical career—which included practicing, teaching, serving as an administrator, and participating in professional organizations—she built a political career by starting as a member of the League of Communists of Yugoslavia. She held a variety of posts within the party and continued to do so when she joined the Socialist Party of Serbia in 1990. Dejanović went on to serve two terms in the National Assembly and as the federal deputy. During the interim government, she was the minister of family care. In 2008, she was elected as the president of the National Assembly. When Boris Tadić resigned as president, Dejanović became the acting president. Her time in office ended with the election of Tomislav Nikolić to the office of president.

Fernández, Rosario (November 9, 1955–)
Prime Minister of Peru (March 19, 2011–July 28, 2011)
Appointed, Political Career Path
Fernández studied law at Pontifical Catholic University of Peru. While serving as the vice chairman of the Lima Stock Exchange and treasurer of the board of the Lima Bar Association, she also held various committee positions within the Peruvian government. In 2007, Fernández was named the minister of justice. She resigned in 2009 but returned to replace Victor Garcia Toma in 2011. After Prime Minister Javier Velásquez resigned to run for president, President Alan Garcia appointed Minister of Education José Antonio Chang prime minister, but he chose to return to his university in March 2011. At that point, Fernández was appointed as prime minister until Salomón Lerner Ghitis received the post after the election of President Ollanta Humala in the 2011 election.

Frederiksen, Mette (November 19, 1977–)
Prime Minister of Denmark (June 27, 2019–)
Elected, Political Career Path
Frederiksen has degrees in social sciences and public administration. She joined the Social Democratic Party and was elected to the parliament when she was twenty-four years old. She was promoted within the party to the position of party spokesperson. When the Social Democrats came to power in 2011, she served as the minister of employment and, later, as the minis-

ter of justice. She became the main opposition leader before winning the 2019 election by a narrow margin to become prime minister.

Gherman, Natalia (March 20, 1969–)
Prime Minister of Moldova (June 22, 2015–July 30, 2015)
Interim, Family Path
Gherman is the daughter of the first president of Moldova, Mircea Snegur. She received her BA from Moldova State University and an MA in war studies from Kings' College London. Her professional career began when she entered into the Moldovan diplomatic service in 1991. She rose through the ranks, eventually becoming the Moldovan ambassador to Austria and the permanent representative to the Organization for Security and Co-operation in Europe and various UN agencies. Her political career began when she was appointed the deputy minister of foreign affairs and European integration in June 2009. She was promoted to minister of that department in 2013. In 2014, Gherman was elected to parliament. She served as the prime minister of Moldova for roughly a month after the resignation of Chiril Gaburici. Gherman was later appointed the Moldovan permanent representative to the UN in 2016.

Grabar-Kitarović, Kolinda (April 29, 1968–)
President of Croatia (February 19, 2015–February 18, 2020)
Elected, Political Career Path
Grabar-Kitarović has undergraduate and graduate degrees from the University of Zagreb. She began her political career holding a variety of bureaucratic and diplomatic posts. From 2003 to 2005, she served as the minister of European affairs and became the first female minister of foreign affairs and European integration in 2005. She was named the Croatian ambassador to the United States in 2008. She served in that post until being named the assistant secretary general for public diplomacy at NATO in 2011. In 2014, she ran for president and was elected by just under a 1.5 percent margin over incumbent President Ivo Josipović. In 2019, she ran for reelection. In the first round, Grabar-Kitarović became the first incumbent president not to finish in first place. In the second round, she was defeated by Prime Minister Zoran Milanović.

Guillaume, Florence Duperval (Birth Date Unknown–)
Prime Minister of Haiti (December 20, 2014–January 16, 2015)
Interim, Political Career Path
Guillaume led an established career within the health sector that culminated in her appointment as the minister of public health and population. In that role, she oversaw efforts to increase medical services to the people of Haiti, including building new hospitals after a devastating earthquake, combating cholera, and treating HIV/AIDS. She was appointed prime minister by the Council of Ministers to replace Laurent Lamothe, who resigned after several weeks of antigovernment protests and warnings from the United States and the United Nations that the country was on the brink of political chaos. Parliament was dissolved in January 2015 after its term expired, and Guillaume was succeeded by Evans Paul.

Gurib-Fakim, Ameenah (October 17, 1959–)
President of Mauritius (June 5, 2015–March 23, 2018)
Appointed, Political Career Path
Gurib-Fakim received her degrees in chemistry, including her PhD from Exeter University, in the UK. She worked as a scholar, chair, and dean at the University of Mauritius in addition to holding other administrative positions in international scientific organizations. She was nominated and elected unanimously as the first female president by the National Assembly that was having disputes over constitutional reforms. Before she could complete her term, she was charged with financial misconduct and resigned from her position.

Heine, Hilda (April 6, 1951–)
President of the Marshall Islands (January 28, 2016–January 14, 2020)
Appointed, Political Career Path
Heine has degrees from the University of Oregon, the University of Hawaii, and the University of Southern California. Her professional career began within the field of education where she was a high school teacher and director of the Pacific Resources for Education and Learning at the Pacific Comprehensive Assistance Center. After being elected to parliament, she became the minister of education. Heine was elected president by parliament after a vote of no confidence ousted Casten Nemra from office just two weeks after his installment. Heine is the first woman president of the Marshall Islands and is one of very few women in parliament.

Jahjaga, Atifete (April 20, 1975–)
President of Kosovo (April 7, 2011–April 7, 2016)
Appointed, Political Career Path
Jahjaga received a law degree in Kosovo and has graduate training in police management and criminal law from the University of Leicester in the UK and the FBI National Academy in the United States. She started her career in law enforcement and reached the top bureaucratic position of general director in 2010. Her name came up as a nonpartisan, consensus candidate when the country was experiencing political turmoil due to the resignation of President Fatmir Sejdiu and the Constitutional Court's decision that ruled against the election of Behgjet Pacolli. Jahjaga was elected by the parliament with 80 of the 100 votes. She emphasized improvement of relations with the European Union, women's rights, and empowerment during her tenure.

Jakobsdóttir, Katrín (February 1, 1976–)
Prime Minister of Iceland (November 30, 2017–)
Elected, Political Career Path
Jakobsdóttir has degrees from the University of Iceland. She began her professional career working in broadcast and print media and serving as a lecturer at multiple universities. In 2009, she was appointed the minister of education, science, and culture. Prior to becoming prime minister, she was the chair of the Left-Green Movement. After the 2017 parliamentary election,

President Guðni Jóhannesson tasked Jakobsdóttir with forming a coalition government consisting of the Left-Green Movement, the Progressive Party, the Social Democratic Alliance, and the Pirate Party. She eventually negotiated a three-party coalition with the Left-Green Movement, the Independence Party, and the Progressive Party. At that time, President Jóhannesson officially installed Jakobsdóttir as prime minister. Jakobsdóttir is the second woman to serve as prime minister of Iceland. Her administration is known for opposing Iceland's participation in NATO and the European Union.

Jara, Ana (May 11, 1968–)
Prime Minister of Peru (July 22, 2014–April 2, 2015)
Appointed, Political Career Path
Jara has degrees in law and political science from Saint Aloysius Gonzaga National University. Before entering the political arena, she worked as an attorney and notary public. In 2011, she was elected to parliament to represent Ica as a member of the Peruvian Nationalist Party. Later that year, she was named the minister of women and social development. She remained in that post until becoming minister of labor and employment promotion in 2014. That same year she also became prime minister after the resignation of Prime Minister René Cornejo. Her term ended in 2015 when Congress voted to censure her and her cabinet for spying against lawmakers, journalists, business leaders, and other citizens.

Kaljulaid, Kersti (December 30, 1969–)
President of Estonia (October 10, 2016–)
Appointed, Political Career Path
Kaljulaid has degrees from the University of Tartu in biology and business management. Her professional career began by working mostly for the state-owned telecom and energy companies. From 1999 to 2002 she served as an economic adviser for Prime Minister Mart Laar. In 2004, she was appointed as Estonia's representative to the European Court of Auditors. As she began working more closely with government in the early 2000s, she joined the Pro Patria Union political party. While continuing to serve on the European Court of Auditors, parliament asked for her consent to be put forward as a presidential candidate after several candidates failed to receive the required two-thirds vote of support. Most objections around her candidacy had to do with the fact that she was relatively unknown. Regardless, she garnered the support needed in parliament to become Estonia's first female president and its youngest.

Kopacz, Ewa (December 3, 1956–)
Prime Minister of Poland (September 22, 2014–November 16, 2015)
Elected, Political Career Path
Trained as a medical doctor, Kopacz specialized in pediatrics and family medicine. She was elected to parliament in 2005 and served as the minister of health from 2007 to 2011 in Prime Minister Donald Tusk's government. She expressed concerns over the way in which pharmaceutical companies

were handling the flu pandemics in the world. At the time, Tusk was the chairperson of the pro-EU political party called the Civic Platform. By the end of 2014, Kopacz had secured the party chair position in Civic Platform. She had an openly pro-NATO position, particularly after the Russian aggression in Ukraine. After being elected prime minister, she stepped down prematurely due to her party's poor performance in local elections. In 2019, she became the vice president of the European Parliament.

Kuugongelwa-Amadhila, Saara (October 12, 1967–)
Prime Minister of Namibia (March 21, 2015–)
Appointed, Political Career Path
Kuugongelwa-Amadhila has undergraduate and graduate degrees in economics. She served as a bureaucrat in various capacities, including economic adviser to the Office of the President and director of the National Planning Commission. She was elected to the parliament in the 1990s and served as the minister of finance from 2003 to 2015. She became the first woman prime minister of Namibia in 2015, where she prioritized gender parity, women's political representation, youth unemployment, and climate change.

Marin, Sanna (November 16, 1985–)
Prime Minister of Finland (December 10, 2019–)
Elected, Political Career Path
Marin received her college degree in public administration. She joined the Social Democratic Party at a young age by participating in their youth branches. She gradually moved up both within the party rank and file and in elected offices. In 2012, she was elected to the Tampere City Council. She would go on to be elected to parliament in 2015 and secure a cabinet position in 2019 as the minister of transportation and communication. She is known to have a progressive stance on women's and LGBT rights. When she became the leader of a center-left coalition in 2019, she secured the title as the youngest prime minister in the world.

May, Theresa (October 1, 1956–)
Prime Minister of the United Kingdom (July 13, 2016–July 24, 2019)
Elected, Political Career Path
May received her undergraduate degree in geography before starting her business career in the financial sector. She joined the Conservative Party and moved up the ranks starting as a member of parliament until she became the party spokesperson in the 2000s. She served in multiple shadow ministry positions, and when Conservatives came to power in 2010 she became the home secretary for six years, which is among the top four most powerful positions in the cabinet. She became the leader of the Conservative Party in 2016 and served as the second woman prime minister of the UK. Her tenure was marked by the Brexit negotiations, and she eventually resigned. She was succeeded by Boris Johnson, who took over the task of leading the UK's exit from the European Union.

Mottley, Mia (October 1, 1965–)
Prime Minister of Barbados (May 25, 2018–)
Elected, Political Career Path
Mottley received her education in Barbados, New York, and the UK. She has her law degree from the London School of Economics. Growing up, there were some political figures in her family: a grandfather who served as a mayor and an uncle who was briefly a political party leader. However, she did not have an immediate family member who held a high national office, such as the presidency or a cabinet position. She became a senator and, later, the youngest cabinet minister of all time in 1994 when she took over as the education, youth affairs, and culture minister. Subsequently, she became the leader of the Labor Party and served as the first woman attorney general. She would also become the first female prime minister after winning the 2018 election.

Nandigna, Maria Adiatu Djaló (November 6, 1958–)
Prime Minister of Guinea-Bissau (February 10, 2012–April 12, 2012)
Interim, Political Career Path
Prior to Nandigna becoming Guinea-Bissau's interim prime minister, she was the minister of culture, youth, and sports. She came to power when Guinea-Bissau was going through significant political turmoil and the military was directly intervening in politics. In fact, the previous government had been deposed by a military coup. Her tenure as the first woman prime minister of Guinea-Bissau lasted for two months as her government was also brought down by military intervention. She would go on to serve as the minister of defense in Prime Minister Carlos Correia's cabinet in 2015.

Park Geun-hye (February 2, 1952–)
President of South Korea (February 25, 2013–March 10, 2017)
Elected, Family Path
Park Geun-hye comes from a deeply political family. Her father was a coup leader in the 1960s and ruled South Korea for nearly two decades with an iron fist. After her mother was assassinated, Park Geun-hye served as first lady alongside her father. She got elected to the National Assembly before becoming the leader of the right-wing Liberty Korea Party. She became the first woman executive of South Korea in 2013. Toward the end of her term, she became embroiled in corruption scandals and other controversies that involved cult leaders who served as her confidants and obtained access to state secrets. Eventually, she was impeached and was sentenced to twenty-four years in prison.

Rousseff, Dilma (December 14, 1947–)
President of Brazil (January 1, 2011–August 31, 2016)
Elected, Political Activist Path
Rousseff took up arms against the military dictatorship during the 1970s. She was captured by authorities and jailed for three years. During this period, she was subjected to torture. Upon her release, she worked in public

bureaucracy in various capacities as a trained economist. She also served as the energy minister during Lula da Silva's (Workers' Party) presidency and became his handpicked successor when he could no longer run due to term limits. She won the presidential election twice and focused on social policies, poverty reduction, and social justice issues. She also addressed the human rights abuses that took place during military rule. However, her second term was marred with a series of scandals, involving politicians, large contractors, and Petrobras, Brazil's largest public oil company. While she was not personally charged with corruption, she ended up getting impeached by Congress for charges of mishandling the federal budget.

Sahle-Work, Zewde (February 21, 1950–)
President of Ethiopia (October 25, 2018–)
Appointed, Political Career Path
Sahle-Work studied natural science in France before pursuing a career in diplomacy. She went on to serve as the ambassador of Ethiopia in Senegal and Djibouti and worked as a seasoned diplomat in the United Nations. She worked in various capacities, particularly on peacebuilding operations in Africa. She was eventually promoted to the level of Undersecretary-General of the United Nations before returning to Ethiopia. Long respected as a successful career diplomat, her nomination to the office of the presidency was unanimously approved by members of the parliament. She prioritizes gender parity in her policy agenda.

Sakellaropoulou, Katerina (May 30, 1956–)
President of Greece (March 13, 2020–)
Appointed, Political Career Path
Sakellaropoulou has undergraduate and graduate degrees in law. She served as a judge and held several high-profile leadership positions in the high courts. Notably, she became the first woman to serve as the general secretary, vice president, and president of the highest administrative court in Greece. She was associated with more progressive positions during her tenure, but also did not openly endorse any political party and remained independent. She is a strong advocate of human rights and environmental protections. She also stood up for the elimination of the religion category on the national identification cards in Greece when this position was not palatable for the vast majority of conservative citizens and the Greek Orthodox Church. The parliament elected her the first female president of Greece with a historically large margin.

Samba-Panza, Catherine (June 26, 1956–)
President of the Central African Republic (January 23, 2014–March 30, 2016)
Interim, Political Career Path
Prior to her career in politics, Samba-Panza worked as a corporate lawyer. She was appointed as mayor of Bangui, the capital of the Central African Republic, since she was considered acceptable to both sides involved in

the country's conflict. At a time when religious conflicts flared between minority Muslims and majority Christians, she emphasized her role as a caring woman leader who could better reconcile differences. She urged the militias to drop their arms and called them "my children." Samba-Panza was selected by a national transitional council after the rebel leader behind the March 2013 coup stepped aside due to international criticism about his inability to control his fighters and decrease violence. During her interim mandate, she tried to boost the economy and bring back stability, reconciliation, and rule of law. After approximately two years of interim rule, she lost the next presidential election.

Sandu, Maia (May 24, 1972–)
Prime Minister of Moldova (June 8, 2019–November 14, 2019)
Elected, Political Career Path
Sandu has degrees in economics, management, and international relations. She worked as an adviser at the World Bank and subsequently served as the minister of education. She was elected after the Constitutional Court suspended President Igor Dodon and named then Prime Minister Pavel Filip acting president. She had a pro-democracy and pro-EU platform with a strong emphasis on anticorruption and cleaning up the banking sector. Her Harvard education and work experience at the World Bank supported her reformist agenda. She ruled for about five months until her government was also brought down by a vote of no confidence.

Shinawatra, Yingluck (June 21, 1967–)
Prime Minister of Thailand (August 5, 2011–May 7, 2014)
Elected, Family Path
Yingluck's older brother was the prime minister between 2001 and 2006. He was pushed out of office by a bloodless coup. Her father was an affluent businessman who served as a parliamentarian in the 1960s and 1970s. Yingluck held several executive positions in family businesses prior to her career in politics. Her political career started abruptly when her brother was banned from politics and forced into exile. After winning the election and forming a government as prime minister, she continued to face charges that she was a proxy for her brother. Her tenure was marked by serious controversies and challenges. She was eventually pushed out of office, charged with corruption, and banned from politics.

Siber, Sibel (December 13, 1960–)
Prime Minister of Northern Cyprus (June 13, 2013–September 2, 2013)
Interim, Political Career Path
Siber was trained as a medical doctor in Istanbul, Turkey, and specialized in internal medicine before starting her political career. She was elected to parliament in 2009 with record high support from voters. She became the first female prime minister of Northern Cyprus in 2013 after the ruling party was ousted via a vote of no confidence. Siber was the consensus name for three of the opposition parties. She agreed to form a cabinet and serve as the

prime minister on an interim basis until new elections were held in two months. Following her time as prime minister, she was again elected to parliament and began serving as the president of the parliament.

Sidibé, Cissé Mariam Kaïdama (January 4, 1948–)
Prime Minister of Mali (April 3, 2011–March 22, 2012)
Appointed, Political Career Path
Sidibé has a degree in civil administration from the Malian National School for Administration. She began her political career working as a civil servant in the Ministry of Oversight for State Companies and Societies in 1974. In 1987 she became the department's minister. In 1991, she was named special adviser to President Amadou Toumani Touré and minister of planning and international cooperation. She served as minister of agriculture in 1992. From 1993 to 2000, Sidibé was the executive secretary of the Interstate Committee on the Fight Against Desertification in the Sahel. In 2001, she was named special counselor to the president. She added another ministerial position to her resumé in 2003: Rural Development. Sidibé became the president of Mali's government tobacco corporation in 2003. In 2011, Prime Minister Modibo Sidibé resigned and dissolved the government. President Touré appointed Cissé Sidibé his successor by decree. She was relatively unknown to the public, and many speculated if her appointment was an effort to reach female voters in time for the 2012 election. Before the election could be held, soldiers seized power in a coup d'état because of their displeasure with President Touré's handling of the Tuareg rebellion. Sidibé and the rest of the cabinet were captured and detained by junta forces. They are currently being held at a military camp in Kati.

Solberg, Erna (February 24, 1961–)
Prime Minister of Norway (October 16, 2013–)
Elected, Political Career Path
Solberg has degrees in social sciences and started her political career in local government. She served on the Bergen city council and chaired local and municipal charters of the Young Conservatives and the Conservative Party. She would go on to become a party leader, serve in parliament, and act as the minister of local government and regional development. Solberg was elected president in 2013. During her time as president, she has focused on finding global solutions for development, growth, and conflict resolution.

Sommaruga, Simonetta (May 14, 1960–)
President of Switzerland (January 1, 2015–December 31, 2015;
** January 1, 2020–)**
Elected, Political Career Path
Sommaruga was trained as a musician and concert pianist at an early age. She was involved in politics within the ranks of the Social Democratic Party at the local level when she got elected to the municipal government as a city council member of Bern. Eventually, she became the representative of Bern

at the Federal Assembly. She served in various committees involving environment and energy. Sommaruga also headed the Department of Justice and Police and the Department of Environment, Transport, Energy, and Communications. She was elected as the president of Switzerland by the Federal Council twice, first in 2015 and again in 2020.

Straujuma, Laimdota (February 24, 1951–)
Prime Minister of Latvia (January 22, 2014–February 11, 2016)
Elected, Political Career Path
An economist by training, Straujuma held a variety of positions within the Ministry for Agriculture before being appointed as minister of the department in 2011. Prior to assuming power, Latvia was struggling with multiple problems. Nationalist and pro-Russia groups were having politically charged discussions over the official language, and, in 2013, a supermarket collapsed in Riga, killing more than fifty civilians. This spurred the resignation of Prime Minister Valdis Zatlers. Straujuma was nominated by the Unity Party to fill the post of prime minister given her support from farmers during her time as the agriculture minister. She remained in office as the first female prime minister of Latvia for about two years and resigned after increasing pressure due to the migration crisis in Europe.

Szydło, Beata (April 15, 1963–)
Prime Minister of Poland (November 16, 2015–December 11, 2017)
Elected, Political Career Path
Szydło studied ethnography, social sciences, and economics in college and graduate school. Her political career started with local politics when she was elected as the mayor of Gmina Brzeszcze. She joined the conservative right-wing Law and Justice Party and was elected to the parliament from among their ranks. She was considered skilled but not charismatic. She replaced another female, Prime Minister Ewa Kopacz, when she won the election in 2015. She ran on a conservative platform promising tougher approaches on immigration and the expansion of state benefits. In 2017, she survived a no confidence vote after her government's position on immigration and Brexit was considered untenable by some in parliament and her party. She resigned from office along with her cabinet. Her deputy prime minister and finance minister Mateusz Morawiecki was named prime minister. He named Szydło his deputy prime minister. She continued in this post until she resigned to take the seat she won in the European Parliament in the 2019 election.

Thanou-Christophilou, Vassiliki (November 3, 1950–)
Prime Minister of Greece (August 27, 2015–September 21, 2015)
Interim, Political Career Path
Thanou-Christophilou received her degrees and training in law and served in various levels of the judicial system, including as president of the Greek Supreme Civil and Criminal Court. As the senior member of the Supreme Court, she was also the president of the Supreme Electoral Court. She was

invited to serve as the interim prime minister in a caretaker capacity for less than a month after the resignation of Prime Minister Alexis Tsipras due to the economic and political turmoil the country was facing. This made her the first female prime minister of Greece. In this role, she defined her position as ensuring fair and smooth elections.

Thịnh, Đặng Thị Ngọc (December 25, 1959–)
President of Vietnam (September 21, 2018–October 23, 2018)
Interim, Political Career Path

Thịnh started her political career by joining the Communist Party of Vietnam in November 1979. She went on to serve in the 11th and 13th National Assemblies. In April 2016, she was elected vice president. As vice president, she served as the acting president after the death of President Trần Đại Quang in 2018. In doing so, she became the first female executive in Vietnamese history. Her time as acting president came to an end after the election and swearing in of President Nguyễn Phú Trọng in October 2018.

Thorning-Schmidt, Helle (December 14, 1966–)
Prime Minister of Denmark (November 2, 2011–June 28, 2015)
Elected, Political Career Path

Thorning-Schmidt received undergraduate and graduate degrees in political science from the University of Copenhagen. She began her career by joining the Social Democratic Party and served as an administrator at the European Parliament. Prior to her election to the European Parliament in 2005, she also worked as a consultant for the Danish Confederation of Trade Unions. Thorning-Schmidt eventually became the first female leader of her party. As the leader of the social democratic bloc, she came to power as the first female prime minister by forming a minority center-left coalition in 2011 with an agenda focused on anti-austerity and tax reform. Her term in office was marked by fiscal challenges and scandals that involved her family being brought up on tax evasion charges. After the Social Democrats lost the general elections in 2015, Thorning-Schmidt resigned as prime minister and leader of the Social Democrats.

Touré, Aminata (October 12, 1962–)
Prime Minister of Senegal (September 3, 2013–July 8, 2014)
Appointed, Political Career Path

Touré has degrees in economics, finance, and business administration, including a PhD in international financial management from the International School of Management. Prior to entering the political arena, she worked with family planning and reproductive health programs in Senegal, Burkina Faso, and Côte d'Ivoire. She later went on to serve as a gender and HIV program coordinator for the UN Population Fund. Prior to her appointment as prime minister, she served as the minister of justice. Throughout her political career, she campaigned on anticorruption and women's rights platforms. Her term as the second female prime minister of Senegal was cut short due to her poor electoral performance in local elections in 2014.

Tsai, Ing-wen (August 31, 1956–)
President of Taiwan (May 20, 2016–)
Elected, Political Career Path
Tsai has degrees in law from National Taiwan University, Cornell University, and the London School of Economics and Political Science. She became a law professor at Soochow University and National Chengchi University. In 1993, she was appointed to a variety of governmental positions, such as trade negotiator for World Trade Organization affairs. In 2000, she was named the minister of the Mainland Affairs Council and joined the Democratic Progressive Party (DPP). She briefly served in parliament in 2004 until being appointed vice premier. Tsai became the DPP's chair in 2008, but she resigned that post after losing her 2012 presidential election bid. While serving as the DPP chair, she also ran unsuccessfully for mayor of New Taipei City in 2010. In 2016, she was elected in a landslide with over 50 percent of the vote to become president and was reelected in 2020. Tsai's administration has focused on a host of issues, such as building and maintaining strong relationships with the United States and China, advocating for disadvantaged populations, advancing renewable energy, and reforming labor practices.

Weekes, Paula-Mae (December 23, 1958–)
President of Trinidad and Tobago (March 19, 2018–)
Appointed, Political Career Path
Justice Weekes had a long and distinguished legal career as a lawyer in private practice and a judge in various levels of the judicial branch, including acting chief justice of the Supreme Court. She also served as a judicial educator and developed training programs for new judges. She was nominated to the position of the presidency and claimed the position unopposed in 2018. Despite multimillion-dollar restorations to the presidential palace, she stays with her mother and uses the palace only for official functions. She supports girls' education and gender parity in politics.

Widmer-Schlumpf, Eveline (March 16, 1956–)
President of Switzerland (January 1, 2012–December 31, 2012)
Elected, Family Path
Widmer-Schlumpf has law degrees and a doctorate from the University of Zurich. She worked as a lawyer and public notary before starting her political career in the conservative Swiss People's Party. She served as a cantonal legislative representative from Grison, which was the same canton her father represented before becoming the president of the Swiss Confederation in 1984. Widmer-Schlumpf would go on to serve as the minister of justice and later the finance minister. She was elected to the presidency in 2012 and is the third woman to hold that position.

Wilmès, Sophie (January 15, 1975–)
Prime Minister of Belgium (October 27, 2019–)
Appointed, Political Career Path
Wilmès received college degrees in communication and finance and worked in a law firm as the banking and finance adviser. Her political

career started at the local level when she was elected to the city council of Uccle. Subsequently, she became a representative to the lower chamber of the national parliament. She served as the minister of budget before becoming the first woman prime minister of Belgium. While the Belgian king appointed her to the office, it is a ceremonial process and her appointment is based on getting elected to the parliament from the ranks of the French-speaking liberal party. She is leading a caretaker government and does not have a full mandate due to the highly divided results of the 2019 election.

Yacob, Halimah (August 23, 1954–)
President of Singapore (September 14, 2017–)
Elected, Political Career Path
Yacob received her degrees in law and served as a legal officer and union leader. Her political career consisted of getting elected to the Parliament of Singapore in 2001 and serving in multiple cabinet positions. She became the Speaker of the Parliament in 2013. Her candidacy as a Muslim woman leader from the minority Malay ethnicity was praised by some as a testimony to the democratic aspirations of the multiracial island nation. However, others criticized her campaign as another highly doctored attempt to keep the same party in power for more than five decades. She was the only candidate who could meet the eligibility requirements during the presidential election and became the first female president of Singapore.

Zourabichvili, Salomé (March 18, 1952–)
President of Georgia (December 16, 2018–)
Elected, Political Career Path
Zourabichvili is the daughter of Georgian immigrants from France. She has undergraduate and graduate degrees in political science and pursued a career as a diplomat in France. She was appointed as the ambassador of France in Georgia soon after the invasion of Georgia by Russia. While representing France in Georgia, she was granted Georgian citizenship and was appointed as Georgia's minister of foreign affairs. Politically, she stands for greater democracy in Georgia and stronger links with Europe, instead of Russia. Her political support stems from pro-Europe and pro-democracy parties in Georgia. She was elected to the Georgian parliament as an independent in 2016 and was elected president in 2018.

Sources: BBC, Council of Women World Leaders, *Encyclopedia Britannica, Time,* and Reuters.

References

Abramson, Paul R., John H. Aldrich, and David W. Rohde. 2010. *Change and Continuity in the 2008 Elections.* Washington, DC: CQ Press.

Adler, Nancy. 1996. "Global Women Political Leaders: An Invisible History, an Increasingly Important Future." *Leadership Quarterly* 7, no. 1: 133–161.

Agence France-Presse. 2018. "Marine Le Pen Charged for Posting Violent Isis Images on Twitter." March 1.

Alba, Monica, Frank Thorp V, and Phil McCausland. 2016. "FBI Completes Review of Newly Revealed Hillary Clinton Emails, Finds No Evidence of Criminality." NBC News, November 6.

Aldrich, Andrea S., and Nicholas J. Lotito. 2020. "Pandemic Performance: Women Leaders in the Covid-19 Crisis." *Politics and Gender*: 1–9. https://doi.org/10.1017/S1743923X20000549.

Allen, Jonathan, and Amie Parnes. 2014. *HRC: State Secrets and the Rebirth of Hillary Clinton.* New York: Crown Publishers.

Allen, Peter, David Cutts, and Rosie Campbell. 2016. "Measuring the Quality of Politicians Elected by Gender Quotas: Are They Any Different?" *Political Studies* 64, no. 1: 143–163.

Amaro, Silvia. 2017. "Defeated Conservative Fillon Calls on Supporters to Choose Macron over Le Pen." CNBC, April 23.

Arkin, Daniel, and Corky Siemaszko. 2016. "2016 Election: Donald Trump Wins the White House in Upset." NBC News, November 9.

Baker, Peter. 2014. "3 Presidents and a Riddle Named Putin." *New York Times*, March 23.

Barnes, Tiffany D., and Emily Beaulieu. 2014. "Gender Stereotypes and Corruption: How Candidates Affect Perceptions of Election Fraud." *Politics and Gender* 10, no. 3: 365–391.

Barrington, Lowell. 2012. *Comparative Politics: Structures and Choices.* 2nd ed. Boston: Cengage.

Barro, Josh. 2016. "The Polls Are Swinging Against Hillary Clinton Because She Gave Voters Reason to Distrust Her." *Business Insider*, July 14.

233

Barrow-Giles, Cynthia, ed. 2011. *Women in Caribbean Politics*. Miami, FL: Ian Randle Publishers.

Bassett, Laura, and Jonathan Cohn. 2016. "Female Trump Supporters Don't Really Care About His Sexism." *Huffington Post*, October 4.

Baturo, Alexander, and Julia Gray. 2018. "When Do Family Ties Matter? The Duration of Female Suffrage and Women's Path to High Political Office." *Political Research Quarterly* 71, no. 3: 695–709.

Bauer, Gretchen. 2016. "'What Is Wrong with a Woman Being Chief?': Women Chiefs and Symbolic and Substantive Representation in Botswana." *Journal of Asian and African Studies* 51, no. 2: 222–237.

Bauer, Gretchen, and Manon Tremblay, eds. 2011. *Women in Executive Power*. London: Routledge.

Baynes, Chris. 2019. "Marine Le Pen Ordered to Stand Trial for Tweeting Pictures of Isis Killings." *The Independent*, June 2019.

BBC. 2007. "Attack on Bhutto Convoy Kills 130." October 19.

———. 2010. "The Women Presidents of Latin America." October 31.

———. 2015. "Mauritius Profile—Leader, President: Ameenah Gurib-Fakim." June 5.

———. 2016. "18 Revelations from Wikileaks' Hacked Clinton Emails." October 27.

———. 2017. "Thailand Announces 2018 General Election." October 10.

Beardsley, Eleanor. 2017. "Marine Le Pen's 'Brutal' Upbringing Shaped Her Worldview." NPR, April 21.

Beckwith, Karen. 2000. "Beyond Compare? Women's Movements in Comparative Perspective." *European Journal of Political Research* 37, no. 4: 431–468.

———. 2010. "Someday My Chance Will Come: Women Contesting for Executive Leadership in West Europe." Paper presented at the Annual Meeting of the American Political Science Association, Washington, DC.

Bego, Ingrid. 2014. "Accessing Power in New Democracies: The Appointment of Female Ministers in Postcommunist Europe." *Political Research Quarterly* 67, no. 2: 347–360.

Bevan, Tom. 2017. "Sexism Did Not Cost Hillary the Election." *Real Clear Politics*, June 1.

Bixby, Scott, and Tom McCarthy. 2016. "Donald Trump on Benghazi Attack: 'Clinton Was Sleeping'—as It Happened." *The Guardian*, May 25.

Bjarnegård, Elin, and Pär Zetterberg. 2019. "Political Parties, Formal Selection Criteria, and Gendered Parliamentary Representation." *Party Politics* 25, no. 3: 325–335.

Blake, Aaron. 2016. "Voters Strongly Reject Hillary Clinton's 'Basket of Deplorables' Approach." *Washington Post*, September 26.

Bond, Jon R., Cary Covington, and Richard Fleisher. 1985. "Explaining Challenger Quality in Congressional Elections." *Journal of Politics* 47, no. 2: 510–529.

Booth, John A., and Patricia Bayer Richard. 2015. *Latin American Political Culture: Public Opinion and Democracy*. Los Angeles: Sage, CQ Press.

Bormann, Nils-Christian, and Matt Golder. 2013. "Democratic Electoral Systems Around the World, 1946–2011." *Electoral Studies* 32, no. 2: 360–369.

Borrelli, MaryAnne, and Janet M. Martin, eds. 1997. *The Other Elites: Women, Politics, and Power in the Executive Branch*. Boulder, CO: Lynne Rienner Publishers.

Boutchie, Jessica. 2017. "Marine Le Pen's Journey to Failure." *Harvard Political Review*, September 7.

Bowden, Mark. 2012. *The Finish: The Killing of Osama Bin Laden*. New York: Atlantic Monthly Press.

Bradley, Matt. 2017. "French Election: Marine Le Pen Loses but Propels Far-Right to Mainstream." NBC News, May 9.

Brady, Jonann. 2008. "A Look Back at Hillary's Year in Pantsuits." *Good Morning America*, August 26.

Bremmer, Ian. 2015. "Marine Le Pen Lost a Battle but May Win the War in France." *Time*, December 14.

Britannica. 2020. "Jean-Marie Le Pen." June 16.

Burden, Barry. 2009. "The Nominations: Rules, Strategies, and Uncertainty." In *The Elections of 2008*, edited by Michael Nelson, 22–44. Washington, DC: CQ Press.

Burkett, Elinor. 2008. *Golda Meir: The Iron Lady of the Middle East.* New York: Gibson Square Books.

Bystrom, Dianne. 2010. "18 Million Cracks in the Glass Ceiling: The Rise and Fall of Hillary Rodham Clinton's Presidential Campaign." In *Cracking the Highest Glass Ceiling: A Global Comparison of Women's Campaigns for Executive Office*, edited by Rainbow Murray, 69–90. Santa Barbara, CA: Praeger.

Calabresi, Massimo. 2011. "Hillary Clinton and the Rise of Smart Power." *Time*, November 7.

Caldwell, Patrick. 2013. "Future Superdelegates Are Already Kissing Up to Hillary." *Mother Jones*, November 8.

Cameron, A. Colin, and Pravin K. Trivedi. 1998. *Regression Analysis of Count Data.* New York: Cambridge University Press.

Caraway, Teri L. 2004. "Inclusion and Democratization: Class, Gender, Race, and the Extension of Suffrage." *Comparative Politics* 36, no. 4: 443–460.

Carlin, Diana B., and Kelly L. Winfrey. 2009. "Have You Come a Long Way, Baby? Hillary Clinton, Sarah Palin, and Sexism in 2008 Campaign Coverage." *Communication Studies* 60, no. 4: 326–343.

Carlin, Ryan E., Miguel Carreras, and Gregory J. Love. 2019. "Presidents' Sex and Popularity: Baselines, Dynamics and Policy Performance." *British Journal of Political Science*: 1–21. https://doi.org/10.1017/S0007123418000364.

Carroll, Susan J. 2009. "Reflections on Gender and Hillary Clinton's Presidential Campaign: The Good, the Bad, and the Misogynic." *Politics and Gender* 5, no. 1: 1–20.

Carroll, Susan, and Richard Fox, eds. 2018. *Gender and Elections: Shaping the Future of American Politics.* 4th ed. New York: Cambridge University Press.

Cauterucci, Christina. 2016. "Helpful Critiques of Hillary Clinton's Mouth Shape from Men Watching the Debate." *Slate*, September 27.

Center for American Women and Politics (CAWP). 2017. "The Gender Gap: Voting Choices in Presidential Elections." https://www.cawp.rutgers.edu/sites/default/files/resources/gg presvote.pdf.

Chamorro, Violeta Barrios. 1996. *Dreams of the Heart: The Autobiography of President Violeta Barrios de Chamorro of Nicaragua.* New York: Simon and Schuster.

Chaney, Elsa M. 2014 [1979]. *Supermadre: Women in Politics in Latin America.* Austin: University of Texas Press.

Chozick, Amy. 2015. "Hillary Clinton Announces 2016 Presidential Bid." *New York Times*, April 12.

———. 2016. "Hillary Clinton Calls Many Trump Backers 'Deplorables,' and GOP Pounces." *New York Times*, September 10.

Chozick, Amy, and Patrick Healy. 2016. "Hillary Clinton Has Clinched Democratic Nomination, Survey Reports." *New York Times*, June 6.

Chozick, Amy, and Megan Thee-Brennan. 2016. "Poll Finds Voters in Both Parties Unhappy with Their Candidates." *New York Times*, July 14.

Chrisafis, Angelique. 2011. "Marine Le Pen Emerges from Father's Shadow." *The Guardian*, March 21.

———. 2015. "Marine Le Pen Not Guilty of Inciting Religious Hatred." *The Guardian*, December 15.

———. 2016a. "Jean-Marie Le Pen Fined Again for Dismissing Holocaust as 'Detail.'" *The Guardian*, April 6.

———. 2016b. "The Fear of Marine Le Pen—Will the Next Political Earthquake Happen in France?" *The Guardian*, December 14.

———. 2017a. "'Penelopegate' Casts Dark Shadow over Fillon's Presidential Prospects." *The Guardian*, January 27.

———. 2017b. "Marine Le Pen: The Estranged Daughter Tied to a Very Public Life." *The Guardian*, April 14.

———. 2017c. "Marine Le Pen Under Formal Investigation over Use of EU Funds." *The Guardian*, June 30.

———. 2017d. "French Election: Macron Hailed as Winner of Bruising Le Pen TV Debate." *The Guardian*, May 4.

Christensen, Martin K. I. 2011. "Worldwide Guide to Women in Leadership." June 9. http://www.guide2womenleaders.com/index.html.

Cillizza, Chris. 2016. "The Worst Candidate of 2016." *Washington Post*, December 20.

Cizre, Umit. 2002. "From Ruler to Pariah: The Life and Times of the True Path Party." In *Political Parties in Turkey*, edited by Barry Rubin and Metin Heper, 82–101. London: Frank Cass.

Clarke, Seán, and Josh Holder. 2017. "French Presidential Election May 2017—Full Second Round Results and Analysis." *The Guardian*, May 26.

Clemens, Clay. 2006. "From the Outside In: Angela Merkel as Opposition Leader, 2002–2005." *German Politics and Society* 24, no. 3: 41–81.

CNN. 2008. "Election Center 2008 Primaries and Caucuses: Results: Democratic Scorecard." August 20.

———. 2016a. "Democratic Party: CNN Delegate Estimate," n.d.

———. 2016b. "Exit Polls 2016," November 23.

Cohen, Nancy L. 2016. "Sexism Did Not Cost Hillary Clinton the Election." *Washington Post*, November 16.

Collison, Stephen. 2016. "Outsiders Sweep to Victory in New Hampshire." CNN, February 10.

Confessore, Nicholas, and Jason Horowitz. 2016. "Hillary Clinton's Paid Speeches to Wall Street Animate Her Opponents." *New York Times*, January 21.

Cooper, Helene, and Steven Lee Myers. 2011. "Obama Takes Hard Line with Libya After Shift by Clinton." *New York Times*, March 18.

Coppedge, Michael, and John Gerring, with David Altman, Michael Bernard, Steven Fish, Allen Hicken, Matthew Kroenig, Staffan I. Lindberg, Kelly McMann, Pamela Paxton, Holli A. Semetko, Svend-Erik Skaaning, Jeffrey K. Staton, and Jan Teorell. 2011. "Conceptualizing and Measuring Democracy: A New Approach." *Perspectives on Politics* 9, no. 2: 247–267.

Cox, Douglas. 2015. "Hillary Clinton Email Controversy: How Serious Is It?" CNN, July 27.

Cracolici, Maria Francesca, Miranda Cuffaro, and Peter Nijkamp. 2010. "The Measurement of Economic, Social, and Environmental Performance of Countries: A Novel Approach." *Social Indicators Research* 95, no. 2: 339–356.

Cummings, William. 2016. "'Deplorable' and Proud: Some Trump Supporters Embrace the Label." *USA Today*, September 12.

Darcy, R., Susan Welch, and Janet Clark. 1994. *Women, Elections, and Representation*. Lincoln: University of Nebraska Press.

Davidson-Schmich, Louise K. 2006. "Implementation of Political Party Gender Quotas: Evidence from the German Lander 1990–2000." *Party Politics* 12, no. 2: 211–232.

Dearden, Lizzie. 2017. "French Elections: Marine Le Pen Vows to Suspend Immigration to 'Protect France.'" *The Independent*, April 18.

Debenedetti, Gabriel. 2016. "Clinton Blames Comey Letters for Defeat." *Politico*, November 12.

Della Porta, Donatella. 2006. *Social Movements, Political Violence, and the State: A Comparative Analysis of Italy and Germany*. New York: Cambridge University Press.

Dilanian, Ken. 2016. "Clinton Emails Held Indirect References to Undercover CIA Officers." NBC News, February 4.

Dinan, Stephen. 2016. "Hillary Clinton 'Secret' Email Count Doubles as Latest Batch Is Released." *Washington Times*, February 29.

Dolan, Julie, Melissa M. Deckman, and Michele I. Swers. 2016. *Women and Politics: Paths to Power and Political Influence*. 3rd ed. Maryland: Rowman & Littlefield.

Duerst-Lahti, Georgia. 1997. "Reconceiving Theories of Power: Consequences of Masculinism in the Executive Branch." In *The Other Elites*, edited by Mary Anne Borelli and Janet M. Martin, 11–32. Boulder, CO: Lynne Rienner.

———. 2006. "Presidential Elections: Gendered Space and the Case of 2004." In *Gender and Elections: Shaping the Future of American Politics*, edited by Susan J. Carroll and Richard L. Fox, 12–42. New York: Cambridge University Press.

Duverger, Maurice. 1955. *The Political Role of Women*. Paris: UNESCO.

El Amraoui, Ahmed. 2017. "Fillon and Le Pen: A Tale of Two Scandals." Al Jazeera, April 18.

Embury-Dennis, Tom. 2017. "Emmanuel Macron Leads Marine Le Pen by at Least 20 Points in Every French Election Poll Since End of First Round." *The Independent*, April 25.

Erlanger, Steven. 2010. "Child of France's Far Right Prepares to Be Its Leader." *New York Times*, May 21.

Esarey, Justin, and Leslie Schwindt-Bayer. 2017. "Women's Representation, Accountability, and Corruption in Democracies." *British Journal of Political Science* 48, no. 3: 659–690.

Escobar-Lemmon, Maria, and Michelle M. Taylor-Robinson. 2005. "Women Ministers in Latin American Government: When, Where, and Why?" *American Journal of Political Science* 49, no. 4: 685–699.

———. 2009. "Getting to the Top: Career Paths of Women in Latin American Cabinets." *Political Research Quarterly* 62, no. 4: 685–699.

——— (eds). 2014. *Representation: The Case of Women*. New York: Oxford University Press.

Evans, Jocelyn, and Gilles Ivaldi. 2018. *The 2017 French Presidential Elections: A Political Reformation?* New York: Palgrave.

Falk, Erika. 2008. *Women for President: Media Bias in Eight Campaigns*. Chicago: University of Illinois Press.

Faris, Robert, Hal Roberts, Bruce Etling, Nikki Bourassa, Ethan Zuckerman, and Yochai Benkler. 2017. *Partisanship, Propaganda, and Disinformation: Online Media and the 2016 U.S. Presidential Election*. Cambridge, MA. https://dash.harvard.edu/bitstream/handle/1/33759251/2017-08_electionReport_0.pdf.

Federal Election Commission. 2017. *Federal Elections 2016: Election Results for the U.S. President, the U.S. Senate and the U.S. House of Representatives*. Washington, DC. https://www.fec.gov/resources/cms-content/documents/federalelections2016.pdf.

Fieldstadt, Elisha. 2016. "Donald Trump Consistently Made Lewd Comments on 'The Howard Stern Show,'" NBC News, October 8.

Flegenheimer, Matt. 2016. "Hillary Clinton Says 'Radical Fringe' Is Taking Over G.O.P. Under Donald Trump." *New York Times*, August 25.

Folke, Olle, Johanna Karin Rickne, and Daniel M. Smith. 2020. "Gender and Dynastic Political Selection." *Social Science Research Network*. https://ssrn.com/abstract=2985230.

Fox, Richard L., and Zoe M. Oxley. 2003. "Gender Stereotyping in State Executive Elections: Candidate Selection and Success." *Journal of Politics* 65, no. 3: 833–850.

Franceschet, Susan, Mona Lena Krook, and Jennifer M. Piscopo, eds. 2012. *The Impact of Gender Quotas*. New York: Oxford University Press.

Franceschet, Susan, and Jennifer M. Piscopo. 2013. "Equality, Democracy, and the Broadening and Deepening of Gender Quotas." *Politics and Gender* 9, no. 3: 310–316.

Freedom House. 2018. "Freedom in the World Report 2018." https://freedomhouse .org/report/freedom-world/freedom-world-2018.

Gallagher, Michael. 2018. Election Indices Dataset. http://www.tcd.ie/Political_Science /people/michael_gallagher/EISystems/index.php.

Genovese, Michael A. 1993a. "Women as National Leaders: What Do We Know?" In *Women as National Leaders*, edited by Michael A. Genovese, 211–217. London: Sage.

———, ed. 1993b. *Women as National Leaders*. London: Sage.

Gerstein, Josh, and Rachel Bade. 2016. "22 Hillary Clinton Emails Declared 'Top Secret' by State Dept." *Politico*, January 31.

Geske, Mary, and Susan C. Bourque. 2001. "Grassroots Organizations and Women's Human Rights: Meeting the Challenge of the Global-Local Link." In *Women, Gender, and Human Rights: A Global Perspective*, edited by Marjorie Agosin, 246–262. New Brunswick, NJ: Rutgers University Press.

Ghattas, Kim. 2013. *The Secretary: A Journey with Hillary Clinton from Beirut to the Heart of American Power*. New York: Times Books.

Givhan, Robin. 2007a. "Hillary Clinton's Tentative Dip into New Neckline Territory." *Washington Post*, July 20.

———. 2007b. "Wearing the Pants: Envisioning a Female Commander-in-Chief." *Washington Post*, December 9.

Goldberg, Michelle. 2008. "Three A.M. Feminism." *New Republic*, June 25.

———. 2016. "The Hillary Haters." *Slate*, July 24.

Goldmacher, Shane, and Ben Schreckinger. 2016. "Trump Pulls Off Biggest Upset in U.S. History." Politico, November 9.

Goldstein, Joshua S. 2010. "On Asterisk Inflation." *PS: Political Science and Politics* 43, no. 1: 59–61.

Gottlieb, Karla. 2011. "Queen Nanny of the Jamaican Maroons." In *Women in Caribbean Politics*, edited by Cynthia Barrow-Giles. Miami, FL: Ian Randle Publishers.

Green, December, and Laura Luehrmann. 2017. *Comparative Politics of the Global South: Linking Concepts and Cases*. 4th ed. Boulder, CO: Lynne Rienner.

Greene, William. 2008. *Econometric Analysis*. 6th ed. Upper Saddle River, NJ: Prentice Hall.

Hagen, Lisa. 2016. "Supporters Join Trump on Stage: We Are Not Deplorable." *The Hill*, September 10.

Hartig, Hannah, John Lapinski, and Stephanie Psyllos 2016. "Hillary Clinton Holds Slim National Lead over Donald Trump: Poll." NBC News, May 15.

Hayden, Michael Edison. 2016. "5 Missteps That May Have Doomed the Clinton Campaign." ABC News, November 9.

Healy, Patrick. 2007a. "The Resume Factor: Those Two Terms First Lady." *New York Times*, December 26.

———. 2007b. "The Clinton Conundrum: What's Behind the Laugh?" *New York Times*, December 12.

Healy, Patrick, and Amy Chozick. 2016. "Minority Voters Push Hillary Clinton to Victories." *New York Times*, March 1.

Henderson, Sarah L., and Alana S. Jeydel. 2007. *Participation and Protest: Women and Politics in a Global World*. New York: Oxford University Press.

———. 2014. *Women and Politics in a Global World*. New York: Oxford University Press.

Henley, Jon. 2012. "Marine Le Pen's 17.9% Is Not a Breakthrough for the Far Right." *The Guardian*, April 25.

———. 2017. "Marine Le Pen Promises Liberation from the EU with France-First Policies." *The Guardian*, February 5.

Hepker, Aaron. 2016. "All Precincts Reported: Clinton Defeats Sanders by Historically Small Margin." *WHO-TV*, February 2.

Hinojosa, Magda. 2012. *Selecting Women, Electing Women: Political Representation and Candidate Selection in Latin America*. Philadelphia, PA: Temple University Press.

Hodson, Piper. 1997. "Routes to Power: An Examination of Political Change, Rulership, and Women's Access to Executive Office." In *Other Elites*, edited by Mary Anne Borelli and Janet M. Martin, 33–47. Boulder, CO: Lynne Rienner.

Htun, Mala. 2016. *Inclusion Without Representation: Gender Quotas and Ethnic Reservations in Latin America*. New York: Cambridge University Press.

Htun, Mala N., and Mark P. Jones. 2002. "Engendering the Right to Participate in Decision-Making: Electoral Quotas and Women's Leadership in Latin America." In *Gender and the Politics of Rights and Democracy in Latin America*, edited by Nikki Craske and Maxine Molyneux, 32–54. New York: Palgrave.

Htun, Mala, and Jennifer Piscopo. 2014. "Women in Politics and Policy in Latin America and the Caribbean." Conflict Prevention and Peace Forum Working Paper on Women in Politics No. 2, Social Science Research Council. https://webarchive.ssrc.org/working-papers/CPPF_WomenInPolitics_02_Htun_Piscopo.pdf.

Huang, Peter H. 2020. "Put More Women in Charge and Other Leadership Lessons from COVID-19." Florida International University Law Review 15(3): 1–102 (Forthcoming).

Huddy, Leonie, and Tony E. Carey. 2009. "Group Politics Redux: Race and Gender in the 2008 Democratic Presidential Primaries." *Politics and Gender* 5, no. 1: 81–96.

Huddy, Leonie, and Nayda Terkildsen. 1993. "Gender Stereotypes and the Perception of Male and Female Candidates." *American Journal of Political Science* 37, no. 1: 119–147.

Hughes, Melanie M., Pamela Paxton, and Mona Lena Krook. 2017. "Gender Quotas for Legislatures and Corporate Boards." *Annual Review of Sociology* 43, no. 1: 331–353.

Idea Gender Quota Database. 2020. https://www.idea.int/data-tools/data/gender-quotas.

The Independent. 2004. "Maria de Lourdes Pintasilgo." July 14.

Inglehart, Ronald, and Pippa Norris. 2003. *The Rising Tide: Gender Equality and Cultural Change Around the World*. New York: Cambridge University Press.

Jalalzai, Farida. 2004. "Women Political Leaders: Past and Present." *Women and Politics* 26, no. 3–4: 85–108.

———. 2008. "Women Rule: Shattering the Executive Glass Ceiling." *Politics and Gender* 4, no. 2: 1–27.

———. 2013. *Shattered, Cracked, or Firmly Intact? Women and the Executive Glass Ceiling Worldwide*. New York: Oxford University Press.

———. 2016a. "Shattered Not Cracked: The Effect of Women's Executive Leadership. *Journal of Women, Politics and Policy* 37, no. 4: 439–463.

———. 2016b. *Women Presidents in Latin America: Beyond Family Ties?* London: Routledge.

———. 2017. "Global Trends in Women's Executive Leadership." In *Women Presidents and Prime Ministers in Post-Transition Democracies*, edited by Veronica Montecinos, 59–79. London: Palgrave.

———. 2018. "A Comparative Assessment of Hillary Clinton's 2016 Presidential Race." *Socios: Sociological Research for a Dynamic World* 4, no. 1: 1–11.

Jalalzai, Farida, and Mona Lena Krook. 2010. "Beyond Hillary and Benazir: Women's Political Leadership Worldwide." *International Political Science Review* 31, no. 1: 5–21.

Jalalzai, Farida, and Meg Rincker. 2018. "Blood Is Thicker Than Water: Family Ties to Political Power Worldwide." *Historical Social Research* 43, no. 4: 54–72.

Jensen, Jane. 2008. *Women Political Leaders*. New York: Palgrave Macmillan.

Jones, Mark P. 1998. "Gender Quotas, Electoral Laws, and the Election of Women: Lessons from the Argentine Provinces." *Comparative Political Studies* 31, no. 1: 3–21.

Katzenstein, Mary Fainsod. 1978. "Towards Equality? Cause and Consequences of the Political Prominence of Women in India." *Asian Survey* 18, no. 5: 473–486.

Keneally, Meghan, and Ryan Struyk. 2016. "Tim Kaine Nominated as Democratic Vice Presidential Candidate." ABC News, July 27.

Kessler, Glenn. 2016. "How Did 'Top Secret' Emails End Up on Hillary Clinton's Server?" *Washington Post*, February 4.

Kincaid, Diane D. 1978. "Over His Dead Body: A Positive Perspective on Widows in the U.S. Congress." *Western Political Quarterly* 31, no. 1: 96–104.

King, Anthony. 2002. "The Outsider as Political Leader: The Case of Margaret Thatcher." *British Journal of Political Science* 32, no. 3: 435–454.

Kittilson, Miki Caul. 1999. "Women's Representation in Parliament: The Role of Political Parties." *Party Politics* 5, no. 1: 79–98.

Kittilson, Miki Caul, and Kim Fridkin. 2008. "Gender, Candidate Portrayals and Election Campaigns: A Comparative Perspective." *Politics and Gender* 4, no. 3: 371–392.

Kittilson, Miki Caul, and Leslie Schwindt-Bayer. 2012. *The Gendered Effects of Electoral Institutions: Political Engagement and Participation*. New York: Oxford University Press.

Klein, Joe. 2009. "The State of Hillary: A Mixed Record on the Job." *Time*, November 5.

Kohler, Ulrich, and Frauke Kreuter. 2009. *Data Analysis Using Stata*. 2nd ed. College Station, TX: Stata Press.

Kollman, Ken, Allen Hicken, Daniele Caramani, David Backer, and David Lublin. 2018. Constituency-Level Elections Archive. Produced and distributed by the Center for Political Studies, University of Michigan, Ann Arbor.

Kroet, Cynthia. 2017. "Marine Le Pen Steps Down as Party Leader Until Election Runoff." Politico, April 24.

Krook, Mona Lena. 2009. *Quotas for Women in Politics: Gender and Candidate Selection Reform Worldwide*. New York: Oxford University Press.

Laakso, Markku, and Rein Taagepera. 1979. "'Effective' Number of Parties: A Measure with Application to West Europe." *Comparative Political Studies* 12, no. 1: 3–27.

Labott, Elise. 2012. "Clinton: I'm Responsible for Diplomats' Security." CNN, October 16.

Landler, Mark. 2016. "H Is for Hawk." *New York Times Magazine*, April 24.

Lauter, David. 2016. "Trump Takes Lead over Clinton as GOP Convention Generates a Bounce for Its Nominee." *Los Angeles Times*, July 25.

Lawless, Jennifer L. 2009. "Sexism and Gender Bias in Election 2008: A More Complex Path for Women in Politics." *Politics and Gender* 5, no. 1: 70–80.

Lawless, Jennifer L., and Richard L. Fox. 2010. *It Still Takes a Candidate: Why Women Don't Run for Office*. New York: Cambridge University Press.

———. 2018. *Women, Men and U.S. Politics: Ten Big Questions*. New York: W. W. Norton.

Lawrence, Regina G., and Melody Rose. 2010. *Hillary Clinton's Race for the White House: Gender Politics and the Media on the Campaign Trail*. Boulder, CO: Lynne Rienner.

Leonnig, Carol D., Rosalind S. Helderman, and Anne Gearan. 2015. "Clinton E-mail Review Could Find Security Issues." *Washington Post*, March 6.

Leroux, Thibault. 2011. "Marine Le Pen, France Far-Right Presidential Candidate, Advocates Euro Exit." *Huffington Post*, November 19.

Lewis-Beck, Michael S. 1995. *Data Analysis: An Introduction*. Thousand Oaks, CA: Sage.

Lima, Christiana. 2017. "Brazile: I Found 'No Evidence' Democratic Primary Was Rigged." Politico, November 5.

Linz, Juan J. 1990. "The Perils of Presidentialism." *Journal of Democracy* 1, no. 1: 51–69.

———. 1994. "Presidential or Parliamentary Democracy: Does It Make a Difference?" In *The Failure of Presidential Democracy: Comparative Perspective*, vol. 1, edited by Juan J. Linz and Arturo Valenzuela, 3–87. Baltimore: Johns Hopkins University Press.

Liswood, Laura A. 2007. *Women World Leaders: Great Politicians Tell Their Stories*. Washington, DC: Council Press.

Long, Ray. 2016. "Why Did Hillary Clinton Lose? Simple. She Ran a Bad Campaign." *Chicago Tribune*, November 14.

Long, J. Scott, and Jeremy Freese. 2005. *Regression Models for Categorical Outcomes Using Stata*. 2nd ed. College Station, TX: Stata Press.

Lovenduski, Joni. 1993. "Introduction: The Dynamics of Gender and Party." In *Gender and Party Politics*, edited by Joni Lovenduski and Pippa Norris, 1–15. London: Sage.

Lovenduski, Joni, and Pippa Norris, eds. 1993. *Gender and Party Politics*. London: Sage.

Luhiste, Maarja, and Meryl Kenny. 2016. "Pathways to Power: Women's Representation in the 2014 European Parliament Elections." *European Journal of Political Research* 55, no. 3: 626–641.

Macaulay, Fiona. 2017. "Dilma Rousseff (2011–2016): A Crisis of Governance and Consensus in Brazil." In *Women Presidents and Prime Ministers in Post-Transition Democracies*, edited by Verónica Montecinos, 123–140. London: Palgrave Macmillan.

Maeda, Ko, and Misa Nishikawa. 2006. "Duration of Party Control in Parliamentary and Presidential Governments: A Study of 65 Democracies, 1950 to 1998." *Comparative Political Studies* 39, no. 3: 352–374.

March, James, and Johan Olsen. 2011. "Elaborating the 'New Institutionalism.'" In *Oxford Handbook of Political Science*, edited by Robert Goodin, 159–175. New York: Oxford University Press.

Marquand, Robert. 2010. "France's National Front: Will Marine Le Pen Take the Reins?" *Christian Science Monitor*, June 25.

Martin, Cathi Jo, and Duane Swank. 2008. "The Political Origins of Coordinated Capitalism: Business Organizations, Party Systems, and State Structure in the Age of Innocence." *American Political Science Review* 102, no. 2: 181–198.

Martin, Janet, and MaryAnne Borrelli, eds. 2016. *The Gendered Executive: A Comparative Analysis of Presidents, Prime Ministers, and Chief Executives*. Philadelphia: Temple University Press.

Masters, James, and Margaux Deygas. 2017. "Marine Le Pen Sparks Outrage over Holocaust Comments." CNN, April 10.

Matland, Richard E. 1993. "Institutional Variables Affecting Female Representation in National Legislature: The Case of Norway." *Journal of Politics* 55, no. 3: 737–755.

———. 1998a. "Women's Representation in National Legislatures: Developed and Developing Countries." *Legislative Studies Quarterly* 23, no. 1: 109–125.

———. 1998b. "Enhancing Women's Political Participation: Legislative Recruitment and Electoral Systems." In *Women in Parliament: Beyond Numbers*, edited by Azza Karam, 65–86. Stockholm: International IDEA.

Matland, Richard E., and Michelle M. Taylor. 1997. "Electoral System Effects on Women's Representation: Theoretical Arguments and Evidence from Costa Rica." *Comparative Studies* 30, no. 2: 186–210.

Matthews, Chris. 2008. "Hardball with Chris Matthews for Jan. 29." MSNBC, January 29.

Maxwell, Fiona. 2017. "Right-Winger Dupont-Aignan Endorses Le Pen for French President." Politico, April 29.

McCarthy, Justin. 2016. "Americans' Reactions to Trump, Clinton Explain Poor Images." Gallup, September 8.

McDonagh, Eileen. 2009. The Motherless State: Women's Political Leadership and American Democracy. Chicago: University of Chicago Press.

McThomas, Mary, and Michael Tesler. 2016. "The Growing Influence of Gender Attitudes on Public Support for Hillary Clinton, 2008–2012." Politics and Gender 12, no. 1: 28–49.

Meir, Golda. 1975. My Life. New York: Dell Publishing.

Melander, Ingrid. 2017. "Le Pen's Run-off Campaign Targets Far Left and Right." Reuters, April 24.

Menard, Scott W. 1995. Applied Logistic Regression Analysis. Thousand Oaks, CA: Sage.

Mendoza, Diana, and Maria Elissa Jayme Lao. 2017. "Corazon Aquino: The Reluctant First Female President of the Philippines." In Women Presidents and Prime Ministers in Post-Transition Democracies, edited by Verónica Montecinos, 205–219. London: Palgrave Macmillan.

Miller, Melissa K., Jeffrey Peake, and Brittany Ann Boulton. 2010. "Testing the Saturday Night Live Hypothesis: Fairness and Bias in Newspaper Coverage of Hillary Clinton's Campaign." Politics and Gender 6, no. 2: 169–198.

Montanaro, Domenico. 2016. "Hillary Clinton's 'Basket of Deplorables,' in Full Context of This Ugly Campaign." NPR, September 10.

Montecinos, Veronica, ed. 2017a. Women Presidents and Prime Ministers in Post-Transition Democracies. London: Palgrave Macmillan.

———. 2017b. "Michelle Bachelet: Engendering Chile's Democratization." In Women Presidents and Prime Ministers in Post-Transition Democracies, edited by Veronica Montecinos, 141–163. London: Palgrave Macmillan.

Morgan, Jana, and Melissa Buice. 2013. "Latin American Attitudes Toward Women in Politics: The Influence of Elite Cues, Female Advancement, and Individual Characteristics." American Political Science Review 107, no. 4: 644–662.

Murray, Rainbow, ed. 2010. Cracking the Highest Glass Ceiling: A Global Comparison of Women's Campaigns for Executive Office. Santa Barbara, CA: Praeger.

Myers, Steven Lee. 2016. "22 Clinton Emails Deemed Too Classified to Be Made Public." New York Times, January 30.

Myers, Steven Lee, and Julie Hirschfeld Davis. 2016. "Last Batch of Hillary Clinton's Emails Is Released." New York Times, February 29.

Nagelkerke, Nico J. D. 1991. "A Note on a General Definition of the Coefficient of Determination." Biometrika 78, no. 3: 691–692.

Nelson, Michael. 2009. "The Setting." In The Elections of 2008, edited by Michael Nelson, 1–21. Washington, DC: CQ Press.

Newport, Frank. 2016. "Eight Things We Learned in This Election." Gallup, November 10.

Noonan, Peggy. 2016. "The High Cost of a Bad Reputation." Wall Street Journal, January 14.

Norris, Pippa, and Ronald Inglehart. 2011. Sacred and Secular: Religion and Politics Worldwide. 2nd ed. New York: Cambridge University Press.

Norris, Pippa, and Joni Lovenduski. 2010. "Puzzles in Political Recruitment." In Women, Gender, and Politics: A Reader, edited by Mona Lena Krook and Sarah Childs, 135–140. New York: Oxford University Press.

Nossiter, Adam. 2017. "Marine Le Pen Loses French Parliamentary Immunity over Tweets." New York Times, November 9.

————. 2018. "Approaching 90, and Still the 'Devil of the Republic.'" *New York Times*, March 16.

Noymer, Andrew. 2008. "Alpha, Significance Level of Test." In *Encyclopedia of Survey Research Methods,* edited by Paul J. Lavrakas, 18. Thousand Oaks, CA: Sage.

O'Brien, Richard. 2018. *Women Presidents and Prime Ministers 2018.* Washington, DC: Double Bridge Publishing.

O'Brien, Robert M. 2007. "A Caution Regarding Rules of Thumb for Variance Inflation Factors." *Quality and Quantity* 41, no. 5: 673–690.

Opfell, Olga S. 1993. *Women Prime Ministers and Presidents.* Jefferson, NC: McFarland.

Orin, Deborah. 1999. "Trump Toyz with Prez Run." *New York Post*, July 12.

Pace, Julie. 2016. "For Some Americans, Politician's Promises of Change and Disruption Have Come Too Slowly, or Failed Altogether." *USA Today*, January 30.

Paquette, Danielle. 2016. "What We Mean When We Say Hillary Clinton 'Overprepared' for the Debate." *Washington Post*, September 27.

Pasha-Robinson, Lucy. 2016. "Marine Le Pen Takes Huge Lead over Nicolas Sarkozy in French First Round Presidential Election Poll." *The Independent*, November 20.

Patterson, Thomas E. 2016a. "Pre-Primary News Coverage of the 2016 Presidential Race: Trump's Rise, Sanders' Emergence, Clinton's Struggle." Shorenstein Center on Media, Politics, and Public Policy, June 13.

————. 2016b. "News Coverage of the 2016 Presidential Primaries: Horse Race Reporting Has Consequences." Shorenstein Center on Media, Politics, and Public Policy, July 11.

————. 2016c. "News Coverage of the 2016 National Conventions: Negative News, Lacking Context." Shorenstein Center on Media, Politics, and Public Policy, September 21.

————. 2016d. "News Coverage of the 2016 General Election: How the Press Failed the Voters." Shorenstein Center on Media, Politics, and Public Policy, December 7.

Paxton, Pamela. 1997. "Women in National Legislatures: A Cross-National Analysis." *Social Science Research* 26, no. 4: 442–464.

Paxton, Pamela, Jennifer Green, and Melanie M. Hughes. 2008. Women in Parliament Dataset, 1893–2003. [Computer file]. Ann Arbor, MI: Inter-university Consortium for Political and Social Research [distributor], 2008-12-22. doi:10 .3886/ICPSR24340.v1.

Paxton, Pamela, Melanie M. Hughes, and Tiffany D. Barnes. 2020. *Women, Politics, and Power: A Global Perspective.* 4th ed. Lanham, MD: Rowman and Littlefield.

Payne, Richard J., and Jamal R. Nassar. 2015. *Politics and Culture in the Developing World.* 5th ed. New York: Routledge.

Peck, Emily. 2017. "Hillary Clinton Says Misogyny Played a Part in Her Loss. She's Right." *Huffington Post*, May 2.

Perez, Evan, and Pamela Brown. 2016a. "Comey Notified Congress of Email Probe Despite DOJ Concerns." CNN, October 29.

————. 2016b. "FBI Discovered Clinton-Related Emails Weeks Ago." CNN, October 31.

Pew Research Center. 2015. "Women and Leadership: Public Says Women Are Equally Qualified, but Barriers Persist." January 14.

Pignataro, Adrián, and Michelle M. Taylor-Robinson. 2019. "Party Competition, Gender Quotas, and Enhanced Inclusiveness in the Selection of Vice-Presidential Candidates." *Politics, Groups, and Identities*: 1–18. https://doi.org/10.1080/21565503 .2019.1637354.

Piscopo, Jennifer M. 2015. "States as Gender Equality Activists: The Evolution of Quota Laws in Latin America." *Latin American Politics and Society* 57, no. 3: 27–49.

Pottier, Jean-Marie. 2014. "Five Frenchmen, Including Marine Le Pen, in the 2014 Foreign Policy List." *Slate*, November 26.

Quigley, Aidan. 2017. "Trump Expresses Support for Le Pen." Politico, April 21.

Rappeport, Alan, Yamiche Alcindor, and Jonathan Martin. 2016. "Democrats Nominate Hillary Clinton Despite Sharp Divisions." *New York Times*, July 26.

Reyes, Raul A. 2015. "Clinton Testimony Upstages GOP's 2016 Field." *The Hill*, October 26.

Reyes-Housholder, Catherine. 2016. "Presidentas Rise: Consequences for Women in Cabinets?" *Latin American Politics and Society* 58, no. 3: 3–25.

Reynolds, Andrew. 1999. "Women in the Legislatures and Executives of the World: Knocking at the Highest Glass Ceiling." *World Politics* 51, no. 4: 547–572.

Richter, Linda K. 1991. "Explaining Theories of Female Leadership in South and South East Asia." *Pacific Affairs* 63, no. 1: 524–540.

Richter, Paul. 2009. "World Breathes Sigh of Relief, Hillary Clinton Says." *Los Angeles Times*, January 28.

Robbins, Mel. 2017. "Hillary Clinton Lost Because of Sexism." CNN, May 3.

Rosen, Jennifer. 2013. "The Effects of Political Institutions on Women's Political Representation: A Comparative Analysis of 168 Countries from 1992 to 2010." *Political Research Quarterly* 66, no. 2: 306–321.

Rubin, Alissa J., and Aurelien Breeden. 2015. "Far-Right Party in France Tries to Push Jean-Marie Le Pen, Provocative Founder, to the Margins." *New York Times*, May 4.

Rucker, Philip. 2017. "Donna Brazile: I Considered Replacing Clinton with Biden as 2016 Democratic Nominee." *Washington Post*, November 4.

Rule, Wilma. 1985. "Twenty-Three Democracies and Women's Parliamentary Representation." Paper presented at the Annual Meeting of the International Political Science Association, Paris.

Rule, Wilma, and Joseph F. Zimmerman, eds. 1994. *Electoral Systems in Comparative Perspective: Their Impact on Women and Minorities.* Westport, CT: Greenwood Press.

Sachar, Jasmine, and Bob Cusack. 2014. "60 Dems Endorse Hillary for 2016." *The Hill*, January 28.

Saint-Germain, Michelle A. 1993. "Women in Power in Nicaragua: Myth and Reality." In *Women as National Leaders*, edited by Michael A. Genovese, 70–102. London: Sage.

Salmond, Rob. 2006. "Proportional Representation and Female Parliamentarians." *Legislative Studies Quarterly* 31, no. 2: 175–204.

Salo, Elaine. 2010. "South African Feminism: A Coming of Age?" In *Women's Movements in the Global Era: The Power of Local Feminisms*, edited by Amrita Basu, 29–55. Boulder, CO: Westview Press.

Samprit, Chatterlee, Ali S. Hadi, and Bertram Prince. 2000. *Regression Analysis by Example.* 3rd ed. New York: John Wiley and Sons.

Samuel, Henry. 2012. "Marion Le Pen Becomes Youngest French MP in Modern History." *The Telegraph*, June 17.

———. 2014a. "Far-Right Front National Makes Historic Gains in French Municipal Elections." *The Telegraph*, March 23.

———. 2014b. "Marine Le Pen 'Has the Stuff of Thatcher.'" *The Telegraph*, November 28.

———. 2017. "Emmanuel Macron Accuses Marine Le Pen of 'Peddling the Same Lies as Your Father': What We Learnt from the French Presidential TV Debate." *The Telegraph*, April 5.

Satlin, Alana Horowitz. 2016. "MSNBC Interrupts Hillary Clinton's Speech to Complain About Her Voice." *Huffington Post*, March 7.

Schemo, Diana Jean. 1997. "Ecuadorean Is Again Elected Interim President, Five Days Later." *New York Times*, February 12.

Schmidt, Gregory D., and Kyle L. Saunders. 2004. "Effective Quotas, Relative Party Magnitude, and the Success of Female Candidates: Peruvian Municipal Elections in Comparative Perspective." *Comparative Political Studies* 37, no. 6: 704–734.

Schofield, Hugh. 2012. "What Next for Marine Le Pen's National Front." *BBC News*, April 24.

Schwindt-Bayer, Leslie. 2009. "Making Quotas Work: The Effect of Gender Quota Laws on the Election of Women." *Legislative Studies Quarterly* 34, no. 1: 5–28.

———. 2011. "Women Who Win: Social Backgrounds, Paths to Power, and Political Ambition in Latin American Legislatures." *Politics and Gender* 7, no. 1: 1–33.

Schwindt-Bayer, Leslie, and Catherine Reyes-Housholder. 2017. "Gender Institutions in Post-Transition Executives." In *Women Presidents and Prime Ministers in Post-Transition Democracies*, edited by Veronica Montecinos, 81–100. London: Palgrave Macmillan.

Scicluna, Rachel. 2018. "Agatha: Malta's First Female Socialist and Feminist Role Model." *Isles of the Left*, March 7.

Sczesny, Sabine, Janine Bosak, Daniel Neff, and Birgit Schyns. 2004. "Gender Stereotypes and the Attribution of Leadership Traits: A Cross-Cultural Comparison." *Sex Roles* 41, no. 11: 631–645.

Sen, Amartya. 1990. "More Than 100 Million Women Are Missing." *New York Review of Books*, December 20.

Serhan, Yasmeen. 2017. "Emmanuel Macron's Unexpected Shot at the French Presidency." *The Atlantic*, February 8.

Shane, Scott, and Michael S. Schmidt. 2015. "Hillary Clinton Emails Take Long Path to Controversy." *New York Times*, August 8.

Shields, James. 2007. *The Extreme Right in France: From Pétain to Le Pen*. New York: Routledge.

Shugart, Matthew Soberg, and John M. Carey. 1992. *Presidents and Assemblies: Constitutional Design and Electoral Dynamics*. New York: Cambridge University Press.

Simon, Roger. 2008. "Lost in Hillaryland." Politico, August 25.

Singer, Paul. 2016. "Analysis: House Benghazi Committee Report Was Drowned by Politics." *USA Today*, June 28.

Skard, Torild. 2014. *Women of Power: Half a Century of Female Presidents and Prime Ministers Worldwide*. Bristol, UK: Policy Press.

Stokols, Eli. 2016. "Trump Ignores Advice and Launches Bill Clinton Attack." Politico, September 29.

Styrkársdóttir, Auður. 2013. "Iceland: Breaking Male Dominance by Extraordinary Means." In *Breaking Male Dominance in Old Democracies*, edited by Drude Dahlerup and Monique Levenaar, 124–139. Oxford: Oxford University Press.

Taagepera, Rein. 1994. "Beating the Law of Minority Attrition." In *Electoral Systems in Comparative Perspective: Their Impact on Women and Minorities*, edited by Wilma Rule and Joseph F. Zimmerman, 235–245. Westport, CT: Greenwood Press.

Tarrow, Sidney. 2011. *Power in Movement: Social Movements and Contentious Politics*. 3rd ed. Cambridge: Cambridge University Press.

Taub, Amanda. 2017. "France's Far Right, Once Known for Anti-Semitism, Courts Jews." *New York Times*, April 5.

Thames, Frank, and Margaret Williams. 2013. *Contagious Representation: Women's Political Representation in Democracies Around the World*. New York: New York University Press.

Thompson, Mark R. 2002/2003. "Female Leadership of Democratic Transitions in Asia." *Pacific Affairs* 75, no. 4: 535–555.

Thompson, Mark R., and Ludmilla Lennartz. 2006. "The Making of Chancellor Merkel." *German Politics* 15, no. 1: 99–110.

Thrush, Glenn. 2011. "Hillary Clinton Plays Key Role in Dance with Hosni Mubarak." Politico, February 2.

Thrush, Glenn, and Annie Karni. 2016. "How Clinton Hit the Reset Button on 2016." Politico, March 3.

Time. 2016. "Here's Donald Trump's Presidential Announcement Speech." June 16.

Tripp, Alli Mari. 2001. "Women and Democracy: The New Political Activism in Africa." *Journal of Democracy* 12, no. 3: 141–155.

Tumulty, Karen, Philip Rucker, and Anne Gearan. 2016. "Donald Trump Wins the Presidency in Stunning Upset over Clinton." *Washington Post*, November 9.

Valdini, Melody Ellis. 2012. "A Deterrent to Diversity: The Conditional Effect of Electoral Rules on the Nomination of Women Candidates." *Electoral Studies* 31, no. 4: 740–749.

———. 2013. "Electoral Institutions and the Manifestation of Bias: The Effect of the Personal Vote on the Representation of Women." *Politics and Gender* 9, no. 1 (March): 76–92.

Vinocur, Nicholas. 2015. "National Front Ousts Jean-Marie Le Pen." Politico, August 20.

———. 2017. "François Fillon Fights Growing 'Penelopegate' Scandal." Politico, January 26.

———. 2017b. "Marine Le Pen's Moment of Truth." Politico, May 7.

Von Drehle, David. 2014. "Can Anyone Stop Hillary?" *Time*, January 27.

Wagner, Meg, Fernando Alfonso III, Mike Hayes, and Veronica Rocha. 2020. "The 2020 New Hampshire Primary." CNN, February 12.

Wagner, Meg, Amanda Willis, Veronica Rocha, and Mike Hayes. 2020. "The 2020 Iowa Caucuses." CNN, February 5.

Wall, Irwin. 2014. *France Votes: The Election of François Hollande*. New York: Palgrave.

Walt, Vivienne. 2017. "The Power of Le Pen." *Time*, March 16.

Watson, Robert P., Alicia Jencik, and Judith A. Selzer. 2005. "Women World Leaders: Comparative Analysis and Gender Experiences." *Journal of International Women's Studies* 7, no. 2: 53–76.

Watson, Russell. 1994. "'Dynasty' Meets 'Family Feud.'" *Newsweek*, January 23. https://www.newsweek.com/dynasty-meets-family-feud-187370.

Welle, Deutsche. 2018. "European Union Court Rules Marine Le Pen Must Repay $350,000 in Misspent Funds." *USA Today*, June 19.

Whicker, Marcia Lynne, and Hedy Leonie Isaacs. 1999. "The Maleness of the American Presidency." In *Women in Politics: Outsiders or Insiders*, edited by Lois Duke Whitaker, 221–232. Upper Saddle River, NJ: Prentice Hall.

Willsher, Kim. 2017a. "François Fillon Sinks in Polls After 'Penelopegate' Scandal." *The Guardian*, February 4.

———. 2017b. "Fears That Paris Shooting Will Affect Presidential Election as First Round Looms." *The Guardian*, April 21.

———. 2017c. "Marine Le Pen Accused of Plagiarising François Fillon in May Day Speech." *The Guardian*, May 2.

World Bank. 2019. "World Development Indicators." http://www.data.worldbank.org.

World Economic Forum. 2018. "Global Gender Gap Report 2018." http://reports .weforum.org/ global-gender-gap-report-2018/.

Yoon, Mi Yung. 2010. "Explaining Women's Legislative Representation in Sub-Saharan Africa." In *Women, Gender, and Politics: A Reader*, edited by Mona Lena Krook and Sarah Childs, 167–173. New York: Oxford University Press.

Zapotosky, Matt, and Rosalind S. Helderman. 2016. "FBI Recommends No Criminal Charges in Clinton Email Probe." *Washington Post*, July 5.

Zetlin, Diane. 2014. "Women in Parliaments in the Pacific Region." *Australian Journal of Political Science* 49, no. 2: 252–266.

Index

About the Book

From Brazil to Bangladesh, Liberia to Switzerland, Malta to the Marshall Islands, more and more women are rising to the top level of political leadership. What can we learn from this? What kinds of conditions and political institutions pave the way for a woman's ascendance to power? Are there common pathways to power? How much do family ties matter? Is political activism and important factor?

Evren Celik Wiltse and Lisa Hager answer these questions, and more, in their comprehensive study encompassing all the women presidents and prime ministers around the world from the 1960s through 2020.

Evren Celik Wiltse is associate professor of political science and **Lisa Hager** is assistant professor of political science at South Dakota State Unviersity.